LEVEL II PRACTICE EXAMS – VOLUME

D0536257

SCHWESER 2012 CFA LEVEL II PRACTICE EXAMS VOLUME 1

©2011 Kaplan, Inc. All rights reserved.

Published in 2011 by Kaplan Schweser.

Printed in the United States of America.

ISBN: 978-1-4277-3688-8 / 1-4277-3688-X

PPN: 3200-1743

If this book does not have a front and back cover, it was distributed without permission of Kaplan Schweser, and is in direct violation of global copyright laws. Your assistance in pursuing potential violators of this law is greatly appreciated.

Required CFA Institute® disclaimer: "CFA® and Chartered Financial Analyst® are trademarks owned by CFA Institute. CFA Institute (formerly the Association for Investment Management and Research) does not endorse, promote, review, or warrant the accuracy of the products or services offered by Kaplan Schweser."

Certain materials contained within this text are the copyrighted property of CFA Institute. The following is the copyright disclosure for these materials: "Copyright, 2012, CFA Institute. Reproduced and republished from 2012 Learning Outcome Statements, Level I, II, and III questions from CFA® Program Materials, CFA Institute Standards of Professional Conduct, and CFA Institute's Global Investment Performance Standards with permission from CFA Institute. All Rights Reserved."

These materials may not be copied without written permission from the author. The unauthorized duplication of these notes is a violation of global copyright laws and the CFA Institute Code of Ethics. Your assistance in pursuing potential violators of this law is greatly appreciated.

Disclaimer: The Schweser Notes should be used in conjunction with the original readings as set forth by CFA Institute in their 2012 CFA Level II Study Guide. The information contained in these Notes covers topics contained in the readings referenced by CFA Institute and is believed to be accurate. However, their accuracy cannot be guaranteed nor is any warranty conveyed as to your ultimate exam success. The authors of the referenced readings have not endorsed or sponsored these Notes.

HOW TO USE THE LEVEL II PRACTICE EXAMS

Thank you for purchasing the Schweser Practice Exams. We hope that you find this volume effective and user-friendly. The following suggestions are designed to help you get the most out of these practice exams and prepare for the actual Level II Exam.

Save the practice exams for last. Save the practice exams for the last month before the exam. A good strategy would be to take one exam in each of the three weeks leading up to the test. Do your best to mimic actual exam conditions for at least one of the practice exams (e.g., time yourself, have someone turn the heat down and up so that you go from freezing to boiling, hire a construction crew to do some blasting outside your window).

Remember, no matter how challenging we make our practice exams, the actual exam will be different. Also, mainly due to the stress of the day, your perception will be that the actual exam was much more difficult than any practice exam or old exam you have ever seen.

Then, use your results as a diagnostic tool to help you identify areas in which you are weak. One good way to accomplish this is to use your online access to Performance Tracker. This is a tool that will provide you with exam diagnostics to target your study and review effort, and allow you to compare your scores on practice exams to those of other candidates.

Make sure you understand the mistake(s) you made on every question you got wrong. Make a flashcard that illustrates that particular concept, carry it around with you, and read it until you are confident you have mastered the concept. Also, make sure that for every correct answer, you got it right for the right reason. This "feedback" loop (practice exam, diagnosis of results, identification of concepts yet to be mastered, more study of those concepts, and then another practice exam) is a very effective study strategy in the last month before exam day.

Be ready for a new format. The format of the Level II exam is different from Level I. The exam consists of item sets, which are vignettes or short cases followed by six multiple-choice questions (CFA Institute calls these "mini-cases"). There will be 20 item sets (120 questions) on the exam: 10 item sets (60 questions) in the morning and 10 more item sets (60 more questions) in the afternoon. Each question is worth 3 points (and 3 minutes), and there are 360 total points available. Each selected-response question will have three possible choices (A, B, or C).

Any topic can be tested in the morning and/or the afternoon, so you might have an economics item set in the morning and another one in the afternoon. Don't spend a lot of time guessing which topics might appear in which session.

Topic Area	Guideline Topic Area Weight	
Ethical and Professional Standards (total)		10%
Quantitative Methods	5 to 10%	
Economics	5 to 10%	
Financial Reporting and Analysis	15 to 25%	
Corporate Finance	5 to 15%	
Investment Tools (total)		30 to 60%
Equity Investments	20 to 30%	
Fixed Income	5 to 15%	
Derivatives	5 to 15%	
Alternative Investments	5 to 15%	
Asset Classes (total)		35 to 75%
Portfolio Management (total)		5 to 15%
TOTAL		100%

Expect the unexpected. Be prepared for difficult questions on unexpected topics. Only one thing is certain about the exam: you will be surprised by some of the questions.

Guess if you must. It should take you approximately 18 minutes to read the vignette and answer the six questions that make up each item set. Don't fall behind: the successful candidates know when to cut their losses by guessing and moving on. Try to eliminate one of the incorrect answers, and then pick one of the remaining choices. If you eliminate one choice you know is wrong, you have a 50/50 chance of selecting the correct answer. There is no penalty for guessing.

Be ready for more than just number-crunching. Your reading comprehension ability is a very important component of success on the Level II exam. The vignettes will be long and full of information. Your job is to focus on finding the important pieces of information and answer the questions correctly.

There are two approaches to these item sets. You can read the vignette first and then answer the questions, or you can read the questions first. We recommend the second approach because it saves time and helps you to focus on the details you need. When taking the practice exams, experiment with both techniques and do what works best for you!

 ©2011 Kaplan, Inc.

My thanks to the Schweser team. I would like to thank all of my colleagues at Schweser for their incredible work ethic and commitment to quality. Kaplan Schweser would not be the company it is, nor could it provide the quality products you see, without the help of these content and editing professionals.

You may expect me to end this introduction with a "good luck on the exam." To me, that suggests you need to be lucky to pass Level II. With your hard work and our assistance, luck will have nothing to do with it. Instead, I'll simply say, "See you next year at Level III."

Best Regards,

Bijesh Tolia

Dr. Bijesh Tolia, CFA, CA
Vice President and Level II Manager

Kaplan Schweser

Exam 1
Morning Session

Question	Topic	Minutes (Points)
1 to 6	Fixed Income Investments	18
7 to 12	Portfolio Management	18
13 to 18	Equity Investments	18
19 to 24	Equity Investments	18
25 to 30	Quantitative Methods	18
31 to 36	Alternative Investments	18
37 to 42	Portfolio Management	18
43 to 48	Derivative Investments	18
49 to 54	Fixed Income Investments	18
55 to 60	Fixed Income Investments	18

Test Answers

#	A	B	C		#	A	B	C
1.	A	B	C		41.	A	B	C
2.	A	B	C		42.	A	B	C
3.	A	B	C		43.	A	B	C
4.	A	B	C		44.	A	B	C
5.	A	B	C		45.	A	B	C
6.	A	B	C		46.	A	B	C
7.	A	B	C		47.	A	B	C
8.	A	B	C		48.	A	B	C
9.	A	B	C		49.	A	B	C
10.	A	B	C		50.	A	B	C
11.	A	B	C		51.	A	B	C
12.	A	B	C		52.	A	B	C
13.	A	B	C		53.	A	B	C
14.	A	B	C		54.	A	B	C
15.	A	B	C		55.	A	B	C
16.	A	B	C		56.	A	B	C
17.	A	B	C		57.	A	B	C
18.	A	B	C		58.	A	B	C
19.	A	B	C		59.	A	B	C
20.	A	B	C		60.	A	B	C
21.	A	B	C					
22.	A	B	C					
23.	A	B	C					
24.	A	B	C					
25.	A	B	C					
26.	A	B	C					
27.	A	B	C					
28.	A	B	C					
29.	A	B	C					
30.	A	B	C					
31.	A	B	C					
32.	A	B	C					
33.	A	B	C					
34.	A	B	C					
35.	A	B	C					
36.	A	B	C					
37.	A	B	C					
38.	A	B	C					
39.	A	B	C					
40.	A	B	C					

Exam 1
Morning Session

Questions 1-6 relate to Susan Evermore.

The Wyroman International Pension Fund includes a $65 million fixed-income portfolio managed by Susan Evermore, CFA, of Brighton Investors. Evermore is in the process of constructing a binomial interest-rate tree that generates arbitrage-free values for on-the-run Treasury securities. She plans to use the tree to value more complex bonds with embedded options. She starts out by observing that the yield on a one-year Treasury security is 4.0%. She determines in her initial attempt to price the two-year Treasury security that the value derived from the model is higher than the Treasury security's current market price.

After several iterations Evermore determines that the interest rate tree that correctly values the one and two-year Treasury securities has a rate of 5.0% in the lower node at the end of the first year and a rate of 7.5% in the upper node at the end of the first year. She uses this tree to value a two-year 6% coupon bond with annual coupon payments that is callable in one year at $99.50. She determines that the present value at the end of the first year of the expected value of the bond's remaining cash flows is $98.60 if the interest rate is 7.5% and $100.95 if the interest rate is 5.0%.

Note: Assume Evermore's calculations regarding the two-year 6% callable bond are correct.

Evermore also uses the same interest rate tree to price a 2-year 6% coupon bond that is putable in one year, and value the embedded put option. She concludes that if the yield volatility decreases unexpectedly, the value of the putable bond will increase and the value of the embedded put option will also increase, assuming all other inputs are unchanged.

Evermore also uses the interest rate tree to estimate the option-adjusted spreads of two additional callable corporate bonds, as shown in the following figure.

Issuer	Option-Adjusted Spread
AA-rated issuer	53 basis points
BB-rated issuer	–18 basis points

Evermore concludes, based on this information, that the AA-rated issue is undervalued, and the BB-rated issue is overvalued.

At a subsequent meeting with the trustees of the fund, Evermore is asked to explain what a binomial interest rate model is and how it was used to estimate effective duration and effective convexity. Evermore is uncertain of the exact methodology because the actual calculations were done by a junior analyst, but she tries to provide the trustees with a reasonably accurate step-by-step description of the process:

Step 1: Given the bond's current market price, the on-the-run Treasury yield curve, and an assumption about rate volatility, create a binomial interest rate tree.

Step 2: Add 100 basis points to each of the 1-year rates in the interest rate tree to derive a "modified" tree.

Step 3: Compute the price of the bond if yield increases by 100 basis points using this new tree.

Step 4: Repeat Steps 1 through 3 to determine the bond price that results from a 100 basis point decrease in rates.

Step 5: Use these two price estimates, along with the original market price, to calculate effective duration and effective convexity.

Lucas Davenport, a trustee and university finance professor, immediately speaks up to disagree with Evermore. He claims that a more accurate description of the process is as follows:

Step 1: Given the bond's current market price, the Treasury yield curve, and an assumption about rate volatility, create a binomial interest rate tree and calculate the bond's option-adjusted spread (OAS) using the model.

Step 2: Impose a parallel upward shift in the on-the-run Treasury yield curve of 100 basis points.

Step 3: Build a new binomial interest rate tree using the new Treasury yield curve and the original rate volatility assumption.

Step 4: Add the OAS from Step 1 to each of the 1-year rates on the tree to derive a "modified" tree.

Step 5: Compute the price of the bond using this new tree.

Step 6: Repeat Steps 1 through 5 to determine the bond price that results from a 100 basis point decrease in rates.

Step 7: Use these two price estimates, along with the original market price, to calculate effective duration and effective convexity.

At the meeting with the trustees, Evermore also presents the results of her analysis of the effect of changing market volatilities on a 1-year convertible bond issued by Highfour Corporation. Each bond is convertible into 25 shares of Highfour common stock. The bond is also callable at 110 at any time prior

©2011 Kaplan, Inc.

to maturity. She concludes that the value of the bond will decrease if either (1) the volatility of returns on Highfour common stock decreases or (2) yield volatility decreases.

Davenport immediately disagrees with her by saying "changes in the volatility of common stock returns will have no effect on the value of the convertible bond, and a decrease in yield volatility will result in an increase in the value of the bond."

1. The value of the 2-year 6% callable bond today using the interest rate tree is *closest* to:
   A. $95.24.
   B. $101.01.
   C. $102.21.

2. Is Evermore correct in her analysis of the effect of a change in yield volatility?
   A. Incorrect on the puttable bond only.
   B. Incorrect on the put option only.
   C. Incorrect on both the bond and the option.

3. What are the benchmark interest rates Evermore uses to estimate the option-adjusted spreads?
   A. Treasuries.
   B. AA and BB-related issues.
   C. LIBOR.

4. Is Evermore correct in her analysis of the relative valuation of the bonds?
   A. Correct on both issues.
   B. Correct on the AA issue only.
   C. Correct on the BB issue only.

5. Which of the following statements regarding the methodologies for estimating effective duration and convexity is *most accurate*?
   A. Davenport's description is a more accurate depiction of the appropriate methodology than Evermore's.
   B. The two methodologies will result in the same effective duration and convexity estimates only if the same rate volatility assumption is used in each.
   C. The two methodologies will result in the same effective duration and convexity estimates only if the same rate volatility assumption is used in each and the bond's OAS is equal to zero.

6. For this question, analyze each effect separately. Is Davenport correct in disagreeing with Evermore's conclusions regarding the effect on the value of the convertible bond resulting from a change in volatility?
   A. Davenport is correct on both conclusions.
   B. Davenport is correct on stock return volatility only.
   C. Davenport is correct on yield volatility only.

Questions 7–12 relate to Factor Analytics Capital Management.

Factor Analytics Capital Management makes portfolio recommendations using various factor models. Mauricio Rodriguez, a Factor Analytics research analyst, is examining the prospects of two portfolios, the FACM Century Fund (CF) and the FACM Esquire Fund (EF).

The variance of returns are identical for the two funds. The estimates in Exhibit 1 were derived for CF and EF using monthly data for the past five years.

Exhibit 1: Market Model Estimates for CF and EF

Market model for CF: $R_{CF} = 0.05 + 0.70 R_M + \varepsilon_{CF}$

Market model for EF: $R_{EF} = 0.02 + 1.50 R_M + \varepsilon_{EF}$

where:
R_{CF} = return on the CF fund
R_{EF} = return on the EF fund
R_M = return on the market portfolio
ε_{CF} = regression error term for CF
ε_{EF} = regression error term for EF

Supervisor Barbara Woodson asks Rodriguez to use the Capital Asset Pricing Model (CAPM) and a multifactor model (APT) to make a decision to continue or discontinue the EF fund. The two factors in the multifactor model are not identified. To help with the decision, Woodson provides Rodriguez with the capital market forecasts in Exhibit 2.

Exhibit 2: Capital Market Forecasts

Treasury bond yield	4%
Market portfolio risk premium	8%
APT factor 1	5%
APT factor 2	2%
Inflation rate	3%
Market portfolio standard deviation	20%

After examining the prospects for the EF portfolio, Rodriguez derives the forecasts in Exhibit 3.

©2011 Kaplan, Inc.

Exhibit 3: EF Forecasts

Return for EF	0.12
Portfolio beta*	0.80
APT factor 1 sensitivity	1.50
APT factor 2 sensitivity	2.00

*Relative to the market portfolio

Rodriguez also develops a 2-factor macroeconomic factor model for the EF portfolio. The two factors used in the model are the surprise in GDP growth and the surprise in Investor Sentiment. The equation for the macro factor model is:

$$R_{EF} = a_{EF} + b_{EF,1}F_{GDP} + b_{EF,2}F_{IS} + \varepsilon_{EF}$$

During an investment committee meeting, Woodson makes the following statements related to the 2-factor macroeconomic factor model.

Statement 1:   An investment combination in CF and EF that provides a GDP growth factor beta equal to one and an Investor Sentiment factor beta equal to zero will have ~~lower~~ higher active factor risk than a tracking portfolio consisting of CF and EF.

Statement 2:   When markets are in equilibrium, no combination of CF and EF will produce an arbitrage opportunity.

In their final meeting, Rodriguez informs Woodson that the CF portfolio consistently outperformed its benchmark over the past five years. Rodriguez makes the following comments to Woodson: "The consistency with which CF outperformed its benchmark is amazing. The difference between the CF monthly return and its benchmark return was nearly always positive and varied little over time."

7.   Using the market model estimates for CF and EF, which fund has higher:

	Systematic risk?	Unsystematic risk?
A.	CF	CF
B.	CF	EF
C.	EF	CF

8.   Based on the data provided in Exhibits 2 and 3, should Rodriguez
     recommend that Factor Analytics continue to invest in the EF fund using
     the:

     CAPM?   2-factor APT?
     A. Yes   Yes
     B. Yes   No
     C. No   Yes

9.   Are Woodson's Statements 1 and 2 regarding the macro factor model
     correct?
     A. Both statements are correct.
     B   Only Statement 1 is correct.
     C. Only Statement 2 is correct.

10. Using data provided in Exhibit 2, the intercept and slope of the Security
     Market Line (SML) are *closest* to:

     Intercept   Slope
     A. 0.03   0.04
     B. 0.03   0.08
     C. 0.04   0.08

11. The intercept for the 2-factor macroeconomic model employed by
     Rodriguez for the EF portfolio, using the GDP growth and Investor
     Sentiment risk factors, is *closest* to:
     A. 0.040.
     B. 0.080.
     C. 0.155.

12. The historical performance of the CF portfolio is *best* summarized as:
     A. high active risk.
     B. high tracking risk.
     C. high information ratio.

©2011 Kaplan, Inc.

Questions 13–18 relate to O'Connor Textiles, Part 1.

Emily De Jong, CFA, works for Charles & Williams Associates, a medium-sized investment firm operating in the northeastern United States. Emily is responsible for producing financial reports to use as tools to attract new clients. It is now early in 2009, and Emily is reviewing information for O'Connor Textiles and finalizing a report that will be used for an important presentation to a potential investor at the end of the week.

Following an acquisition of a major competitor in 1992, O'Connor went public in 1993 and paid its first dividend in 1999. Dividends are paid at the end of the year. After 2008, dividends are expected to grow for three years at 11%: $2.13 in 2009, $2.36 in 2010, and $2.63 in 2011. The average of the arithmetic and compound growth rates are given in Exhibit 1. Dividends are then expected to settle down to a long-term growth rate of 4%. O'Connor's current share price of $70 is expected to rise to $72.92 by the end of the year according to the consensus of analysts' forecasts.

O'Connor's annual dividend history is shown in Exhibit 1.

Exhibit 1: O'Connor Textiles Dividend History

Year	Dividend ($)	% Change		
1999	0.76			
2000	0.76	0.000		
2001	0.76	0.000		
2002	0.82	7.895		
2003	0.91	10.976		
2004	1.03	13.187		
2005	1.16	12.621	Arithmetic mean growth	11.1%
2006	1.34	15.517	Compound growth	10.9%
2007	1.52	13.433		
2008	1.92	26.316		

De Jong is also considering whether or not she should value O'Connor using a free cash flow model instead of the dividend discount model.

In addition, De Jong observes that the current return on 3-month T-bills is 3% and determines that the expected return on the market portfolio is 7%. She has gathered monthly data on company stock returns ($R_{i,t}$) and market returns ($R_{M,t}$) and has decided to run an ordinary least squares regression according to the model $R_{i,t} = \alpha_i + \beta_i R_{M,t} + \varepsilon_t$. De Jong uses the S&P 500 as the proxy for the market portfolio.

The output from the regression appears in Exhibit 2.

Exhibit 2: Summary Output

Dependent Variable = $R_{i,t}$

Regression Statistics	
Multiple R-Squared	0.6275
R-Squared	0.3938
Adjusted R-Squared	0.3891
Standard Error	0.0572
Observations	132

ANOVA

	df	SS	MS	F	Significance F
Regression	1	0.2764	0.2764	8.4437	<0.0001
Residual	130	0.4256	0.0033		
Total	131	0.7020			

	Coefficients	Adjusted Standard Error	t-Stat	P-value	Lower 95%	Upper 95%
Intercept	0.0062	0.0051	1.2067	0.2297	–0.0039	0.0163
$R_{M,t}$	1.0400	0.1136	9.1549	<0.0001	0.8190	1.2685

De Jong determines that employing the CAPM to estimate the required return on equity suffers from the following sources of error:

- Estimation of the model's inputs (e.g., the market risk premium).
- The company's dividend payment schedule.
- The accuracy of the beta estimate.
- Whether or not the model is the appropriate one to use.

De Jong observes that two reputable statistical analysis firms estimate betas for O'Connor stock at 0.85 and 1.10. She concludes that the differences between her beta estimate and the published estimates resulted from her use of standard errors in her regression to correct for serial correlation; the other firms did not make a similar adjustment.

De Jong considers using adjusted beta in her analysis. Typically, her company uses 1/3 for the value of α_0. However, in this case, she is considering using $\alpha_0 = 1/2$. She determines that her adjusted beta forecast will be closer to the mean reverting level using this value than it would be using a value of 1/3.

 ©2011 Kaplan, Inc.

13. The required return on equity (according to the CAPM) for O'Connor is *closest* to:
   A. 4.2%.
   B. 7.2%.
   C. 9.2%.

For Questions 14 and 15 only, use the required return on equity from Question 13 as the discount rate.

14. The value of one share of O'Connor stock in early 2009 using the two-stage dividend discount model (DDM) is *closest* to:
   A. $58.55.
   B. $75.68.
   C. $85.63.

15. Assuming the market has also applied a two-stage DDM, and the market's consensus estimate of dividend growth and required return are the same as De Jong's, the market's consensus estimate of the duration of the high-growth period is *most likely*:
   A. less than three years.
   B. equal to three years.
   C. greater than three years.

16. In what situation is it *most appropriate* for De Jong to employ a:

Dividend discount model?	FCFE model?
A. Non-control perspective	FCFE aligned with profitability
B. Control perspective	FCFE aligned with profitability
C. Non-control perspective	FCFE aligned with dividend policy

17. Is De Jong correct about the sources of error in the CAPM?
   A. Yes.
   B. No, because model appropriateness is not a source of error.
   C. No, because the company's dividend payment schedule is not a source of error.

18. Is De Jong correct with respect to her conclusions regarding the causes of the differences between her beta estimate for O'Connor and the published beta estimates, and her strategy for adjusting her beta estimate to more quickly approach the mean reverting level of beta?
   A. Yes on both counts.
   B. Yes on one count, and no on the other.
   C. No on both counts.

Questions 19–24 relate to O'Connor Textiles, Part 2.

De Jong continues her analysis of O'Connor. She is concerned that along with a dividend discount model approach she would also like to get a measure of the contribution that the key managers, Melanie and Arthur O'Connor, have made to the company's apparent ongoing success.

She considers using NOPAT and EVA to assess management performance. She believes that increasing invested capital to take advantage of projects with positive net present values increases both NOPAT and EVA.

However, De Jong decides to use residual income analysis instead. She provides the following justification for using the residual income model:

- The calculation of residual income depends primarily on readily available accounting data.
- The residual income model can be used even when cash flow is difficult to forecast.
- The residual income model does not depend on dividend payments or on positive free cash flows in the near future.
- The residual income model depends on the validity of the clean surplus relation.

She also considers the following assumptions about continuing residual income:

Assumption 1:   Residual income is positive and continues at the same level year after year.

Assumption 2:   ROE declines over time to the cost of equity.

Assumption 3:   Residual income declines to zero immediately.

De Jong gathers recent financial information data on O'Connor, as shown in Exhibit 1.

©2011 Kaplan, Inc.

Exhibit 1: O'Connor Textiles, Inc. Summary Income Statement (U.S. $ thousands, except per share data)

	2008	2009
	Actual	*Projection*
Sales	$509,447	$529,429
Cost of sales	398,100	405,068
Selling and administrative expenses	49,608	59,378
Depreciation and amortization	18,562	22,979
Total operating expenses	466,270	487,425
Earnings from operations	43,177	42,004
Interest expense	28,004	28,906
Earnings before income taxes	15,173	13,098
Provision for income taxes	5,138	4,453
Net earnings for the year	10,035	8,645
Earnings per share: basic	$0.59	$0.51
Fully diluted	$0.56	*

*Non-dilutive

De Jong has also determined that at the beginning of 2008, O'Connor had total capital of $324,000,000, of which $251,000,000 was debt and $73,000,000 was equity. The company's cost of debt before taxes is 7%, and the cost of equity capital is 8%. The company has a tax rate of approximately 34%. Weighted average cost of capital is 5.4%. Net operating profit after tax (before any adjustments) is $28,517,640.

De Jong is interested in obtaining the market's assessment of the implied growth rate in residual income and notes that the book value per share for O'Connor at the beginning of 2009 was $4.29, and the current market price is $70. She forecasts the return on equity (ROE) for 2009 to be 11.84%.

De Jong discusses her analyses with a colleague, who makes the following general statements:

Statement 1: It is usually the case that value is recognized later in the residual income model than in the dividend discount model.

Statement 2: When the present value of expected future residual income is negative, the justified P/B based on fundamentals is less than one.

19. Is De Jong correct about the *likely* effects on NOPAT and EVA from increasing invested capital to take advantage of projects with positive net present values?
   A. Yes in both cases.
   B. Yes in one case, and no in the other.
   C. No in both cases.

20. Are De Jong's justifications for using the residual income model correct?
   A. Yes.
   B. No, because the residual income model should be not be used when cash flows are difficult to forecast.
   C. No, because the residual income model depends on positive free cash flows in the near future.

21. Which of De Jong's assumptions about continuing residual income will lead to the highest persistence factor?
   A. Assumption 1.
   B. Assumption 2.
   C. Assumption 3.

22. O'Connor's residual income and economic value added (EVA) for 2008 are *closest* to:

	Residual income	EVA
A.	$6.1 million	$11.0 million
B.	$4.2 million	$11.0 million
C.	$4.2 million	$2.6 million

23. The implied residual income growth rate for 2009, based on the residual income model, is *closest* to:
   A. 7.75%.
   B. 8.16%.
   C. 8.82%.

24. Are the statements made by De Jong's colleague correct?
   A. Both statements are correct.
   B. Only Statement 1 is correct.
   C. Only Statement 2 is correct.

©2011 Kaplan, Inc.

Questions 25–30 relate to Goldensand Jewelry, Ltd.

Introduction

Rajesh Singh is the CFO of Goldensand Jewelry, Ltd, a London-based retailer of fine jewelry and watches. Singh has noticed that the price of gold has begun to increase. If economic activity continues to pick up, the price of gold is likely to accelerate its rate of increase as both the level of demand and inflation rates increase.

Implications of Rising Gold Price

Singh has become concerned about the cost implications for Goldensand if gold prices continue to rise. He has requested a meeting with Anita Biscayne, Goldensand's COO. In preparation for the meeting, Singh asked one of his staff, Yasunobu Hara, to prepare a regression analysis comparing the price of gold to the average cost of Goldensand's purchases of finished gold jewelry. Hara provides the regression results as shown in Exhibit 1.

Exhibit 1: 1979–2009 Annual Data (31 Observations)

Variable	Coefficient	Standard Error of the Coefficient
Intercept	11.06	7.29
Cost of gold	2.897	0.615
standard error of the forecast = 117.8		

Exhibit 2: Partial Student's *t*-distribution Table

	Level of Significance for One-Tailed Test					
df	0.100	0.050	0.025	0.010	0.005	0.0005
	Level of Significance for Two-Tailed Test					
df	0.200	0.100	0.050	0.020	0.010	0.001
29	1.311	1.699	2.045	2.462	2.756	3.659
30	1.310	1.697	2.042	2.457	2.750	3.646
31	1.309	1.696	2.040	2.453	2.744	3.636

Reviewing the regression results, Biscayne becomes concerned about the implications for the cost of finished jewelry to Goldensand if the price of gold continues to rise. To remain profitable, the cost of finished jewelry should not exceed $2,000.

Regression Concerns

Overall Concerns

Singh's principal concern about the regression is whether the time period chosen is a good predictor of the current situation. He makes the following statement:

Statement 1:   We may have a problem with parameter instability if the relationship between gold prices and jewelry costs has changed over the past 30 years.

Singh also focuses on the value of the slope coefficient. He expected it to be 4.0 based on his experience in the industry. Hara computes the appropriate test statistic and reports the following:

Statement 2:   We fail to reject the null hypothesis that the slope coefficient is equal to 4.0 at the 5% level of significance.

Testing for Heteroskedasticity

Biscayne remarks that the dramatic increase in the price level over the past 30 years leads her to suspect heteroskedasticity in the regression results. She suggests to Singh that they should conduct a Breusch-Pagan chi-square test for heteroskedasticity by calculating the following test statistic:

$$n \times R^2 \text{ with k degrees of freedom}$$

where:
n   = number of observations
R^2 = R^2 of the regression of jewelry prices on gold prices
k   = number of independent variables

Model Misspecification

Biscayne and Singh have various views on the potential for model misspecification and the effect of any such misspecification.

- Biscayne worries that the regression model is misspecified because it does not include a variable to measure the cost of the highly specialized labor used by manufacturing jewelers. She points out that the effect of omitting an important variable in a regression analysis is that the regression coefficients will be unbiased and inconsistent.
- Singh adds that another common consequence of misspecifying a regression analysis is creating undesired stationarity.

©2011 Kaplan, Inc.

Multiple Regression

Hara conducts a series of regression analyses using all possible combinations of the suggested independent variables based on their average quarterly values. He returns with the following regression results as shown in Exhibit 3 for the equation which uses all suggested independent variables.

Exhibit 3: 1999–2009 Quarterly Data (44 Observations)

Independent Variables	Coefficient	t-Statistic
Intercept	–3.9	3.7
Gold price	4.7	14.5
Silver price	1.2	7.8
Platinum price	3.5	3.1
Labor costs	0.82	2.4
GDP (EU)	0.000274	5.7
GDP (Middle East)	0.000049	3.6
Personal income (EU)	0.000314	2.1
Personal income (Middle East)	0.009876	2.2

R^2: 0.55

Durbin-Watson: 3.89

Hara is concerned about the equation described in Exhibit 3. He makes the following statement:

Statement 3:   The Durbin-Watson statistic indicates the presence of positive [*Negative*] autocorrelation at the 5% level.

Biscayne responds with the following statement:

Statement 4:   An autocorrelation problem can be addressed by using the Hansen method to adjust the R^2.

Exhibit 4: Partial Durbin-Watson Table

Critical Values for the Durbin-Watson Statistic (a = 0.05)

	K = 3		K = 4		K = 5	
n	d_l	d_u	d_l	d_u	d_l	d_u
39	1.33	1.66	1.27	1.72	1.22	1.79
40	1.34	1.66	1.29	1.72	1.23	1.79
45	1.38	1.67	1.34	1.72	1.29	1.78

25. The per ounce price of gold that corresponds to the $2,000 cost of finished jewelry is *closest* to:
    A. $687.
    B. $712.
    C. $3,240.

26. Are Singh (Statement 1) and Hara (Statement 2) correct or incorrect regarding the usefulness of regression results described in Exhibit 1 and the value of the slope coefficient?
    A. Both are correct.
    B. One is correct, the other is incorrect.
    C. Both are incorrect.

27. Is Biscayne correct with regard to the specification of the Breusch-Pagan test?
    A. No, because it is an *F*-test.
    B. No, because the wrong R^2 is used.
    C. No, because the degrees of freedom are equal to k and n – k – 1.

28. Regarding the comments on the potential consequences of misspecification in the simple linear regression, is Singh correct or incorrect regarding his comment on his concern over stationarity, and is Biscayne correct or incorrect about the effect of omitting an important variable?
    A. Only Singh is incorrect.
    B. Only Biscayne is incorrect.
    C. Both are incorrect.

29. Is Hara correct regarding his statement concerning autocorrelation?
    A. Yes.
    B. No, because in this case the Durbin-Watson test is inconclusive.
    C. No, because in this case the Durbin-Watson statistic indicates the presence of negative autocorrelation.

©2011 Kaplan, Inc.

30. Is Biscayne correct regarding his statement concerning how to correct for autocorrelation?
    A. No, because the White method is used to adjust the R^2.
    B. No, because the Hansen method adjusts the coefficient standard errors.
    C. No, because the Hansen method is used to address the problem of multicollinearity.

Questions 31–36 relate to Akshay Nagoree.

Akshay Nagoree, Chief Investment Officer of a large private university endowment fund, is perplexed with the performance of the fund over the past two years. He schedules a meeting with Vijay Tendulkar, CFA, who works for Magnestar Advisors, consultants to the fund. Nagoree provides details of the fund's performance and composition over the past two years to Tendulkar (shown in Exhibits 1 & 2).

Exhibit 1: Monthly Returns and Standard Deviation from 2009-2010 (annualized)

	Endowment Fund	Benchmark
Return	−6.9%	−1.7%
Standard deviation	15.6%	7.9%

Exhibit 2: Average Weights by Asset Class (from 2009-2010)

	Endowment Fund	Benchmark
Stocks	57%	83%
Bonds	16%	17%
Hedge funds	27%	—

Nagoree notes that over the past five years, the endowment has increased its portfolio allocation to alternative investments, primarily hedge funds, to diversify and to seek superior returns. However, lately the performance of the endowment's investments has been far from good, and risk seems to differ significantly from expectations. Nagoree indicates a willingness to change fund managers but wishes to maintain exposure to hedge funds.

At their meeting, Tendulkar makes the following statements:

Statement 1: The endowment fund should take on an exposure to equity market neutral funds, because these funds hedge risk exposures to market, size, and industry.

Statement 2: Zeta fund has delivered consistent and attractive returns. Their managers actively trade on mispriced securities in the market. However, some analysts have compared Zeta's strategy to selling insurance.

Statement 3: Standard deviation is an inadequate measure of risk for evaluating the performance of hedge funds, because hedge funds' return distributions exhibit negative skewness and negative excess kurtosis.

 ©2011 Kaplan, Inc.

Nagoree feels that the fees charged by hedge funds are excessive. He would prefer a fee structure that requires a minimum return before an incentive fee is payable, and that such incentive fees should not accrue more than once on the same dollar of return.

One of the funds that Nagoree is considering is Neptune—a fund of hedge funds. Based on Nagoree's information, Neptune has delivered strong returns during the past bear market. However, Nagoree is concerned about any biases present in such reported returns.

31. An excessive portfolio allocation to hedge funds is *most likely* to result from:
   A. low measured hedge fund standard deviation due to stale pricing.
   B. consideration of higher moment risk exposures in hedge fund return distributions.
   C. hedge funds taking large traditional market exposures.

32. Based on the information provided, Nagoree's preference for a fee structure would be for one that has:
   A. a hurdle rate arrangement only.
   B. a high-water mark provision only.
   C. both a hurdle rate and a high-water mark provision.

33. Neptune's past performance is *most likely* biased due to:
   A. selection bias, survivorship bias, and instant history bias.
   B. selection bias and survivorship bias.
   C. none of the above biases.

34. Tendulkar's Statement 1 is *most likely*:
   A. correct.
   B. incorrect about identifying the type of hedge fund strategy.
   C. incorrect regarding the risk exposures being hedged.

35. Zeta fund as described by Tendulkar is *most likely* following a:
   A. fixed income arbitrage strategy.
   B. merger arbitrage strategy.
   C. medium volatility strategy.

36. Tendulkar's Statement 3 is *most likely*:
   A. correct.
   B. incorrect because hedge fund return distributions exhibit negative skewness and positive excess kurtosis.
   C. incorrect because hedge fund return distributions exhibit positive skewness and positive excess kurtosis.

Questions 37–42 relate to Tamara Ogle and Isaac Segovia.

Tamara Ogle, CFA, and Isaac Segovia, CAIA, are portfolio managers for Luca's Investment Management (Luca's). Ogle and Segovia both manage large institutional investment portfolios for Luca's and are researching portfolio optimization strategies.

Ogle and Segovia begin by researching the merits of active versus passive portfolio management. Ogle advocates a passive approach, pointing out that on a risk-adjusted basis, most managers cannot beat a passive index strategy. Segovia points out that there will always be a need for active portfolio managers because as prices deviate from fair value, active managers will bring prices back into equilibrium. They determine that Treynor-Black models permit active management within the context of normally efficient markets.

Ogle decides to implement Treynor-Black models in her practice and starts the implementation process. In conversations with her largest client's risk manager, Jim King, FRM, she is asked about separation theorem in relation to active portfolio management. She responds that separation theorem more properly relates to asset prices deviating from and gravitating toward their theoretical fair price. King next asks Ogle about the differences between the Sharpe ratio and the information ratio and the difference between the security market line (SML) and the capital market line (CML).

After reallocating her client portfolios based on using the Treynor-Black model, Ogle discusses the results with Segovia. Ogle states that she is satisfied with the current methodology, but given her preference for passive management, she is still concerned about relying on analyst's forecasts. Segovia tells Ogle that he will research methods for modifying the Treynor-Black model to account for analyst forecasts.

37. The optimal portfolio for an investor under the Treynor-Black model:
    A. depends on analyst forecast accuracy.
    B. depends on the unsystematic risk of mispriced securities.
    C. is not sensitive to a change in the risk-free rate of interest.

38. Which of the following is *most accurate* regarding the separation theorem?
    A. An investor's optimal portfolio is independent of the investor's risk aversion.
    B. The expected alpha of an actively managed portfolio should be maximized, regardless of the risk-free rate.
    C. An investor's choice of risky assets does not depend on his degree of risk aversion.

 ©2011 Kaplan, Inc.

39.   The information ratio for a tracking portfolio is:
        A. expected to be zero.
        B. an indicator of a manager's systematic risk exposure.
        C. an indicator of a manager's pure stock selection ability.

40.   The optimal risky portfolio determined by the Treynor-Black model
        has an allocation of 30% to the active portfolio and a Sharpe ratio
        of 0.45. Given that the risk-free rate is 3%, the standard deviation of
        the market (passive) portfolio is 20%, and the expected return on the
        optimal risky portfolio is 10%, the standard deviation of an investor's
        optimal portfolio that is allocated 70% to the risk-free asset is *closest*
        to:
        A. 4.7%.
        B. 5.2%.
        C. 6.0%.

41.   When using the Treynor-Black model, the weight of a security in the
        actively managed portfolio is:
        A. positively related to its alpha and negatively related to its
            systematic risk.
        B. positively related to its alpha and negatively related to the alpha of
            other securities in the actively managed portfolio.
        C. positively related to its alpha and negatively related to its total risk.

42.   Modifying a Treynor-Black model to account for a lack of precision in
        an analyst's forecast is *most likely* to include:
        A. a correction to the analyst's forecast of alphas based on their prior
            bias.
        B. adjusting the Treynor-Black actively managed portfolio weights
            using the square of the correlation between the analyst's forecast
            and realized alphas.
        C. reducing portfolio weights by the reciprocal of the analyst's
            average alpha forecast error as a percentage of expected excess
            returns.

Questions 43–48 relate to Jonathan Adams.

Jonathan Adams, CFA, is doing some scenario analysis on forward contracts. The process involves pricing the forward contracts and then estimating their values based on likely scenarios provided by the firm's forecasting and strategy departments. The forward contracts with which Adams is most concerned are those on fixed income securities, interest rates, and currencies.

The first contract he needs to price is a 270-day forward on a $1 million Treasury bond with ten years remaining to maturity. The bond has a 5% coupon rate, has just made a coupon payment, and will make its next two coupon payments in 182 days and in 365 days. It is currently selling for 98.25. The effective annual risk-free rate is 4%. Adams is also analyzing forward rate agreements (FRAs).

The LIBOR spot curve is as follows:

30-day: 3.12%	60-day: 3.32%	90-day: 3.52%
120-day: 3.72%	150-day: 3.92%	180-day: 4.12%

Adams determines the price of a 2×5 FRA from the spot yield curve using the following calculation:

$$\left[\frac{1+0.0352\left(\frac{90}{360}\right)}{1+0.0332\left(\frac{60}{360}\right)} - 1 \right]\left(\frac{360}{90}\right)$$

Finally, Adams wants to price and value a currency forward on euros. The euro spot rate is $1.1854. The dollar risk-free rate is 3%, and the euro risk-free rate is 4%.

43. The no-arbitrage price for the forward contract on the Treasury bond is *closest* to:
    A. 98.54.
    B. 98.57.
    C. 98.62.

44. If the Treasury bond price decreases to 98.11 (including accrued interest) over the next 60 days, the value of a short position in the 270-day forward contract on a $10 million bond is *closest* to:
    A. $76,500.
    B. $76,800.
    C. $78,000.

©2011 Kaplan, Inc.

45. How many of the following terms are correct in the calculation of the FRA price: 0.0352, 0.0332, 60/360, 90/360?
    A. Two.
    B. Three.
    C. Four.

46. After 30 days, Adams wants to value a $10 million short position in the 2×5 FRA. The 90-day forward rate in 30 days is now 4.14%, and the original price of the FRA was 4.30%. 120-day LIBOR has changed to 3.92%. The current value of the $10 million FRA to the short position under this scenario is *closest* to:
    A. $15,794.
    B. $3,948.
    C. −$15,794.

47. The no-arbitrage price for a 1-year forward contract on euros is *closest* to:
    A. $1.1401.
    B. $1.1740.
    C. $1.1969.

48. Suppose that at maturity of the forward contract on euros the spot rate is greater than the forward rate at the initiation of the contract. Which party is exposed to credit risk, and why?

Exposed to credit risk	Reason
A. Long position	Long position value < 0
B. Long position	Short position value < 0
C. Short position	Long position value < 0

Questions 49–54 relate to Wendall Wayne.

Wendall Wayne is a fixed income portfolio manager with Skyline Investments. Until recently he has focused almost exclusively on residential mortgage-backed securities (MBS). However, two weeks ago he was given approval to begin purchasing asset-backed securities (ABS) and commercial MBS as well. Wayne has forecasted that interest rates will decrease by approximately 100 basis points over the next month.

Wayne first completes an analysis of two tranches (a PAC I tranche and a support tranche) from a collateralized mortgage obligation (CMO) that was issued 18 months ago. When the CMO was issued, the initial collar of the PAC I tranche was 150 – 400 PSA. He estimates the change in the average life of each tranche as the prepayment speed varies, assuming the prepayment speed stays at that speed until the tranche matures. The results are shown in Exhibit 1.

Exhibit 1: Average Life of Tranches XX and YY for Varying Prepayment Speeds

PSA Speed	Tranche XX Average Life	Tranche YY Average Life
0	21.9	12.2
50	17.5	8.9
100	13.2	5.1
150	9.1	5.1
200	4.3	5.1
250	3.6	5.1
300	2.9	5.1
350	2.0	4.7
400	1.4	3.9

In his report, Wayne makes the following statements regarding the CMO:

Statement 1: The CMO is structured so that the support tranche has more extension risk, and the PAC I tranche has more contraction risk.

Statement 2: The cash flows of the PAC I tranche will be less affected by the change in interest rates I have forecast than the cash flows of the support tranche.

©2011 Kaplan, Inc.

Wayne has pushed for approval to begin trading ABS because he is particularly interested in collateralized debt obligations (CDOs). However, he doesn't know a lot about them, so he first does some reading and prepares some key points related to CDOs to guide his analysis.

Statement 3: CDOs are typically collateralized by emerging market bond issues, home equity bank loans, and high-yield corporate bond issues.

Statement 4: One advantage of issuing a synthetic CDO versus a cash CDO is that credit risk is lower with a synthetic CDO because the junior note holders also sell a credit default swap.

Statement 5: Some CDOs include an equity tranche to provide payment and credit protection to the senior and mezzanine tranches, but for most issues, credit protection is provided by external credit enhancements.

Wayne wants to understand the distinction between amortizing and non-amortizing assets that are securitized by ABS transactions, as well as the appropriate spread measures to use for various types of fixed-income securities. He asks a colleague, Martin Freed, to explain to him the difference between the two and how the payment structure of the ABS is affected by whether the assets in the pool are amortizing or non-amortizing. Freed replies:

Statement 6: An auto loan is an example of an amortizing asset, and a credit card receivable is an example of a non-amortizing asset.

Statement 7: For amortizing assets, the composition of the loans in the asset pool doesn't change once the assets are securitized. For non-amortizing assets, the composition of the asset pool does change.

Freed also tells Wayne that the credit analysis of commercial mortgage-backed securities (CMBS) should focus on the credit risk of the property, not the borrower. Freed also says that two key ratios useful for assessing the credit risk of the property are the debt service coverage ratio (net operating income/debt service) and the loan-to-value ratio (current mortgage amount/current appraised value). Wayne concludes that both of the ratios Freed recommends for credit analysis of CMBS are positively related to credit risk: the higher the ratio, the more risky the loan.

Finally, Wayne is trying to determine the most appropriate spread measure for valuing callable corporate bonds and high-quality home equity loan ABS. He plans to choose from the following measures: the zero-volatility spread, the OAS from the binomial model, and the OAS from the Monte Carlo model.

49. Which of the two tranches (XX or YY) is *most likely* the support tranche, and what is the effective collar of the PAC I tranche?

Support tranche	Effective collar of PAC I tranche
A. XX	100 – 300 PSA
B. XX	0 – 400 PSA
C. YY	100 – 300 PSA

50. Regarding the CMO, are Wayne's statements correct?
    A. Both statements are correct.
    B. Only Statement 1 is correct.
    C. Only Statement 2 is correct.

51. How many of Wayne's observations related to CDOs (Statement 3, Statement 4, and Statement 5) are correct?
    A. None.
    B. One.
    C. Two.

52. Based on the material he has read concerning ABS, Wayne disagrees with Freed's Statement 6 but agrees with Statement 7. In fact:
    A. both statements are correct.
    B. only Statement 6 is correct.
    C. only Statement 7 is correct.

53. Is Wayne correct or incorrect with regard to his analysis of debt service coverage and loan-to-value?
    A. Correct on both.
    B. Correct on debt service coverage only.
    C. Correct on loan-to-value only.

54. What is the *most appropriate* spread measure for valuing callable corporate bonds and high-quality home equity loan ABS?

Callable corporate bond	Home equity loan ABS
A. Zero-volatility spread	OAS from binomial model
B. OAS from binomial model	OAS from binomial model
C. OAS from binomial model	OAS from Monte Carlo model

©2011 Kaplan, Inc.

Questions 55–60 relate to Natalia Berg.

Natalia Berg, CFA, has estimated the key rate durations for several maturities in three of her $25 million bond portfolios, as shown in Exhibit 1.

Exhibit 1: Key Rate Durations for Three Fixed-Income Portfolios

Key Rate Maturity	Portfolio 1	Portfolio 2	Portfolio 3
2-year	2.45	0.35	1.26
5-year	0.20 0.70	0.40 0.90	1.27
10-year	0.15 0.65	4.00 4.50	1.23
20-year	2.20	0.25	1.24
Total	5.00	5.00	5.00

At a fixed-income conference in London, Berg hears a presentation by a university professor on the increasing use of the swap rate curve as a benchmark instead of the government bond yield curve. When Berg returns from the conference, she realizes she has left her notes from the presentation on the airplane. However, she is very interested in learning more about whether she should consider using the swap rate curve in her work.

As she tries to reconstruct what was said at the conference, she writes down two advantages to using the swap rate curve:

Statement 1: The swap rate curve typically has yield quotes at 11 maturities between 2 and 30 years. The U.S. government bond yield curve, however, has fewer on-the-run issues trading at maturities of at least two years.

Statement 2: Swap curves across countries are more comparable than government bond curves because they reflect similar levels of credit risk.

Berg also estimates the nominal spread, Z-spread, and option-adjusted spread (OAS) for the Steigers Corporation callable bonds in Portfolio 2. The OAS is estimated from a binomial interest rate tree. The results are shown in Exhibit 2.

Exhibit 2: Spread Measures for Steigers Corporation Callable Bonds

	Spread Measure	Benchmark
Nominal spread	25 basis points	Steigers Corp yield curve
Z-spread	35 basis points	Steigers Corp spot rate curve
OAS	–20 basis points	Steigers Corp spot rate curve
Nominal spread	120 basis points	Treasury yield curve
OAS	40 basis points	Treasury spot rate curve

Berg determines that to obtain an accurate estimate of the effective duration and effective convexity of a callable bond using a binomial model, the specified change in yield (i.e., Δy) must be equal to the OAS.

Berg also observes that the current Treasury bond yield curve is upward sloping. Based on this observation, Berg forecasts that short-term interest rates will increase.

55. If the spot-rate curve experiences a parallel downward shift of 50 basis points:
    A. all three portfolios will experience the same price performance.
    B. Portfolio 1 will experience the best price performance.
    C. Portfolio 3 will experience the best price performance.

56. If the 5- and 10-year key rates increase by 20 basis points, but the 2- and 20-year key rates remain unchanged:
    A. all three portfolios will experience the same price performance.
    B. Portfolio 1 will experience the best price performance.
    C. Portfolio 2 will experience the best price performance.

57. Are the two observations Berg writes down after the fixed income conference advantages to using the swap rate curve as a benchmark instead of a government bond curve?
    A. Both statements are advantages.
    B. Only Statement 1 is an advantage.
    C. Only Statement 2 is an advantage.

©2011 Kaplan, Inc.

58. The *most appropriate* conclusion to draw from Berg's analysis of the Steigers Corp callable bond is that the bond is relatively:
   A. undervalued, because the OAS relative to the Treasury spot rate curve is positive.
   B. overvalued, because the OAS relative to Steigers' spot rate curve is negative.
   C. undervalued, because the nominal spread and *Z*-spread relative to Steigers' yield curve and spot rate curve, respectively, are positive.

59. Is Berg correct about the specified change in yield needed to obtain an accurate estimate of the effective duration and effective convexity of a callable bond using a binomial model?
   A. No, because the specified change in yield must be larger than the option-adjusted spread (OAS).
   B. No, because the specified change in yield must be smaller than the OAS.
   C. No, because the specified change in yield can be larger than, smaller than, or equal to the OAS.

60. Is Berg's short-term interest rate forecast consistent with the pure expectations theory and the liquidity premium theory?
   A. Consistent with both theories.
   B. Consistent with the pure expectations theory only.
   C. Consistent with the liquidity premium theory only.

End of Morning Session

EXAM 1
AFTERNOON SESSION

Question	Topic	Minutes (Points)
61 to 66	Ethics	18
67 to 72	Ethics	18
73 to 78	Equity Investments	18
79 to 84	Equity Investments	18
85 to 90	Financial Reporting and Analysis	18
91 to 96	Financial Reporting and Analysis	18
97 to 102	Financial Reporting and Analysis	18
103 to 108	Corporate Finance	18
109 to 114	Portfolio Management	18
115 to 120	Economics	18

Test Answers

61.	Ⓐ	Ⓑ	Ⓒ		101.	Ⓐ	Ⓑ	Ⓒ
62.	Ⓐ	Ⓑ	Ⓒ		102.	Ⓐ	Ⓑ	Ⓒ
63.	Ⓐ	Ⓑ	Ⓒ		103.	Ⓐ	Ⓑ	Ⓒ
64.	Ⓐ	Ⓑ	Ⓒ		104.	Ⓐ	Ⓑ	Ⓒ
65.	Ⓐ	Ⓑ	Ⓒ		105.	Ⓐ	Ⓑ	Ⓒ
66.	Ⓐ	Ⓑ	Ⓒ		106.	Ⓐ	Ⓑ	Ⓒ
67.	Ⓐ	Ⓑ	Ⓒ		107.	Ⓐ	Ⓑ	Ⓒ
68.	Ⓐ	Ⓑ	Ⓒ		108.	Ⓐ	Ⓑ	Ⓒ
69.	Ⓐ	Ⓑ	Ⓒ		109.	Ⓐ	Ⓑ	Ⓒ
70.	Ⓐ	Ⓑ	Ⓒ		110.	Ⓐ	Ⓑ	Ⓒ
71.	Ⓐ	Ⓑ	Ⓒ		111.	Ⓐ	Ⓑ	Ⓒ
72.	Ⓐ	Ⓑ	Ⓒ		112.	Ⓐ	Ⓑ	Ⓒ
73.	Ⓐ	Ⓑ	Ⓒ		113.	Ⓐ	Ⓑ	Ⓒ
74.	Ⓐ	Ⓑ	Ⓒ		114.	Ⓐ	Ⓑ	Ⓒ
75.	Ⓐ	Ⓑ	Ⓒ		115.	Ⓐ	Ⓑ	Ⓒ
76.	Ⓐ	Ⓑ	Ⓒ		116.	Ⓐ	Ⓑ	Ⓒ
77.	Ⓐ	Ⓑ	Ⓒ		117.	Ⓐ	Ⓑ	Ⓒ
78.	Ⓐ	Ⓑ	Ⓒ		118.	Ⓐ	Ⓑ	Ⓒ
79.	Ⓐ	Ⓑ	Ⓒ		119.	Ⓐ	Ⓑ	Ⓒ
80.	Ⓐ	Ⓑ	Ⓒ		120.	Ⓐ	Ⓑ	Ⓒ
81.	Ⓐ	Ⓑ	Ⓒ					
82.	Ⓐ	Ⓑ	Ⓒ					
83.	Ⓐ	Ⓑ	Ⓒ					
84.	Ⓐ	Ⓑ	Ⓒ					
85.	Ⓐ	Ⓑ	Ⓒ					
86.	Ⓐ	Ⓑ	Ⓒ					
87.	Ⓐ	Ⓑ	Ⓒ					
88.	Ⓐ	Ⓑ	Ⓒ					
89.	Ⓐ	Ⓑ	Ⓒ					
90.	Ⓐ	Ⓑ	Ⓒ					
91.	Ⓐ	Ⓑ	Ⓒ					
92.	Ⓐ	Ⓑ	Ⓒ					
93.	Ⓐ	Ⓑ	Ⓒ					
94.	Ⓐ	Ⓑ	Ⓒ					
95.	Ⓐ	Ⓑ	Ⓒ					
96.	Ⓐ	Ⓑ	Ⓒ					
97.	Ⓐ	Ⓑ	Ⓒ					
98.	Ⓐ	Ⓑ	Ⓒ					
99.	Ⓐ	Ⓑ	Ⓒ					
100.	Ⓐ	Ⓑ	Ⓒ					

Exam 1
Afternoon Session

Questions 61–66 relate to Mike Zonding.

Mike Zonding, CFA, is conducting a background check on CFA candidate Annie Cooken, a freshly minted MBA who applied for a stock-analysis job at his firm, Khasko Financial. Zonding does not like to hire anyone who does not adhere to the Code and Standards' professional conduct requirements.

The background check reveals the following:

(i)   While doing a full-time, unpaid internship at Kale Investments, Cooken was reprimanded for working a 30-hour-a-week night job as a waitress.

(ii)   As an intern at Lammar Corp., Cooken was fired after revealing to the FBI that one of the principals was embezzling from the firm's clients.

(iii) Cooken performed 40 hours of community service in relation to a conviction on a misdemeanor drug possession charge when she was 16 years old.

(iv)   On her resume, Cooken writes, "Recently passed Level II of the CFA exam, a test that measures candidates' knowledge of finance and investing."

During the interview, Zonding asks Cooken several questions on ethics-related issues, including questions about the role of a fiduciary and Standard III(E) Preservation of Confidentiality. He asks her about her internship at Kale Investments, specifically about the working hours. Cooken replies that the internship turned out to require more time than she originally planned, up to 65 hours per week.

Zonding subsequently hires Cooken and functions as her supervisor. On her third day at the money management boutique firm, portfolio manager Steven Clarrison hands her a report on Mocline Tobacco and tells her to revise the report to reflect a buy rating. Cooken is uncomfortable about revising the report.

To supplement the meager income from her entry-level stock-analysis job, Cooken looks for part-time work. She is offered a position working three hours each Friday and Saturday night tending bar at a sports bar and grill downtown. Cooken does not tell her employer about the job.

During her first week, Cooken has lunch with former MBA classmates, including Taira Basch, CFA, who works for the compliance officer at a large investment bank in town. Basch arrives late, explaining, "What a day, it's only noon and already I have worked on the following requests:

1. A federal regulator called and wanted information on potentially illegal activities related to one of the firm's key clients.

2. A rival company's employee wanted information regarding employment opportunities at the firm.

3. A potential client contacted an employee and wanted detailed performance records of client accounts so he can decide whether to invest with the firm."

Basch goes on to say that she is responsible for developing a presentation on the differences between the Prudent Investor and the Prudent Man rules for managing trust portfolios. Basch explains to Cooken that the Prudent Investor rule requires a trustee to exercise five fiduciary standards in managing the assets of a trust account, including care, skill, caution, loyalty, and impartiality. She states that although there are many differences between the Prudent Man and the newer Prudent Investor rule, one element of continuity is the duty of the trustee to delegate investment authority in the event that the trustee lacks sufficient investment knowledge.

Toward the end of the lunch meeting, Basch suggests that in exchange for research published by Cooken and Khasko, Basch can have portfolio managers at her firm send clients that are too small for their firm to Khasko. Since Khasko specializes in clients with smaller portfolios, the arrangement sounds like a good idea to Cooken. Cooken tells Basch that she will think the arrangement over and get back with her next week with a decision.

61. In the context of the Code and Standards, which of the items from the background check would *most likely* indicate that Zonding should not have hired Cooken?
    A. Item i.
    B. Item ii.
    C. Item iii.

62. Which of the following statements provides the *least appropriate* justification for Cooken's caution about revising the report on Mocline Tobacco?
    A. Cooken knows next to nothing about Mocline stock.
    B. Cooken's uncle, George Whates, is the CFO of Mocline.
    C. In college, Cooken worked for Mocline but never declared the income on her taxes.

 ©2011 Kaplan, Inc.

63. By not telling Zonding about the bartending position, Cooken has *most likely* violated:
    A. no Standards.
    B. Standard IV(B) Additional Compensation Arrangements.
    C. Standard IV(A) Loyalty (to employer) and Standard IV(B) Additional Compensation Arrangements.

64. Which of the requests, if fulfilled, is *most likely* to place Basch in violation of Standard III(E) Preservation of Confidentiality?
    A. Request 1.
    B. Request 2.
    C. Request 3.

65. Is Basch correct or incorrect with regard to her statement about the five required fiduciary standards and her statement about the duty to delegate investment authority?
    A. Incorrect about fiduciary standards only.
    B. Incorrect about delegation of authority only.
    C. Incorrect about fiduciary standards and delegation of authority.

66. According to CFA Institute Standards of Professional Conduct, which of the following statements is *most accurate* with regard to the arrangement proposed by Basch to Cooken?
    A. Under no circumstances may Cooken agree to the arrangement as proposed by Basch.
    B. Cooken may agree to the arrangement only if it is disclosed to her employer, clients, and prospects.
    C. Cooken may agree to the arrangement but need only make appropriate disclosure to prospective clients.

Questions 67–72 relate to Mary Montpier.

Mary Montpier is an equity analyst with World Renowned Advisors. The firm provides investment advice and financial planning services globally to institutional and retail clients. Shortly after the company opened an office in Malaysia, Montpier's supervisor in the New York office, Rick Reynolds, asked her to relocate, and Montpier agreed. The goal of the new Malaysian office is to serve as a source of international investment opportunities for U.S. clients. Montpier's main task is to cover small-cap stocks in the region and develop a network of contacts with other investment firms in the region.

Through her interaction with other analysts in Malaysia, Montpier learns that the use of material nonpublic information is common practice in analyst research reports and recommendations. Such practice is not prohibited by law in Malaysia. Montpier is encouraged by this knowledge because she recently observed several investment bankers meeting numerous times at an exclusive local country club with the CEOs of two Malaysian rival companies. It is public information that one of the companies is searching for potential acquisition targets. She has thought several times about issuing a recommendation on one of the companies but has not done so for fear of breaking the law. After learning of the Malaysian insider trading laws, Montpier recommends the stock of the acquisition target, which she had already established as a good investment through prior research.

Montpier has also learned that Malaysian law is very lax regarding outside consulting arrangements by investment professionals. It is common for analysts and portfolio managers to maintain ongoing consulting contracts with entities other than their primary employer. As a result of this, Montpier has begun financial service consultations for members of a local investment club. The club is developing an appropriate compensation package for her services, which to date have included financial planning activities and investment research. When Montpier established the relationship with the investment club, she informed them that she had a full-time job at World Renowned Advisers, which offers similar services. After a year of consulting with the investment club, Malaysian law changed, requiring investment bankers, securities analysts, and portfolio managers to register with the Malaysian Securities Commission in order to engage in independent consulting practice. Since she is unaware of the change, Montpier does not file the proper registration forms and is later investigated, fined, and temporarily sanctioned by the Malaysian Securities Commission. Montpier is able to have the sanction, but not the fine, removed after appealing the Commission's ruling.

Montpier's counterpart in the New York office is Jim Taylor, who has worked as an analyst at World Renowned Advisors for approximately seven years. Taylor researches health care and biotech stocks for the firm and participates in client meetings when managers are recommending stocks that Taylor

©2011 Kaplan, Inc.

covers. Taylor recently completed Level I of the CFA examination and is waiting for his results so he can register for the Level II examination.

In preparation for a client meeting, Taylor's supervisor, Jessica James, asks him to prepare a research report on attractive companies in the health care industry. Since Taylor is busy preparing for company conference calls, James tells him to "throw something together from the street." To meet James' request, Taylor obtains reports on Immune Healthcare and Remedy Corp., two companies that he has heard about but has not researched. Taylor takes the original reports he obtains from a third-party, adds some general industry information, and submits "strong buy" recommendations to James for the stocks. He does not credit the original authors in the report, which is a violation of copyright law. Taylor includes his qualifications in the report and mentions that he is a "Level II Candidate in the CFA Program." Although written procedures require James to review all analyst reports prior to release, time constraints often prevent her from reviewing the reports prior to distribution. James recommends the stocks to her clients, who then purchase them. Several months later, the clients are able to sell the Immune Healthcare and Remedy Corp. shares at annualized rates of return of 21% and 17%, respectively. James informs Taylor of the clients' successful investments and requests that he begin investigating potential biotech investments for the same group of investors.

To gain insight on biotech stocks, Taylor registers for an upcoming medical study, where he and others will be the subject of testing for the efficacy of several new drugs. On his application, Taylor indicates that he has the appropriate medical condition for the study and signs a confidentiality agreement, but he leaves the question about his occupation blank. During the study, Taylor learns that two of the new drugs on which Next Breakthrough Corp. is awaiting regulatory approval have serious negative side effects in patient testing. This information confirms existing research that Taylor has been working on in the health care sector. At the conclusion of the study, Taylor sends an e-mail to his clients recommending that they "sell" Next Breakthrough Corp. Over the next two weeks, Next Breakthrough releases information that the drugs in question have been held up by a regulatory agency pending additional investigation. The stock plunges over 30% on the news.

67. Has Montpier *likely* violated any CFA Standards of Professional Conduct by recommending the stock of the acquisition target company?
    A. Yes.
    B. No, because she has already researched the company and deemed it a good investment.
    C. No, because she is recommending the stock based on information assembled under the mosaic theory.

68. By not filing the proper registration forms with the Malaysian Securities Commission, did Montpier *likely* violate any CFA Institute Standards of Professional Conduct?
    A. Yes. Montpier attempted to deceive the Malaysian Securities Commission, which violates the Standards.
    B. No. Montpier's sanction was later removed, indicating the Commission did not hold her responsible for the oversight.
    C. Yes. Montpier should have regularly updated her knowledge about local laws and by not doing so violated the Standards.

69. In providing financial planning and investment research services to the investment club, has Montpier *likely* violated any CFA Institute Standards of Professional Conduct?
    A. Yes. She has not received consent from her employer to all of the terms of the arrangement.
    B. Yes. She has not received verbal approval from her employer and written approval from her financial service client.
    C. No. She has not yet received any compensation for her consulting services and has informed her financial service client of her firm and its services.

70. In referencing his participation in the CFA program, has Taylor *likely* violated any CFA Institute Standards of Professional Conduct?
    A. No, since he did not imply superior investment ability as a result of his candidacy.
    B. Yes, since he must refer to himself as a Level I candidate, not a Level II candidate.
    C. No, since he appropriately referenced his candidacy and did not imply a partial designation.

71. In creating his report on Immune Healthcare and Remedy Corp., Taylor *likely* violated the CFA Institute Standards of Professional Conduct for all of the following reasons *except* that he failed to:
    A. give proper credit to the sources of information used in his report.
    B. establish a reasonable and adequate basis for his recommendation.
    C. determine the suitability of the investment for his firm's clients.

72. By using the information obtained as a result of participating in the drug study, did Taylor *likely* violate any CFA Institute Standards of Professional Conduct?
    A. Yes.
    B. No. By participating in the study, Taylor had permission to use the information for the benefit of his clients.
    C. No. The information received supplemented Taylor's existing research and was non-material, nonpublic information.

 ©2011 Kaplan, Inc.

Questions 73–78 relate to Trailblazer, Inc.

Louise Valentine, CFA, is analyzing the financial information of Trailblazer, Inc., a company in the retail sector. She is preparing to write a report on her findings. Valentine is considering various valuation approaches and is convinced that a dividend discount model (DDM) would be among the best choices in this case. She notes that Trailblazer does not vary its dividend payments significantly from year to year.

In preparing to estimate a suitable required rate of return on equity for Trailblazer, Valentine notes that the current T-bill rate is 3.5% and that the yield on the company's 10-year bonds is 7.25%. Additionally, Valentine estimates that the appropriate equity risk premium in excess of the company's cost of debt is 3%.

Valentine also gathers the information shown in Exhibit 1.

Exhibit 1: Trailblazer, Inc. Multifactor Sensitivities (APT)

Factor	Factor Risk Premium	Trailblazer, Inc. Factor Sensitivities
1	1.91%	0.81
2	1.22%	−0.45
3	3.47%	0.24
4	4.15%	0.74

Valentine notes that a share of Trailblazer's stock is currently priced at $32. Moreover, she expects the dividend for next year to be $1.47 and forecasts that the price of one share of Trailblazer stock at the end of the year will be $35.

In her report, Valentine makes the following statements about Trailblazer dividends:

Statement 1:   Trailblazer is expected to pay a dividend next year and will continue to do so for the foreseeable future.

Statement 2:   The required rate of return for Trailblazer stock will likely exceed the growth rate of its dividends.

Statement 3:   Trailblazer is in a mature sector of its industry, and accordingly, I expect dividends to decline to a constant rate of 4% indefinitely.

In speaking to a colleague at her firm, Valentine makes the following additional statements after her report is released:

Statement 4:   Trailblazer has a 10-year history of paying regular quarterly dividends.

Statement 5:   Over a recent 10-year period, Trailblazer has experienced one 3-year period of consecutive losses and another period of two annual losses in a row but has been extremely profitable in the remaining five years.

Valentine is concerned about the theoretical validity of using the APT to obtain an estimate of the required rate of return on equity. She decides to attend a conference dealing specifically with estimation techniques that analysts can employ. At one of the conference seminars, the following points are made:

Statement 6:   The APT is a better approach than the CAPM because even though the factor risk premiums are difficult to estimate, the CAPM is more problematic because it relies on a single market risk premium estimate, which in turn leads to greater input uncertainty.

Statement 7:   Model uncertainty is a problem with the APT but not with the CAPM.

Valentine is also analyzing the stock of Farwell, Inc. Farwell shares are currently trading at $48 based on current earnings of $4 and a current dividend of $2.60. Dividends are expected to grow at 5% per year indefinitely. The risk-free rate is 3.5%, the market risk premium is 4.5%, and Farwell's beta is estimated to be 1.2.

73.   Based on the APT model and the bond yield plus risk-premium (BYPRP) method, the discount rate Valentine should use in valuing the equity of Trailblazer is *closest* to:

Rate based on APT	Rate based on BYPRP
A. 8.40%	10.25%
B. 4.90%	10.25%
C. 8.40%	7.25%

74.   The expected holding period return over the next year is *closest* to:
A. 13.45%.
B. 13.97%.
C. 14.59%.

                    ©2011 Kaplan, Inc.

75. How many of the first three statements Valentine made concerning Trailblazer's dividends are consistent with assumptions of the Gordon growth model (GGM)?
    A. None.
    B. Two.
    C. Three.

76. Do statements 4 and 5 support the decision by Valentine to use a dividend discount model?
    A. Both statements support the use of DDM.
    B. Only Statement 4 supports the use of DDM.
    C. Only Statement 5 supports the use of DDM.

77. Are statements 6 and 7 correct?
    A. Both statements are incorrect.
    B. Only Statement 6 is incorrect.
    C. Only Statement 7 is incorrect.

78. The justified leading and justified trailing P/E ratios of Farwell are *closest* to:

	Justified leading P/E	Justified trailing P/E
A.	16.67	9.42
B.	8.97	17.50
C.	16.67	17.50

Questions 79–84 relate to Tom Vadney.

Tom Vadney, CFA, is president and CEO of Vadney Research and Advisors (VRA), a large equity research firm that specializes in providing international investment and advisory services to global portfolio managers. He has a staff of five junior analysts and three senior analysts covering industries and firms across the Americas, Europe, and Asia-Pacific regions.

In a recent meeting with an institutional portfolio manager, Vadney is asked to review the differences between U.S. GAAP and International Financial Reporting Standards (IFRS) as well as provide a comprehensive industry analysis for the telecommunications sector in Europe and the Asia-Pacific region. Vadney asks Maria Mnoyan, a senior analyst covering the sector, to research the requested information for the client meeting.

Prior to the meeting, Vadney and Mnoyan meet to prepare for the client presentation. They first discuss differences between U.S. GAAP and IFRS. Mnoyan states that although there will be increasing convergence between the two accounting standards, one major difference currently is that IFRS permits either the "partial goodwill" or "full goodwill" method to value the goodwill and the noncontrolling interest under the acquisition method. U.S. GAAP requires the full goodwill method. Vadney adds that U.S. GAAP requires equity method accounting for joint ventures, while under IFRS, proportionate consolidation is preferred, but the equity method is permitted.

Vadney then asks Mnoyan to share her findings on the telecommunications sector. Mnoyan first presents an overview of the competitive forces that characterize the sector in the two regions. In particular, she notes that the sector in both regions is characterized by high switching costs. Vadney asks how high switching costs would affect the bargaining power of buyers and suppliers.

Mnoyan firmly believes that investing in companies located in developing countries provides strong growth potential through technological change and increases in capital, labor, and savings that contribute to higher dividend levels, even if the dividend growth rate is unaffected.

Jimmy Telga is one of the junior analysts working for VRA and is responsible for emerging market equities. Vadney discusses Mnoyan's findings with Telga. Telga states that high inflation complicates valuation in emerging markets. Telga makes the following statements about high inflation's impact on emerging market equity valuations.

©2011 Kaplan, Inc.

Statement 1: Multiples such as P/E ratios and EV/EBITDA would be overstated compared to developed market multiples.

Statement 2: Turnover ratios, return on invested capital, and leverage ratios (Debt/Assets) would be overstated.

Statement 3: To account for country risk, free cash flow to firm valuation models may be adjusted by using a higher discount rate that adds country risk premium to the required return on equity.

79. Are Mnoyan and Vadney correct about differences between U.S. GAAP and IFRS?
    A. Both are correct.
    B. Only Mnoyan is correct.
    C. Only Vadney is correct.

80. Mnoyan's *best* response to Vadney on how high switching costs affect the bargaining power of buyers and suppliers, respectively, should be:
    A. only the bargaining power of buyers will decrease.
    B. only the bargaining power of suppliers will decrease.
    C. the bargaining power of buyers and suppliers will decrease.

81. Mnoyan's description of the growth potential of developing countries is *best* described through the:
    A. new growth theory.
    B. neoclassical growth theory.
    C. multifactor model theory.

82. Telga's Statement 1 is *most likely*:
    A. correct.
    B. incorrect about P/E multiples but correct about EV/EBITDA multiples.
    C. incorrect about both P/E multiples and EV/EBITDA multiples.

83. Telga's Statement 2 is *most likely*:
    A. correct.
    B. incorrect about leverage ratios but correct about turnover ratios and return on invested capital.
    C. incorrect about return on invested capital but correct about turnover and leverage ratios.

84. Telga's Statement 3 is *most likely*:
    A. correct.
    B. incorrect about adding a country risk premium to the required return on equity.
    C. incorrect about a higher discount rate.

Questions 85–90 related to High Plains Tubular.

High Plains Tubular Company is a leading manufacturer and distributor of quality steel products used in energy, industrial, and automotive applications worldwide.

The U.S. steel industry has been challenged by competition from foreign producers located primarily in Asia. All of the U.S. producers are experiencing declining margins as labor costs continue to increase. In addition, the U.S. steel mills are technologically inferior to the foreign competitors. Also, the U.S. producers have significant environmental issues that remain unresolved.

High Plains is not immune from the problems of the industry and is currently in technical default under its bond covenants. The default is a result of the failure to meet certain coverage and turnover ratios. Earlier this year, High Plains and its bondholders entered into an agreement that will allow High Plains time to become compliant with the covenants. If High Plains is not in compliance by year end, the bondholders can immediately accelerate the maturity date of the bonds. In this case, High Plains would have no choice but to file bankruptcy.

High Plains follows U.S. GAAP. For the year ended 2008, High Plains received an unqualified opinion from its independent auditor. However, the auditor's opinion included an explanatory paragraph about High Plains' inability to continue as a going concern in the event its bonds remain in technical default.

At the end of 2008, High Plains' Chief Executive Officer (CEO) and Chief Financial Officer (CFO) filed the necessary certifications required by the Securities and Exchange Commission (SEC).

To get a better understanding of High Plains' financial situation, it is helpful to review High Plains' cash flow statement found in Exhibit 1 and selected financial footnotes found in Exhibit 2.

©2011 Kaplan, Inc.

Exhibit 1: Cash Flow Statement

High Plains Tubular Cash Flow Statement

in thousands	Year ended December 31,	
	2008	**2007**
Net income	$158,177	$121,164
Depreciation expense	34,078	31,295
Deferred taxes	7,697	11,407
Receivables	(144,087)	(24,852)
Inventory	(79,710)	(72,777)
Payables	36,107	22,455
Cash flow from operations	$12,262	$88,692
Cash flow from investing	($39,884)	($63,953)
Cash flow from financing	$82,676	$6,056
Change in cash	$55,054	$30,795

Exhibit 2: Selected Financial Footnotes

1. During 2008, High Plains' sales increased 27% over 2007. Its sales growth continues to significantly exceed the industry average. Sales are recognized when a firm order is received from the customer, the sales price is fixed and determinable, and collectability is reasonably assured.

2. The cost of inventories is determined using the last-in, first-out (LIFO) method. Had the first-in, first-out method been used, inventories would have been $152 million and $143 million higher as of December 31, 2008 and 2007, respectively.

3. Effective January 1, 2008, High Plains changed its depreciation method from the double-declining balance method to the straight-line method in order to be more comparable with the accounting practices of other firms within its industry. The change was not retroactively applied and only affects assets that were acquired on or after January 1, 2008.

4. High Plains made the following discretionary expenditures for maintenance and repair of plant and equipment and for advertising and marketing:

in millions	2008	2007	2006
Maintenance and repairs	$180	$184	$218
Advertising and marketing	94	108	150

5. During the fiscal year ended December 31, 2008, High Plains sold $50 million of its accounts receivable, with recourse, to an unrelated entity. All of the receivables were still outstanding at year end.

6. High Plains conducts some of its operations in facilities leased under noncancelable finance (capital) leases. Certain leases include renewal options with provisions for increased lease payments during the renewal term.

7. High Plains' average net operating assets at the end of 2008 and 2007 was $977.89 million and $642.83 million, respectively.

85. Which of the following is *least likely* to prevent earnings manipulation?
    A. The independent audit.
    B. SEC certification filed by High Plains' CEO and CFO.
    C. High Plains' bond covenants.

86. What is the *most likely* effect of High Plains' revenue recognition policy on net income and inventory turnover?
    A. Net income and inventory turnover are overstated.
    B. Only net income is overstated.
    C. Only inventory turnover is overstated.

87. As compared to the year ended 2007, High Plains' cash flow accrual ratio for the year ended 2008 is:
    A. higher.
    B. lower.
    C. the same.

88. Using only the information found in Exhibit 1 and Exhibit 2, which of the following is *most* indicative of lower earnings quality?
    A. High Plains' discretionary expenses.
    B. The change in High Plains' depreciation method.
    C. High Plains' inventory cost flow assumption.

89. Does High Plains' accounting treatment of its finance (capital) leases and receivable sale lower its earnings quality?
    A. Both treatments lower earnings quality.
    B. The treatment of finance (capital) leases lowers earnings quality.
    C. The treatment of the receivables sale lowers earnings quality.

©2011 Kaplan, Inc.

90. Which of the following statements about evaluating High Plains' financial reporting quality is *least* accurate?
    A. Higher Plains may have manipulated earnings due to the risk of default.
    B. High Plains' extreme revenue growth will likely revert back to normal levels over time.
    C. Because of the estimates involved, a higher weighting should be assigned to the accrual component of High Plains' earnings as compared to the cash component.

Questions 91–96 relate to Stanley Bostwick.

Stanley Bostwick, CFA, is a business services industry analyst with Mortonworld Financial. Currently, his attention is focused on the 2008 financial statements of Global Oilfield Supply, particularly the footnote disclosures related to the company's employee benefit plans. Bostwick would like to adjust the financial statements to reflect the actual economic status of the pension plans and analyze the effect on the reported results of changes in assumptions the company used to estimate the projected benefit obligation (PBO) and net pension cost. But first, Bostwick must familiarize himself with the differences in the accounting for defined contribution and defined benefit pension plans.

Global Oilfield's financial statements are prepared in accordance with International Financial Reporting Standards (IFRS). Excerpts from the company's annual report are shown in the following exhibits.

Exhibit 1: Reconciliation of Projected Benefit Obligation

(in thousands)	2008	2007	2006
Change in projected benefit obligation:			
Benefit obligation at beginning of year	€64,230	€50,534	€39,132
Service cost	8,298	7,290	5,926
Interest cost	4,128	3,906	3,322
Actuarial loss (gain)	(1,932)	5,034	4,590
Benefits paid	(3,824)	(2,534)	(2,436)
Projected benefit obligation at end of year	€70,900	€64,230	€50,534

©2011 Kaplan, Inc.

Exhibit 2: Reconciliation of Fair Value of Plan Assets

(in thousands)	2008	2007	2006
Change in plan assets:			
Fair value of plan assets at beginning of year	€65,164	€44,296	€35,796
Actual return on plan assets	7,084	9,916	(1,868)
Employer contributions	5,000	13,486	12,804
Benefits paid	(3,824)	(2,534)	(2,436)
Fair value of plan assets at end of year	€73,424	€65,164	€44,296

Exhibit 3: Reconciliation of Funded Status and Prepaid Benefit Cost

(in thousands)	2008	2007	2006
Funded status at December 31:	€2,524	€934	(€6,238)
Unrecognized transition asset	–	(76)	(224)
Unrecognized prior service cost	126	88	2
Unrecognized net actuarial loss	4,572	8,980	11,496
Net pension asset	€7,222	€9,926	€5,036

Exhibit 4: Components of Pension Cost

(in thousands)	2008	2007	2006
Service cost	€8,298	€7,290	€5,926
Interest cost	4,128	3,906	3,322
Expected return on plan assets	(4,608)	(3,086)	(2,886)
Amortization of past service cost	(38)	(88)	(88)
Amortization of transition asset	(76)	(148)	(148)
Recognized net actuarial gain	–	724	212
Net pension cost	€7,704	€8,598	€6,338

Exhibit 5: Weighted Average Pension Assumptions

	2008	**2007**	**2006**
Discount rate	6.75%	6.25%	6.75%
Rate of compensation growth	5.00%	5.00%	5.00%
Expected return on plan assets	7.50%	7.50%	9.00%

91. If Global Oilfield's retirement plan is a defined contribution arrangement, which of the following statements would be the *most* correct?
    A. Pension expense and the cash funding amount would be the same.
    B. The potential gains or losses from the assets contributed to the plan are borne by the firm.
    C. The firm would report the difference in the accumulated benefit obligation and the pension assets on the balance sheet.

92. If Global Oilfield were to adopt U.S. pension accounting standards, what adjustment, if any, is necessary to its balance sheet at the end of 2008 assuming no taxes?
    A. Decrease assets by €7,222, decrease liabilities €2,524, and decrease equity by $4,698.
    B   Decrease assets by €4,698 and decrease equity by €4,698.
    C. No adjustment is necessary.

93. What was the *most likely* cause of the actuarial gain reported in the reconciliation of the projected benefit obligation for the year ended 2008?
    A. Increase in the average life expectancy of the participating employees.
    B. Decrease in the expected rate of return.
    C. Increase in the discount rate.

94. Which of the following *best* describes the effects of a decrease in the rate of compensation growth during 2009 all else equal? Global Oilfield's:
    A. service cost is lower and the accumulated benefit obligation is higher.
    B. pension expense is lower and the plan assets are higher.
    C. net income is higher and the funded status is higher.

95. As compared to Global Oilfield's reported pension expense, economic pension expense for the year ended 2008 is:
    A. higher.
    B. lower.
    C. the same.

©2011 Kaplan, Inc.

96. Assume for this question only that economic pension expense for the year ended 2008 was €4,250. Ignoring income taxes, which of the following statements *best* describes the adjustment necessary for analyzing Global Oilfield's cash flow statement?
    A. Increase operating cash flow €750 and decrease financing cash flow €750.
    B. Decrease operating cash flow €2,084 and increase investing cash flow €2,084.
    C. Increase operating cash flow €5,000 and decrease financing cash flow €5,000.

Questions 97–102 relate to Valley Airlines.

Jason Bennett is an analyst for Valley Airlines (Valley), a U.S. firm. Valley owns a stake in Southwest Air Cargo (Southwest), also a U.S. firm. The two firms have had a long-standing relationship. The relationship has become even closer because several of Valley's top executives hold seats on Southwest's Board of Directors.

Valley acquired a 45% ownership stake in Southwest on December 31, 2007. Acquisition of the ownership stake cost $9 million and was paid in cash. Valley's stake in Southwest is such that management can account for the investment using either the equity method or the acquisition method. While Valley's management desires to fairly represent the firm's operating results, they have assigned Bennett to assess the impact of each method on reported financial statements.

Immediately prior to the acquisition, Valley's current asset balance and total equity were $96 million and $80 million, respectively. Southwest's current assets and total equity were $32 million and $16 million, respectively.

While analyzing the use of the equity method versus the acquisition method, Bennett calculates the return on assets (ROA) ratio. He arrives at two conclusions:

Statement 1:   Compared to the acquisition method, the equity method results in a higher ROA because of the higher net income under the equity method.

Statement 2:   Compared to the acquisition method, the equity method results in a higher ROA because of the smaller level of total assets under the equity method.

In order to get a better picture of Valley's operating condition, Bennett is also considering the use of proportionate consolidation to account for Southwest. He makes the following statements regarding the acquisition method and a proportionate consolidation:

Statement 3:   Both methods are widely accepted under the provisions of U.S. GAAP and International Financial Reporting Standards (IFRS).

Statement 4:   Both methods report the same level of assets on the parent's balance sheet.

Statement 5:   Both methods report all of Southwest's liabilities on the parent's balance sheet.

In addition, Valley has always wanted to pursue its goal of vertical integration by expanding its scope of operations to include the manufacturing of airline

©2011 Kaplan, Inc.

parts for its own airplanes. Therefore, it established a subsidiary, Mountain Air Parts (Mountain), in Switzerland on January 1, 2008. Switzerland was chosen as the location for economic and geographical diversification reasons. Mountain will operate as a self-contained, independent subsidiary. Local management in Switzerland will make the majority of operating, financing, and investing decisions.

The Swiss franc (CHF) is the official currency in Switzerland. On January 1, 2008, the USD/CHF exchange rate was 0.77. At December 31, 2008, the exchange rate had changed to 0.85 USD/CHF. The average exchange rate in 2008 was 0.80 USD/CHF. In its first year of operations, Mountain paid no dividends and no taxes. Mountain uses the FIFO assumption for its flow of inventory.

Mountain Air Parts
Balance Sheet

(in CHF thousands)	12/31/2008	1/1/2008
Assets		
Cash and accounts receivable	600	400
Inventory	500	500
Property, plant, and equipment	600	700
Total assets	1,700	1,600
Liabilities and equity		
Accounts payable	200	100
Long-term debt	100	200
Common stock	1,300	1,300
Retained earnings	100	0
Total liabilities and owner's equity	1,700	1,600

Mountain Air Parts
Income Statement for 2008

(in CHF thousands)	
Sales	7,000
COGS	(6,800)
Depreciation	(100)
Net income	100

97. The balance of Valley's current assets as of December 31, 2007, using the acquisition method, is *closest* to:
    A. $87 million.
    B. $119 million.
    C. $128 million.

98. Are Bennett's Statements 1 and 2 regarding ROA correct?

	Statement 1	Statement 2
A.	Yes	Yes
B.	Yes	No
C.	No	Yes

99. How many of Bennett's statements on proportionate consolidation are correct?
   A. None.
   B. Two.
   C. Three.

100. Using the appropriate method of translation, the amount of total assets reported on Mountain's balance sheet at the end of 2008 is *closest* to:
   A. $1,325.
   B. $1,375.
   C. $1,445.

101. Using the appropriate method of translation, the translation gain (loss) for the year ended 2008 is *closest* to:
   A. $99.
   B. $104.
   C. $109.

102. For this question only, assume that Mountain is operating in a highly inflationary environment. Which of the following statements is *least* correct? Mountain's:
   A. nonmonetary assets and nonmonetary liabilities are adjusted for inflation in accordance with U.S. GAAP.
   B. functional currency is the U.S. dollar.
   C. financial statements are adjusted for inflation, and the net purchasing power gain or loss is recognized in the income statement in accordance with IFRS.

©2011 Kaplan, Inc.

Questions 103–108 relate to Alertron.

Alertron is a pharmaceutical company with approximately $3.5 billion in annual sales that specializes in the development, manufacturing, and marketing of neurology and oncology drug therapies. The firm is seeking to achieve more rapid growth, and Alertron's executive management team feels that the company can grow faster by making acquisitions than it can by trying to grow organically. As a result, management asks the firm's Director of Strategic Planning, Kanna Ozer, CFA, to analyze potential alternatives. At Alertron's next executive management team meeting, Ozer presents the report shown in Exhibit 1 concerning four potential acquisition targets:

Exhibit 1: Report 1—Description of Potential Acquisition Targets

Potential Target	Potential Acquisition Description
BriscoePharm	Firm develops, manufactures, and markets prescription drugs for humans and animals. BriscoePharm has annual sales of $1.2 million, but only certain BriscoePharm drugs are attractive cash flow generators.
Carideo	Firm develops and manufactures oncology and neurology drugs in the United States and abroad. Carideo has annual sales of $1.2 million, and all assets and liabilities would likely be absorbed by Alertron in a potential merger.
Dillon Biotech	Firm designs and manufactures analytical instruments used in drug development. Dillon has $3.5 billion in annual sales. A successful acquisition by Alertron would involve combining operations and forming a new company.
Escarigen	Firm is a pharmaceutical company specializing in cardiology medications. Escarigen is well known among heart surgeons and has a blockbuster cholesterol drug called Karlynivus that is well known in the medical community. In an acquisition, Alertron would want to maintain the successful Escarigen brand and operational structure.

Alertron's executive team agrees that the report is helpful for initiating discussion but decides they need more information concerning the form of each potential acquisition and the most appropriate method of payment. Alertron's management is also concerned whether each potential target would view a takeover attempt as friendly or hostile. Paul Mussara, Alertron's CEO, asks Ozer to prepare a second report that specifically describes the transaction characteristics corresponding to each deal. Ozer's second report is shown in Exhibit 2.

Exhibit 2: Report 2—Merger Transaction Characteristics

Potential Target	Optimal Form of Acquisition	Method of Payment	Likely Attitude of Target Management
BriscoePharm	Asset purchase involving 30% of BriscoePharm's assets ~~50%~~	Cash offering	View offer as friendly
Carideo	Stock purchase	Securities offering	View offer as friendly
Dillon Biotech	Stock purchase	Mixed cash and securities offering	View offer as hostile
Escarigen	Stock purchase	Cash offering	View offer as friendly

As Alertron was conducting its analysis, Bhavik Kumar, CEO of Dillon Biotech, hears rumors that Alertron may attempt a hostile takeover of his firm. Kumar calls an emergency meeting with Dillon's four executive vice presidents and expresses his concern that Alertron may attempt a bear hug by submitting a merger proposal directly to the board without informing Dillon's management. Kumar concludes the emergency meeting by asking each executive vice president to brainstorm defense mechanisms that Dillon could employ before a takeover attempt is made and also defenses that could be employed after a hostile takeover offer.

After intense discussions, Alertron decides that a takeover offer for Carideo would be most beneficial due to the net present value of cost reduction synergies of $600 million that Ozer estimates would result from the merger. Mussara asks Ozer to evaluate the deal based on a stock offer in which Alertron would exchange 0.75 shares of Alertron stock for each outstanding share of Carideo stock. Ozer compiles the information shown in Exhibit 3 for her analysis.

Exhibit 3: Merger Evaluation Inputs

	Alertron	Carideo
Pre-merger stock price	$60	$39
Number of shares outstanding (millions)	150	80
Pre-merger market value (millions)	$9,000	$3,120
Estimated NPV of Cost Reduction Synergies	$600 million	

©2011 Kaplan, Inc.

Ozer, and the rest of the executive management team at Alertron, is extremely confident in the $600 million dollar estimate of cost reduction synergies that are likely to result from the merger and feel that the estimate may actually be conservative. However, when analysts at Carideo review the figures, they have a much different opinion and are less certain that $600 million worth of synergies could be realized. While Carideo believes the net present value of synergies from the deal would still be positive, its estimates are much lower than Alertron's.

Carideo's management is also concerned that a merger between Alertron and Carideo could face scrutiny from regulators. Although neither firm is the largest in the pharmaceutical industry, their combined market power could raise antitrust concerns. Phillip Wu, an analyst with Carideo, compiles the following table showing the market share of each of the 12 firms in the pharmaceutical industry to determine whether the concerns were valid. Both Alertron's and Carideo's management teams decide that if regulators are unlikely to challenge the deal, they will proceed with the necessary steps to complete the merger.

Exhibit 4: Market Share of Firms in the Pharmaceutical Industry

Firm Name	Market Share in Pharmaceutical Industry
Munnzer Pharmaceuticals	20%
Spencer Corp.	18%
Alertron	15%
Escarigen	12%
Carideo	10%
Faltysgen	7%
Six other firms	Each have 3% market share

103. Based on Ozer's description of potential acquisition targets, which form of integration and type of merger would *best* describe the transaction if Alertron tried to acquire Escarigen?

	Form of integration	Type of merger
A.	Statutory	Horizontal
B.	Subsidiary	Horizontal
C.	Subsidiary	Vertical

104. Based on the information in Exhibit 2, which of the following statements concerning the transaction characteristics of the potential mergers with Alertron is *most accurate*?
    A. Purchasing Escarigen is likely to reduce Alertron's financial leverage.
    B. Carideo would likely avoid paying corporate taxes in the potential deal with Alertron.
    C. BriscoePharm's shareholders would likely be required to approve the deal with Alertron before any proposed deal is completed.

105. Which of the following *best* satisfies Kumar's request to identify a pair of defense mechanisms that consist of a pre-offer and a post-offer defense?

Pre-offer defense mechanism	Post-offer defense mechanism
A. Poison put	Fair price amendment
B. Greenmail	Restricted voting rights
C. Supermajority voting provision	Leveraged recapitalization

106. Using Ozer's estimates of the cost reduction synergies, the gain that would accrue to Carideo's shareholders as a result of the merger with Alertron is *closest* to:
    A. $108.5 million.
    B. $455.6 million.
    C. $514.2 million.

107. Based on each firm's forecasts of the estimated NPV of synergies from a merger between Alertron and Carideo, what payment method is each firm *likely* to prefer in the deal?
    A. Both firms prefer a cash deal.
    B. Only Alertron prefers a cash deal.
    C. Only Carideo prefers a cash deal.

108. What would be the increase in the Herfindahl-Hirschman Index (HHI) as a result of a merger between Alertron and Carideo, and the *most likely* reaction by regulators to the merger?

Increase in the HHI	Probable response by regulators
A. 75	No antitrust challenge
B. 300	No antitrust challenge
C. 300	Potential antitrust challenge

©2011 Kaplan, Inc.

Questions 109–114 relate to Nigel Holmes.

Nigel Holmes, CFA, is an investment manager for a small money management firm in London. All of Holmes' clients are citizens of the U.K. Holmes urges all of his clients to maintain internationally diversified portfolios. In his efforts to find undervalued securities, he is currently analyzing a Canadian company called Slapshot, Inc. Slapshot produces hockey equipment at its Canadian manufacturing facilities. About 85% of Slapshot's sales are to the U.S. market, and the remainder are domestic (i.e., in Canada). Sales have been growing at 12% per year. Last year's sales were C$68,000,000. Holmes has gathered the following market information (inflation is perfectly predictable):

- £/$ spot exchange rate = 0.8
- £/C$ spot exchange rate = 0.4
- U.K. risk-free rate = 6%
- U.K. expected inflation rate = 4%
- Canadian risk-free rate = 9%
- Canadian expected inflation rate = 7%
- U.S. risk-free rate = 4%
- U.S. expected inflation = 2%

Holmes uses the international CAPM (ICAPM) to value international investments. For Slapshot, Holmes believes that the stock's returns are sensitive to the £/C$ exchange rate. In order to apply the model, he estimates the following parameters using the £ as the base currency:

- World market risk premium = 6%
- Sensitivity of Slapshot to the world market = 1.2
- Sensitivity of Slapshot to changes in the £/C$ exchange rate = 1.4
- Holmes' expectation for the depreciation of the C$ against the £ = 2%
- The ratio of the price of the U.K. consumption basket to the Canadian consumption basket is 0.3.

Holmes adds Slapshot stock to several client portfolios at a purchase price of C$100. One year later, the stock is trading at C$122. There were no dividend payments during the year.

109.   The real £/C$ exchange rate is *closest* to:
    A. 1.00.
    B. 1.33.
    C. 1.54.

110.   If the real exchange rate remained constant, the GBP (£) return on Slapshot for Holmes' clients is *closest* to:
    A. 19%.
    B. 22%.
    C. 25%.

111. If the real exchange rate at the end of the year was 1.41, the GBP (£) return on Slapshot for Holmes' clients is *closest* to:
    A. 16.32%.
    B. 17.37%.
    C. 24.79%.

112. Consider the current U.S. dollar to C$ ($/C$) spot exchange rate. Suppose that after one year, the nominal spot $/C$ exchange rate is 0.350. The *most likely* impact on Slapshot's valuation from the $/C$ exchange rate change is the:
    A. C$ has depreciated in real terms, and the firm will be more competitive in the U.S. market, leading to a higher valuation.
    B. C$ has appreciated in real terms, and the firm will be less competitive in the U.S. market, leading to a lower valuation.
    C. value of the C$ has not changed in real terms, so there should be no real impact on the firm's valuation.

113. Suppose the C$ suddenly depreciates by 10% against the £. Given his estimated parameters, what is *most likely* to happen to the CAD value of Slapshot in response to this sudden exchange rate change?
    A. Local currency value would fall by 10%.
    B. Local currency value would fall by 4%.
    C. Local currency value would be unchanged.

114. If Holmes uses the ICAPM, the required rate of return on Slapshot is *closest* to:
    A. 13.2%.
    B. 14.6%.
    C. 17.4%.

©2011 Kaplan, Inc.

Questions 115–120 relate to Robert Williams.

Robert Williams is a junior analyst at Anderson Brothers, a large Wall Street brokerage firm. He reports to Will McDonald, the chief economist for Anderson Brothers. McDonald provides economic research, forecasts, and interpretation of economic data to all of Anderson's investment departments, as well as the firm's clients. McDonald has asked Williams to analyze economic trends in the country of Bundovia. The currency of Bundovia is the Bunco (BU).

One of Bundovia's major exports is high quality carpets. However, human rights activists have recently begun to complain about child labor practices in the Bundovian carpet industry, and this has resulted in negative publicity for the industry. Several foreign buyers had set up monitoring operations to ensure that the products they are buying are not tainted by such practices. In response, last year, the Bundovian government banned child labor and set up an oversight agency. Inspectors from the agency now have the power to monitor the industry and assess fines on violators. In response, most foreign buyers halted their monitoring operations, which were now considered an unnecessary expense. Unfortunately, many participants in the Bundovian carpet industry simply bribed the regulators and continued their (now illegal) practices.

Recently, the Bundovian economy has experienced higher growth in real terms compared to the growth of the U.S. economy. Williams is concerned about the impact of such growth on the value of Bunco relative to the U.S. dollar.

Bundovia has announced plans to impose either a tariff or a quota on semiconductor imports from the United States. McDonald also asks Williams to analyze the potential effect on Bundovian Semiconductors, the dominant semiconductor manufacturer located in Bundovia. Currently, Bundovian Semiconductors is not competitive in the global semiconductor market because its higher production costs make it unable to generate profits at the current world market price. Williams concludes that the imposition of either a tariff or quotas would benefit Bundovian Semiconductors. The company would become competitive with foreign producers in its domestic semiconductor market because imports would be reduced and domestic production would rise.

A bank is quoting the following exchange rates:

USD/GBP = 2.0010 – 20

USD/SFr = 0.8550 – 60

Williams asks the bank for a GBP/SFr cross rate.

From the same bank, Williams receives the following forward rate quotes in the USD/GBP market:

- 30-day forward rate: USD/GBP = USD/GBP = 2.0045 – 55
- 60-day forward rate: USD/GBP = USD/GBP = 2.0075 – 85

Williams has uncovered a potential arbitrage opportunity in the foreign exchange markets. The current spot rate is $2.00 per BU. The Bundovian risk-free interest rate is 3%, and the one-year forward rate is $2.10 per BU. The U.S. risk-free rate is 5%.

115. The actions of foreign buyers after the new regulations in Buldovia banning child labor practices took effect are *most* consistent with the:
     A. share the gains, share the pains theory.
     B. capture hypothesis.
     C. feedback effect.

116. Is Williams correct in his conclusions that Bundovian Semiconductors would benefit from the imposition of a tariff or quota?
     A. He is correct on both.
     B. He is only correct about the tariff.
     C. He is only correct about the quota.

117. In the short term, higher economic growth in Bundovia would *most likely* lead to a BU/USD exchange rate that is:
     A. higher.
     B. lower.
     C. unchanged.

118. Based on the USD/GBP and USD/SFr quotes, in response to Williams's request, the bank would quote a cross rate *closest* to:
     A. GBP/SFr = 0.4271 – 78.
     B. GBP/SFr = 2.3375 – 14.
     C. GBP/SFr = 0.4273 – 76.

©2011 Kaplan, Inc.

119. Is the USD selling at a 30-day forward premium or discount to the GBP, and what is the size of the 30-day premium or discount in annualized percentage terms?

Premium or discount	Annualized percentage
A. Premium	2.1%
B. Premium	3.9%
C. Discount	2.1%

120. The maximum profit from covered interest arbitrage in the USD/BU market by borrowing $1,000 or the BU equivalent is *closest* to:
    A. $19.05.
    B. $31.50.
    C. $72.50.

End of Afternoon Session

Exam 2
Morning Session

Question	Topic	Minutes (Points)
1 to 6	Ethics	18
7 to 12	Ethics	18
13 to 18	Financial Reporting and Analysis	18
19 to 24	Equity Investments	18
25 to 30	Equity Investments	18
31 to 36	Equity Investments	18
37 to 42	Economics	18
43 to 48	Fixed Income Investments	18
49 to 54	Fixed Income Investments	18
55 to 60	Financial Reporting and Analysis	18

Test Answers

1.	(A)	(B)	(C)		41.	(A)	(B)	(C)
2.	(A)	(B)	(C)		42.	(A)	(B)	(C)
3.	(A)	(B)	(C)		43.	(A)	(B)	(C)
4.	(A)	(B)	(C)		44.	(A)	(B)	(C)
5.	(A)	(B)	(C)		45.	(A)	(B)	(C)
6.	(A)	(B)	(C)		46.	(A)	(B)	(C)
7.	(A)	(B)	(C)		47.	(A)	(B)	(C)
8.	(A)	(B)	(C)		48.	(A)	(B)	(C)
9.	(A)	(B)	(C)		49.	(A)	(B)	(C)
10.	(A)	(B)	(C)		50.	(A)	(B)	(C)
11.	(A)	(B)	(C)		51.	(A)	(B)	(C)
12.	(A)	(B)	(C)		52.	(A)	(B)	(C)
13.	(A)	(B)	(C)		53.	(A)	(B)	(C)
14.	(A)	(B)	(C)		54.	(A)	(B)	(C)
15.	(A)	(B)	(C)		55.	(A)	(B)	(C)
16.	(A)	(B)	(C)		56.	(A)	(B)	(C)
17.	(A)	(B)	(C)		57.	(A)	(B)	(C)
18.	(A)	(B)	(C)		58.	(A)	(B)	(C)
19.	(A)	(B)	(C)		59.	(A)	(B)	(C)
20.	(A)	(B)	(C)		60.	(A)	(B)	(C)
21.	(A)	(B)	(C)					
22.	(A)	(B)	(C)					
23.	(A)	(B)	(C)					
24.	(A)	(B)	(C)					
25.	(A)	(B)	(C)					
26.	(A)	(B)	(C)					
27.	(A)	(B)	(C)					
28.	(A)	(B)	(C)					
29.	(A)	(B)	(C)					
30.	(A)	(B)	(C)					
31.	(A)	(B)	(C)					
32.	(A)	(B)	(C)					
33.	(A)	(B)	(C)					
34.	(A)	(B)	(C)					
35.	(A)	(B)	(C)					
36.	(A)	(B)	(C)					
37.	(A)	(B)	(C)					
38.	(A)	(B)	(C)					
39.	(A)	(B)	(C)					
40.	(A)	(B)	(C)					

Exam 2
Morning Session

Questions 1–6 relate to Glenda Garvey.

Glenda Garvey is interning at Samson Securities in the summer to earn money for her last semester of studies for her MBA. She took the Level III CFA® exam in June but has not yet received her results. Garvey's work involves preparing research reports on small companies.

Garvey is at lunch with a group of co-workers. She listens to their conversation about various stocks and takes note of a comment from Tony Topel, a veteran analyst. Topel is talking about Vallo Engineering, a small stock he has tried repeatedly to convince the investment director to add to the monitored list. While the investment director does not like Vallo, Topel has faith in the company and has gradually accumulated 5,000 shares for his own account. Another analyst, Mary Kennedy, tells the group about Koral Koatings, a paint and sealant manufacturer. Kennedy has spent most of the last week at the office doing research on Koral. She has concluded that the stock is undervalued and consensus earnings estimates are conservative. However, she has not filed a report for Samson, nor does she intend to. She said she has purchased the stock for herself and advises her colleagues to do the same. After she gets back to the office, Garvey purchases 25 shares of Vallo and 50 shares of Koral for herself.

Samson pays its interns very little, and Garvey works as a waitress at a diner in the financial district to supplement her income. The dinner crowd includes many analysts and brokers who work at nearby businesses. While waiting tables that night, Garvey hears two employees of a major brokerage house discussing Metrona, a nanotechnology company. The restaurant patrons say that the broker's star analyst has issued a report with a buy rating on Metrona that morning. The diners plan to buy the stock the next morning. After Garvey finishes her shift, restaurant manager Mandy Jones, a longtime Samson client, asks to speak with her. Jones commends Garvey for her hard work at the restaurant, praising her punctuality and positive attitude, and offers her two tickets to a Yankees game as a bonus.

The next morning, Garvey buys 40 shares of Metrona for her own account at the market open. Soon afterward, she receives a call from Harold Koons, one of Samson's largest money-management clients. Koons says he got Garvey's name from Bertha Witt, who manages the Koons's account. Koons wanted to reward the analyst who discovered Anvil Hammers, a machine-tool company whose stock soared soon after it was added to his portfolio. Garvey prepared the original report on Anvil Hammers. Koons offers Garvey two free round-trip tickets to the city of her choice. Garvey thanks Koons, then asks her immediate supervisor, Karl May, about the gift from Koons but does not mention the gift from Jones. May approves the Koons' gift.

After talking with May, Garvey starts a research project on Zenith Enterprises, a frozen-juice maker. Garvey's gathers quarterly data on the company's sales and profits over the past two years. Garvey uses a simple linear regression to estimate the relationship between GDP growth and Zenith's sales growth. Next she uses a consensus GDP estimate from a well-known economic data reporting service and her regression model to extrapolate growth rates for the next three years.

Later that afternoon, Garvey attends a company meeting on the ethics of money management. She listens to a lecture in which John Bloomquist, a veteran portfolio manager, talks about his job responsibilities. Garvey takes notes that include the following three statements made by Bloomquist:

Statement 1: I'm not a bond expert, and I've turned to a colleague for advice on how to manage the fixed-income portion of client portfolios.

Statement 2: I strive not to favor either the remaindermen or the current-income beneficiaries; instead, I work to serve both of their interests.

Statement 3: All of my portfolios have target growth rates sufficient to keep ahead of inflation.

Garvey is not working at the diner that night, so she goes home to work on her biography for an online placement service. In it she makes the following two statements:

Statement 1: I'm a CFA Level III candidate, and I expect to receive my charter this fall. The CFA program is a grueling, 3-part, graduate-level course, and passage requires an expertise in a variety of financial instruments, as well as knowledge of the forces that drive our economy and financial markets.

Statement 2: I expect to graduate with my MBA from Braxton College at the end of the fall semester. As both an MBA and a CFA, I'll be in high demand. Hire me now while you still have the chance.

©2011 Kaplan, Inc.

1. During the lunch conversation, which CFA Institute Standard of Professional Conduct was *most likely* violated?
    A. III(B) Fair Dealing.
    B. IV(A) Loyalty.
    C. V(A) Reasonable Basis.

2. Does Garvey's acceptance of the gifts from Koons and Jones violate Standard I(B) Independence and Objectivity?
    A. Accepting Koons' gift was a violation.
    B. Accepting Jones' gift was a violation.
    C. Neither gift would result in a violation.

3. Did Garvey violate Standard II(A) Material Nonpublic Information when she purchased Vallo and Metrona?
    A. Buying Vallo was a violation.
    B. Buying Metrona was a violation.
    C. Neither purchase was a violation.

4. In her estimation of Zenith's future growth rate, what standard did Garvey violate?
    A. Standard I(C) Misrepresentation regarding plagiarism.
    B. Standard V(A) Diligence and Reasonable Basis.
    C. Both I(C) and V(A).

5. Which of Bloomquist's statements *most likely* applies to both the Prudent Man Rule and the Prudent Investor Rule?
    A. Statement 1.
    B. Statement 2.
    C. Statement 3.

6. Did the two statements in Garvey's biography violate Standard VII(B) Reference to CFA Institute, the CFA designation, and the CFA program?
    A. Statement 1 is a violation.
    B. Statement 2 is a violation.
    C. Both statements are violations.

Questions 7–12 relate to Maria Harris.

Maria Harris is a CFA® Level III candidate and portfolio manager for Islandwide Hedge Fund. Harris is commonly involved in complex trading strategies on behalf of Islandwide and maintains a significant relationship with Quadrangle Brokers, which provides portfolio analysis tools to Harris. Recent market volatility has led Islandwide to incur record-high trading volume and commissions with Quadrangle for the quarter. In appreciation of Islandwide's business, Quadrangle offers Harris an all-expenses-paid week of golf at Pebble Beach for her and her husband. Harris discloses the offer to her supervisor and compliance officer and, based on their approval, accepts the trip.

Harris has lunch that day with C. K. Swamy, CFA, her old college roommate and future sister-in-law. While Harris is sitting in the restaurant waiting for Swamy to arrive, Harris overhears a conversation between the president and chief financial officer (CFO) of Progressive Industries. The president informs the CFO that Progressive's board of directors has just approved dropping the company's cash dividend, despite its record of paying dividends for the past 46 quarters. The company plans to announce this information in about a week. Harris owns Progressive's common stock and immediately calls her broker to sell her shares in anticipation of a price decline.

Swamy recently joined Dillon Associates, an investment advisory firm. Swamy plans to continue serving on the board of directors of Landmark Enterprises, a private company owned by her brother-in-law, for which she receives $2,000 annually. Swamy also serves as an unpaid advisor to the local symphony on investing their large endowment and receives four season tickets to the symphony performances.

After lunch, Alice Adams, a client, offers Harris a 1-week cruise as a reward for the great performance of her account over the previous quarter. Bert Baker, also a client, has offered Harris two airplane tickets to Hawaii if his account beats its benchmark by more than 2% over the following year.

Juliann Clark, a CFA candidate, is an analyst at Dillon Associates and a colleague of Swamy's. Clark participates in a conference call for several analysts in which the chief executive officer at Dex says his company's board of directors has just accepted a tender offer from Monolith Chemicals to buy Dex at a 40% premium over the market price. Clark contacts a friend and relates the information about Dex and Monolith. The friend promptly contacts her broker and buys 2,000 shares of Dex's stock.

Ed Michaels, CFA, is director of trading at Quadrangle Brokers. Michaels has recently implemented a buy program for a client. This buy program has driven up the price of a small-cap stock, in which Islandwide owns shares, by approximately 5% because the orders were large in relation to the average daily trading volume of the stock. Michaels's firm is about to bring shares of an OTC firm to market in an

©2011 Kaplan, Inc.

IPO. Michaels has publicly announced that, as a market maker in the shares, his trading desk will create additional liquidity in the stock over its first 90 days of trading by committing to minimum bids and offers of 5,000 shares and to a maximum spread of one-eighth.

Carl Park, CFA, is a retail broker with Quadrangle and has been allocated 5,000 shares of an oversubscribed IPO. One of his clients has been complaining about the execution price of a trade Park made for her last month, but Park knows from researching it that the trade received the best possible execution. In order to calm the client down, Park increases her allocation of shares in the IPO above what it would be if he allocated them to all suitable client accounts based on account size. He allocates a pro-rata portion of the remaining shares to a trust account held at his firm for which his brother-in-law is the primary beneficiary.

7. By accepting the trip from Quadrangle, has Harris complied with the CFA Institute Code and Standards?
   A. Harris may accept the trip because she maintains a significant relationship with Quadrangle that contributes to the performance of client accounts.
   B. Harris may accept the trip because she disclosed the trip to her supervisor and compliance officer and accepted based on their approval.
   C. Harris may not accept the trip because the offer from Quadrangle could impede her ability to make objective investment decisions on behalf of the client.

8. Has either Harris or Clark violated Standard II(A) Integrity of Capital Markets: Material Nonpublic Information?
   A. Harris is in violation.
   B. Clark is in violation.
   C. Both are in violation.

9. According to the Standards of Practice, with respect to the two offers from Adams and Baker, Harris:
   A. may accept both offers if she discloses them to her employer.
   B. may accept both gifts only if she discloses them to her employer and receives permission.
   C. must disclose the offer from Adams to her employer if she accepts it but must receive her employer's permission to accept the offer from Baker.

10. Has Michaels violated Standard II(B) Integrity of Capital Markets: Market Manipulation with respect to any of the following?
    A. The buy program is a violation.
    B. The liquidity activity is a violation.
    C. There is no violation.

11. According to Standard IV Duties to Employers, which of the following is *most likely* required of Swamy? Swamy must:
    A. secure written permission from her employer before performing services for the symphony.
    B. inform her immediate supervisor at Dillon in writing that she (Swamy) must comply with the Code and Standards.
    C. disclose to her employer any additional compensation she receives from Landmark Enterprises and secure written permission to serve on the board.

12. Which action by Park violated Standard III(B) Duties to Clients: Fair Dealing?
    A. Increasing allocation to the problem client.
    B. Decreased allocation to the brother-in-law and other firm clients.
    C. Both actions are violations.

©2011 Kaplan, Inc.

Questions 13–18 relate to Snowboards and Skateboards, Inc.

Ota L'Abbe, a supervisor at an investment research firm, has asked one of the junior analysts, Andreas Hally, to draft a research report dealing with various accounting issues.

Excerpts from the request are as follows:

- "There's an exciting company that we're starting to follow these days. It's called Snowboards and Skateboards, Inc. They are a multinational company with operations and a head office based in the resort town of Whistler in western Canada. However, they also have a significant subsidiary located in the United States."
- "Look at the subsidiary and deal with some foreign currency issues, including the specific differences between the temporal and current rate methods of translation, as well as the effect on financial ratios."
- "The attached file contains the September 30, 2008, financial statements of the U.S. subsidiary. Translate the financial statements into Canadian dollars in a manner consistent with U.S. GAAP."

[handwritten margin notes:]
BEG RE 1,350,000
NI
DIV 34250
END RE 1432500

NI = 83,250

The following are statements from the research report subsequently written by Hally:

Statement 1: Subsidiaries whose operations are well-integrated with the parent will use the current rate method of translation.

Statement 2: Self-contained, independent subsidiaries whose operating, investing, and financing activities are primarily located in the local market will use the temporal method of translation.

[handwritten margin note:]
−52050+X =83250

Snowboards and Skateboards, Inc. (U.S.)
Balance Sheet as of 9/30/2008 (U.S. dollars)

	U.S. dollars	
Cash and accounts receivable	775,000	*×1.32* *810k*
Inventory	600,000	
Property, plant, and equipment (PP&E) – net	730,000	*×1.50*
Total assets	2,105,000	*2,928,000*
Accounts payable	125,000	*×1.32*
Long-term debt	400,000	*×1.32*
Common stock	535,000	*×1.50*
Retained earnings	1,045,000	*1,432,000*
Total liabilities and shareholders' equity	2,105,000	*2928,000*

Income Statement for the Year ended 9/30/2008

Sales	1,352,000	*×1.35*
Cost of goods sold	(1,205,000)	*1667250*
Depreciation	(140,000)	*×1.50*
Net income	7,000	*+ PLUG*
		83250

[handwritten:] NET INC =

Other information to be considered:

- *Exchange rates (CAD/USD)*

Fiscal 2007 (average)	1.44
Fiscal 2008 (average)	1.35
October 1, 2004	1.50
September 30, 2007	1.48
June 30, 2008	1.37
September 30, 2008	1.32

- Beginning inventory for fiscal 2008 had been purchased evenly throughout fiscal 2007. The company uses the FIFO inventory value method.

- Dividends of USD 25,000 were paid to the shareholders on June 30, 2008.

- All of the remaining inventory at the end of fiscal 2008 was purchased evenly throughout fiscal 2008.

- All of the PP&E was purchased, and all of the common equity was issued at the inception of the company on October 1, 2004. No new PP&E has been acquired, and no additional common stock has been issued since then. However, they plan to purchase new PP&E starting in fiscal 2009.

- The beginning retained earnings balance for fiscal 2008 was CAD 1,550,000.

- The accounts payable on the fiscal 2008 balance sheet were all incurred on June 30, 2008.

- The U.S. subsidiary's operations are highly integrated with the main operations in Canada.

- The remeasured inventory for 2008 using the temporal method is CAD 810,000.

- All monetary asset and liability balances are the same as they were at the end of the 2007 fiscal year, except that long-term debt was USD 467,700.

- Costs of goods sold under the temporal method in 2008 is CAD 1,667,250.

13. Are Hally's statements regarding foreign currency translation correct?

	Statement 1	Statement 2
A.	Yes	Yes
B.	Yes	No
C.	No	No

©2011 Kaplan, Inc.

14.   Which of the following *best* describes the effect on the parent's fiscal 2008 sales when translated to Canadian dollars? Sales, relative to what it would have been if the CAD/USD exchange rate had not changed, will be:

    A. lower because the U.S. dollar depreciated during fiscal 2008.

    B. higher because the average value of the Canadian dollar depreciated during fiscal 2008.

    C. lower because the U.S. dollar appreciated during fiscal 2008.

15.   As compared to the temporal method, which of the following financial statement elements of the parent are lower under the current rate method?

    A. Cash and accounts receivable.

    B. Depreciation expense and cost of goods sold.

    C. Common stock and dividends paid.

16.   Using the appropriate translation method, which of the following *best* describes the effect of changing exchange rates on the parent's fiscal 2008 financial statements?

    A. An accumulated loss of CAD 242,100 is reported in the shareholders' equity.

    B. A loss of CAD 31,200 is recognized in the income statement.

    C. A gain of CAD 27,400 is recognized in the income statement.

17.   As compared to the temporal method, the parent's fixed asset turnover for fiscal 2008 using the current rate method is:

    A. higher.

    B. lower.

    C. the same.

18.   Suppose the parent uses the current rate method to translate the subsidiary for fiscal 2008. Will return on assets and net profit margin in U.S. dollars before translation be the same as, or different than, the translated Canadian dollar ratios?

	Return on assets	Net profit margin
A.	Same	Same
B.	Different	Different
C.	Different	Same

Temp = Higher

Temp = Lower

Questions 19–24 relate to Lorenz Kummert.

Lorenz Kummert is a junior equity analyst who is following Schubert, Inc. (Schubert), a small publicly traded company in the United States. His supervisor, Markus Alter, CFA, has advised him to use the residual income model to analyze Schubert.

In his preliminary report to Alter, Kummert makes the following statements:

Statement 1: Residual income models are appropriate when expected free cash flows are negative for the foreseeable future.

Statement 2: Residual income models are not applicable when dividends are volatile.

Kummert has determined Schubert's cost of equity, cost of debt, and weighted average cost of capital (WACC) to be 12.8%, 8.4%, and 11.9%, respectively. The current price of the stock is $36 per share and there are 130,000 shares outstanding. The relevant tax rate is 30%, and return on equity (ROE) is expected to be 14%.

Summarized financial information about Schubert for 2008 is provided in Exhibits 1 and 2.

Exhibit 1: Schubert, Inc., Balance Sheet on December 31, 2008

Cash	$ 125,000	Accounts payable	$ 426,000
Accounts receivable	975,000	Accrued liabilities	774,000
Inventory	1,215,000	Long-term debt	6,211,000
Fixed assets (net)	9,277,000		
		Common shares	2,100,000
		Retained earnings	2,081,000
Total assets	$11,592,000	Total liabilities and equity	$11,592,000

©2011 Kaplan, Inc.

Exhibit 2: Schubert, Inc., Income Statement for the year ended December 31, 2008

Sales	$9,423,000
Cost of sales	4,580,000
Selling, general, and administrative	1,230,000
Depreciation	1,745,000
Interest expense	522,000
Income tax expense	403,800
Net income	$942,200

Based on his analysis of several years of financial statements, Kummert notes that 2008 was an exceptionally profitable year for Schubert, and that its dividend payouts are usually low because the funds are mainly reinvested in the firm to promote growth. Furthermore, there are very few nonrecurring items on the income statement. Upon review of Kummert's preliminary report, Alter concurs with his analysis of the financial statements but reminds him that Schubert's long-term debt is currently trading at 95% of its book value. He also cautions Kummert that violations of the clean surplus relation can bias the results of the residual income model.

The consensus annual EPS estimate for 2009 is $4.50, and the dividend payout ratio for 2009 is estimated at 5%.

19. Are Kummert's statements regarding the residual income model correct?
    A. Both statements are incorrect.
    B. Only Statement 1 is correct.
    C. Only Statement 2 is correct.

20. Assuming that Kummert and Alter are correct with their conclusions regarding Schubert's financial statements, which of the following levels would *best* describe the strength of the persistence factor with respect to Schubert's residual income?
    A. Low persistence factor.
    B. Medium persistence factor.
    C. High persistence factor.

21. Which of the following amounts is *closest* to the forecast of Schubert's book value per share and residual income, respectively, for 2009?

	Book value per share	Residual income
A.	$36.43	$0.38
B.	$38.00	$2.32
C.	$36.40	$2.32

22. Which of the following amounts are *closest* to the economic value added (EVA) and market value added (MVA) of Schubert, respectively?

	EVA	MVA
A.	$71,000	$188,450
B.	$23,000	$369,000
C.	($70,900)	$369,000

23. Which of the following amounts is *closest* to Schubert's implied growth rate in residual income?
    A. 0.34%.
    B. 2.75%.
    C. 12.63%.

24. Regarding Alter's caution about violations of the clean surplus relationship, examples of items that can violate this relationship include:
    A. foreign currency gains and losses under the current rate method.
    B. changes in the market value of debt and equity held as trading securities.
    C. changes in net working capital.

©2011 Kaplan, Inc.

Questions 25–30 relate to Ferguson Department Stores, Inc.

Matthew Emery, CFA, is responsible for analyzing companies in the retail industry. He is currently reviewing the status of Ferguson Department Stores, Inc. (FDS). FDS has recently gone through extensive restructuring in the wake of a slowdown in the economy that has made retailing particularly challenging. As part of his analysis, Emery has gathered information from a number of sources.

Ferguson Department Stores, Inc.

FDS went public in 1969 following a major acquisition, and the Ferguson name quickly became one of the most recognized in retailing. Ferguson had been successful through most of its first 30 years in business and has prided itself on being the one-stop shopping destination for consumers living on the West Coast of the United States. Recently, FDS began to experience both top and bottom line difficulties due to increased competition from specialty retailers who could operate more efficiently and offer a wider range of products in a focused retailing sector. When the company's main bank reduced FDS's line of credit, a serious working capital crisis ensued, and the company was forced to issue additional equity in an effort to overcome the problem. FDS has a cost of capital of 10% and a required rate of return on equity of 12%. Dividends are growing at a rate of 8%, but the growth rate is expected to decline linearly over the next six years to a long-term growth rate of 4%. The company recently paid an annual dividend of $1.

At the end of 2008, FDS announced that it would be expanding its retail operations, moving to a warehouse concept, and opening new stores around the country. FDS also announced it would close some existing stores, write-down assets, and take a large restructuring charge. Upon reviewing the prospects of the firm, Emery issued an earnings-per-share forecast for 2009 of $0.90. He set a 12-month share price target of $22.50. Immediately following the expansion announcement, the share price of FDS jumped from $14 to $18.

**Exhibit 1: Summary Income Statement, Ferguson Department Stores, Inc.
(U.S. $ millions, except per share data and shares outstanding)**

	2008	*2007*
Sales	$6,435.9	$6,322.7
Cost of goods sold, operating, administrative, and selling expenses	6,007.9	5,875.9
Depreciation and amortization	148.7	146.6
Interest expense	59.8	59.5
Unusual items—expense	189.1	5.0
Earnings before tax	30.4	235.7
Income taxes—current	49.3	7.5
Income taxes—future	(71.1)	93.5
	(21.8)	101.0
Net earnings for the year	$52.2	$134.7
Earnings per share: Basic	$0.49	$1.26
Fully diluted	$0.49	$1.26
Weighted average shares outstanding	106,530,610	106,530,610

In 2008, FDS also reported an unusual expense of $189.1 million related to restructuring costs and asset write downs.

Exhibit 2: Selected Industry Information for 2008

Estimated earnings growth rate	0.10
Mean trailing price/earnings (P/E) ratio	22.50
Mean price/sales (P/S) ratio	0.50

In response to questions from a colleague, Emery makes the following statements regarding the merits of earnings yield compared to the P/E ratio:

Statement 1: For ranking purposes, earnings yield may be useful whenever earnings are either negative or close to zero.

Statement 2: A high E/P implies the security is overpriced.

25. The value of one share of FDS using the H-model is *closest* to:
    A. $14.50.
    B. $16.50.
    C. $19.33.

©2011 Kaplan, Inc.

26. Given Emery's dividend forecast for FDS, is the H-model the appropriate valuation model to use to value FDS?
    A. Yes.
    B. No, the H-model is appropriate when the dividend growth rate declines at a linear rate for a short period of time during stage one, followed by a 1-year suspension in dividends before the previous dividend is reinstated, and then dividends grow at a long-term constant rate.
    C. No, the H-model is appropriate when the dividend growth rate grows during the first stage followed by a period of stable growth in dividends in stage two, followed by a dividend growth rate that declines linearly in perpetuity.

27. Assuming that the cost of equity for FDS does not change, the present value of growth opportunities in the share price following the announcement that the company would be expanding its retail operations, using Emery's 2009 earnings forecast, is *closest* to:
    A. $9.00.
    B. $10.50.
    C. $12.50.

28. Are Emery's statements regarding the earnings yield and E/P ratio correct?
    A. One statement is correct and the other statement is incorrect.
    B. Both statements are correct.
    C. Both statements are incorrect.

29. Assuming a tax rate of 34%, the underlying earnings per share (EPS) for FDS in 2008 is *closest* to:
    A. $1.26.
    B. $1.36.
    C. $2.27.

30. According to FDS's price-to-sales ratio for 2008, based on the post-expansion announcement stock price, FDS is: $/8
    A. underpriced relative to the industry.
    B. overpriced relative to the industry.
    C. properly priced relative to the industry.

$\frac{P}{E} \downarrow$ under

$\frac{E}{P} \uparrow$ under

Questions 31–36 relate to Universal Home Supplies, Inc.

Michael Robbins, CFA, is analyzing Universal Home Supplies, Inc. (UHS), which has recently gone through some extensive restructuring.

Universal Home Supplies, Inc.

UHS operates nearly 200 department stores and 78 specialty stores in over 30 states. The company offers a wide range of products, including women's, men's, and children's clothing and accessories, as well as home furnishings, electronics, and other consumer goods. The company is considering cutting back on or eliminating its electronics business entirely. UHS manufactures many of its own apparel products domestically in a large factory located in Kentucky. This central location permits shipping to distribution points around the country at reasonable costs. The company operates primarily in suburban shopping malls and offers mid- to high-end merchandise mainly under its own private label. At present, more than 70% of the company's customers live within a 10-minute drive of one of the company's stores. Web site activity measured in dollar sales volume has increased by over 18% in the past year. Shares of UHS stock are currently priced at $25. Dividends are expected to grow at a rate of 6% over the next eight years and then continue to grow at that same rate indefinitely. The company has a cost of capital of 10.2%, a beta of 0.8, and just paid an annual dividend of $1.25.

UHS has faced serious cash flow problems in recent years as a consequence of its strategy to pursue an upscale clientele in the face of increased competition from several "niche retailers." The firm has been able to issue new debt recently and has also managed to extend its line of credit. The two financing agreements required a pledge of additional assets and a promise to install a super-efficient inventory tracking system in time to meet holiday shopping demand.

Exhibit 1: Summary Income Statement for Universal Home Supplies, Inc. (U.S. $ millions, except per share data and shares outstanding)

	2008	2007
Sales	$7,400.1	$7,383.8
Cost of goods sold, operating, administrative, and selling expenses	7,081.3	7,028.9
Depreciation and amortization	157.7	155.6
Earnings before interest expense and income taxes	161.1	199.3
Interest expense	42.6	45.4
Earnings before tax	118.5	153.9
Income taxes—current	40.3	52.3
Net earnings for the year	$78.2	$101.6
Earnings per share: Basic	$0.82	$1.40
Fully diluted	$0.82	$1.34
Weighted average shares outstanding	95,366,000	72,572,000

 ©2011 Kaplan, Inc.

Exhibit 2: Book Value per Share (BVPS in $) and Return on Equity (ROE), Universal Home Supplies, Inc.

Year	2008	2007	2006	2005
BVPS	$25.58	$33.62	$37.54	$32.26
ROE	3.2%	4.0%	4.5%	3.9%

Exhibit 3: 2008 Selected Industry Information

Estimated earnings growth rate	0.10
Mean trailing price/earnings (P/E) ratio	22.50
Mean price/sales (P/S) ratio	0.50

Robbins is asked by his supervisor to carefully consider the advantages and drawbacks of using the price-to-sales ratio (P/S) and to determine the appropriate valuation metrics to use when returns follow patterns of persistence or reversals.

Robbins also estimates a cross-sectional model to predict UHS's P/E:

$$\text{predicted P/E} = 5 - (10 \times \text{beta}) + [3 \times \text{4-year average ROE(\%)}] + [2 \times \text{5-year growth forecast(\%)}]$$

31. Based on the H-model, the implied expected rate of return for UHS is *closest* to:
     A. 8.8%.
     B. 10.2%.
     C. 11.3%.

32. Robbins should conclude that a key drawback to using the price-to-sales (P/S) ratio in the investment process is that P/S is:
     A. positive even when earnings per share is negative.
     B. not appropriate for valuing the equity of mature companies.
     C. susceptible to manipulation with respect to revenue recognition.

33. Is UHS stock, at the end of 2008, *best* described as overvalued or undervalued according to the:

	Trailing PEG ratio?	P/S ratio?
A.	Undervalued	Undervalued
B.	Overvalued	Undervalued
C.	Undervalued	Overvalued

34. Based on the method of average return on equity (ROE), the normalized EPS for UHS is *closest* to:
   A. $0.94.
   B. $1.00.
   C. $1.26.

35. The predicted P/E for UHS using Robbins's model is *closest* to:
   A. 20.7.
   B. 23.6.
   C. 30.5.

36. Robbins should conclude that patterns of persistence or reversals in returns provide the *most appropriate* rationale for valuation using:
   A. unexpected earnings.
   B. relative-strength indicators.
   C. standardized unexpected earnings.

©2011 Kaplan, Inc.

Questions 37–42 relate to Barton Wilson.

Barton Wilson, a junior analyst, is a new hire at a money center bank. He has been assigned to help Juanita Chevas, CFA, in the currency trading department. Together, Wilson and Chevas are working on the development of new trading software designed to detect profitable opportunities in the foreign exchange market. Obviously, they are interested in risk-free arbitrage opportunities. However, they have also been instructed to investigate the possibility of longer-term currency exposures that are not necessarily risk-free. To test the logic of their new software, Wilson gathers the following market data:

- Spot JPY/USD exchange rate = 120.
- Spot EUR/USD exchange rate = 0.7224.
- U.S. risk-free interest rate = 7%.
- Eurozone risk-free rate = 9.08%.
- Japanese risk-free rate = 3.88%.
- Yield curves in all three currencies are flat.

In addition to in-house currency transactions, the new software program is also intended to provide insight into currency exposure and hedging needs for the bank's major customers. These customers typically include large multinational firms. Essentially, the bank wants to provide consulting services to its clients concerning which currency exposures offer the greatest possibility of appreciation. In this process, the bank will rely on deviations from international parity conditions as an indicator of long-term currency movements.

Wilson obtains the following data from the econometrics department:

- JPY/USD spot rate one year ago = 116.
- EUR/USD spot rate one year ago = 0.7200.
- Anticipated and historical U.S. annual inflation = 3%.
- Anticipated and historical Japanese annual inflation = 0%.
- Anticipated and historical Eurozone annual inflation = 5%.

One of the bank's major customers has significant portions of its business in Japan, and the Eurozone and has long exposure to both currencies. The customer has traditionally hedged all currency risk. However, the customer's new risk manager has decided to leave some currency exposure unhedged in an attempt to profit from long-term currency exposure.

37. According to relative purchasing power parity, the expected JPY/EUR spot rate two years from now is *closest* to:
    A. 150.57.
    B. 158.29.
    C. 166.74.

38.   Are the Japanese and Eurozone inflation forecasts provided by the econometrics department consistent with the inflation rates implied by the exact version of the international Fisher relation, given a U.S. inflation rate of 3%?
    A. Both forecasts are consistent.
    B. Neither forecast is consistent.
    C. One forecast is consistent and the other is not.

39.   Wilson wants to approximate the forward discount/premium for the JPY against the USD 12 months from now. According to the approximate version of interest rate parity, the JPY would *most likely* trade at a:
    A. 3.12% forward premium against the USD.
    B. 3.12% forward discount against the USD.
    C. 1.7% forward discount against the USD.

40.   Suppose that Wilson expects the JPY/USD spot rate one year from now to fall by 2% from its current level. The foreign currency risk premium associated with the JPY is *closest* to:
    A. –5.12%.
    B. –1.12%.
    C. +1.12%.

41.   Based on the assumption that international parity conditions will hold in the long run, should the JPY and Euro currency exposures of the bank's major customer be left unhedged?
    A. Both currencies should be left unhedged.
    B. Neither currency should be left unhedged.
    C. One currency should be left unhedged and the other should not.

42.   An unexpected decline in the growth rate of the USD money supply would *most likely* cause:
    A. the real USD interest rate to increase and the value of the USD to depreciate.
    B. the real USD interest rate to increase and the value of the USD to appreciate.
    C. the real USD interest rate to decrease and the value of the USD to appreciate.

©2011 Kaplan, Inc.

Questions 43–48 relate to William Rogers.

William Rogers, a fixed-income portfolio manager, needs to eliminate a large cash position in his portfolio. He would like to purchase some corporate bonds. Two bonds that he is evaluating are shown in Exhibit 1. These two bonds are from the same issuer, and the current call price for the callable bond is 100. Assume that the issuer will call if the bond price exceeds the call price.

Rogers is also concerned about increases in interest rates and is considering the purchase of a putable bond. He wants to determine how assumed increases or decreases in interest rate volatility affect the value of the straight bonds and bonds with embedded options. After Rogers performs some analysis, he and his supervisor, Sigourney Walters, discuss the relative price movement between the two bonds in Exhibit 1 when interest rates change significantly.

During the discussions, Rogers makes the following statements:

Statement 1: If the volatility of interest rates decreases, the value of the callable bond will increase.

Statement 2: The noncallable bond will not be affected by a change in the volatility or level of interest rates.

Statement 3: When interest rates decrease, the value of the noncallable bond increases by more than the callable bond.

Statement 4: If the volatility of interest rates increases, the value of the putable bond will increase.

Walters mentors Rogers on bond concepts and then asks him to consider the pricing of a third bond. The third bond has five years to maturity, a 6% annual coupon, and pays interest semiannually. The bond is both callable and putable at 100 at any time. Walters indicates that the holders of the bond's embedded options will exercise if the option is in-the-money.

Exhibit 1: Bond Descriptions

	Noncallable Bond	Callable Bond
Price	99.77	98.21
Time to maturity (years)	5	5
Time to first call date (years)	n/a	4
Annual coupon	6.00%	6.00%
Interest payment	Semiannual	Semiannual
Yield to maturity	6.0542%	6.4227%

Rogers obtained the prices shown in Exhibit 1 using software that generates an interest rate lattice. He uses his software to generate the interest rate lattice shown in Exhibit 2.

Exhibit 2: Interest Rate Lattice (Annualized Interest Rates)

									15.44%
								14.10%	
							12.69%		12.46%
						11.85%		11.38%	
					9.75%		10.25%		10.05%
				8.95%		9.57%		9.19%	
			7.91%		7.88%		8.28%		8.11%
		7.35%		7.23%		7.74%		7.42%	
	6.62%		6.40%		6.37%		6.69%		6.54%
6.05%		5.95%		5.85%		6.25%		5.99%	
	5.36%		5.17%		5.15%		5.40%		5.28%
		4.81%		4.73%		5.05%		4.83%	
			4.18%		4.16%		4.36%		4.26%
				3.82%		4.08%		3.90%	
					3.37%		3.52%		3.44%
						3.30%		3.15%	
							2.84%		2.77%
								2.54%	
									2.24%
Years 0.5	1.0	1.5	2.0	2.5	3.0	3.5	4.0	4.5	

43. Evaluate Rogers's statements 1 and 3.
    A. Only Statement 1 is correct.
    B. Only Statement 3 is correct.
    C. Both statements are correct.

44. Evaluate Rogers's statements 2 and 4.
    A. Only Statement 2 is correct.
    B. Only Statement 4 is correct.
    C. Both statements are incorrect.

45. The market value of the embedded call option in Exhibit 1 is *closest* to:
    A. 1.56.
    B. 1.65.
    C. 1.79.

©2011 Kaplan, Inc.

46. For this question only, ignore the information from Exhibit 1 and any other calculations in other questions. Rather, assume that the interest rate lattice provided in Exhibit 2 is constructed to be arbitrage-free. However, when Rogers calculates the price of the callable bond using the interest rates in the lattice, he gets a value higher than the market price of the bond.

Is the price of the third callable and putable bond *likely* to be less than, equal to, or greater than 100%, and is the option-adjusted spread (OAS) on the callable bond *likely* to be zero, positive, or negative?

	Price of third bond	OAS of callable bond
A.	Less than 100%	Zero
B.	Equal to 100%	Positive
C.	Greater than 100%	Negative

47. Using the information in the question and the following relevant portion of the interest rate and pricing trees, Rogers calculates the value of the noncallable bond at node A.

Corresponding portion of the interest rate tree:

8.95%

7.91%

7.23%

Years	1.5	2.0

Corresponding portion of the binomial price tree:

91.73%

A ---->

96.17%

Years	1.5	2.0

The price of the noncallable bond at node A is *closest* to:
A. 89.84% of par.
B. 93.26% of par.
C. 96.14% of par.

48.   Using the information in the question and the following relevant portion of the interest rate and pricing trees, Rogers calculates the value of the callable bond at node B.

Corresponding portion of the interest rate tree:

3.44%

3.15%

2.77%

Years	4.0	4.5

Corresponding portion of the callable bond price tree:

$100.00

B ---->

$100.00

Years	4.0	4.5

The price of the callable bond at node B is *closest* to:
A. 100.0% of par.
B. 101.4% of par.
C. 102.5% of par.

©2011 Kaplan, Inc.

Questions 49–54 relate to Marietta Tech, Inc.

Jerry Sanders, CFA, has been asked to analyze the 20-year bonds of Marietta Tech, Inc., which are currently being held in a corporate bond portfolio managed by a colleague, and to recommend whether the bonds should be sold or held. The bonds currently have a yield spread of 1.55% over Treasuries.

Marietta Tech, Inc. designs, manufactures, and markets specialty trucks and truck bodies mounted on new truck chassis produced by others, including concrete mixers, refuse bodies, fire and emergency vehicles, defense trucks, cut-away and dry freight van bodies, refrigerated units, stake bodies, and other specialized trucks. Marietta also manufactures fiberglass wind deflectors, armored trucks, shuttle buses, and cargo vans. Marietta's customers are located in the United States and Canada.

Exhibit 1: Selected Financial Data for Marietta Tech, Inc. (in thousands of $)

Item	2006	2007	2008
Current assets	$400	$600	$900
Net fixed assets	5,000	5,500	6,000
Total assets	5,400	6,100	6,900
Current liabilities	300	350	450
Long-term debt (LTD)	3,200	2,900	3,100
Shareholders' equity	1,900	2,850	3,350
Total liabilities and SH equity	5,400	6,100	6,900
Earnings before interest, taxes, depreciation, and amortization (EBITDA)	1,300	1,900	2,450
Earnings before interest, taxes (EBIT)	700	1,300	1,650
Earnings before taxes (EBT)	400	970	1,270
Net income	280	697	889
Capital expenditures	900	1,100	1,300
Cash flow from operations (CFO)	1,600	1,129	1,489
Interest expense	300	330	380
Free CFO[1]	700	29	189
EBIT/interest expense	2.33	3.94	4.34
EBITDA/interest expense	4.33	5.76	6.45
EBIT/sales	14.0%	18.6%	18.3%
Long-term obligations/capitalization[2]	68.9%	57.8%	59.39%
Free CFO/ long-term obligations	16.7%	0.7%	3.86%
Current ratio	1.33	1.71	
Total liabilities/assets	64.8%	53.3%	

[1] Free CFO = CFO – capital expenditures.

[2] Long-term obligations = LTD + present value of operating leases; Capitalization = LTD + present value of operating leases + shareholders' equity. PV of operating leases for Marietta are $1,000, $1,000, and $1,800, respectively, for 2006, 2007, and 2008.

Exhibit 2: Median Industry Ratios by Industrial Bond Rating (2008)

Ratio	AAA	AA	A	BBB	BB	B	CCC
EBIT/ interest expense	19.6	9.4	5.9	3.2	2.0	0.5	0.2
EBITDA/ interest expense	24.7	12.4	8.8	5.5	3.0	1.6	0.9
EBIT/sales	26.0%	22.9%	18.8%	15.7%	13.3%	10.7%	10.1%
Long-term obligations/ capitalization	15.6%	30.5%	44.2%	56.3%	68.5%	72.0%	73.4%
Free CFO/ Long-term obligations	65.1%	24.8%	12.0%	5.7%	3.4%	(1.4%)	(8.8%)

Exhibit 3: Median 20-Year Yield Spreads by Industrial Bond Rating (2008)

	AAA	AA	A	BBB	BB	B	CCC
Yield spread over Treasuries	0.90%	1.36%	1.52%	1.85%	2.10%	2.56%	4.89%

At lunch Sanders discusses the credit analysis of various types of bonds with Elizabeth Yan, who was just hired as a bond analyst. Yan makes the following statements:

Statement 1: An analysis of the issuer's business and operating risks is important to the analysis of corporate bond credit risk but not important for the credit analysis of asset-backed securities (ABS).

Statement 2: The unique bond covenants in a municipal bond's trust indenture require an additional level of credit analysis not necessary in a corporate credit analysis.

After lunch, Sanders asks Tatiana Petrovich in the municipal bond department for her opinion on the most important factors in the risk assessment of tax-backed municipal debt. Petrovich identifies three factors:

1. A measure of debt burden, such as debt-per-capita in the tax jurisdiction.

2. An evaluation of tax collection rates and intergovernmental revenue ability.

3. Analysis of the municipality's budgetary policies as an indication of financial discipline.

©2011 Kaplan, Inc.

49. Sanders first analyzes Marietta's 2008 EBIT-to-interest expense and EBITDA-to-interest expense and compares them to the median ratios from Exhibit 2. Relative to the BBB medians for the respective ratios:
    A. both ratios are greater than their respective BBB median ratios.
    B. both ratios are less than their respective BBB median ratios.
    C. only one ratio is greater than its respective BBB median ratios.

50. Compare the 2008 free CFO-to-long-term obligations ratio benchmarks to Marietta's ratio. Marietta is between the:
    A. A and BBB benchmark ratios.
    B. BBB and BB benchmark ratios.
    C. BB and B benchmark ratios.

51. Compare the 2008 long-term obligations to capitalization ratio benchmarks to Marietta's ratio. Marietta is between the:
    A. A and BBB benchmark ratios.
    B. BBB and BB benchmark ratios.
    C. BB and B benchmark ratios.

52. Based on the available information, Sanders should:
    A. hold the Marietta bonds because the ratios are consistent with a BBB-rated bond.
    B. sell the Marietta bonds because the ratios are consistent with a BBB-rated bond.
    C. sell the Marietta bonds because the ratios are consistent with a BB-rated bond.

53. Are Statement 1 and Statement 2 made by Yan correct?
    A. Both statements are correct.
    B. Only one of the statements is correct.
    C. Neither statement is correct.

54. In addition to the factors noted by Petrovich, which of the following is *likely* to be the most important in the risk assessment of tax-backed municipal debt?
    A. A measure of the issuer's debt structure, such as debt as a percentage of total real estate value of properties subject to taxation.
    B. An evaluation of any user-charge covenants that specify how prices will be set on the product or service provided by the municipality with the proceeds of the bond issue.
    C. An evaluation of trends in the local employment level and economic environment, which permits an assessment of the stability of the revenue base and the ability of the municipality to service the debt in the future.

Questions 55–60 relate to Wayland, Inc., and Optimax.

Kevin Rathbun, CFA, is a financial analyst at a major brokerage firm. His supervisor, Elizabeth Mao, CFA, asks him to analyze the financial position of Wayland, Inc. (Wayland), a manufacturer of components for high quality optic transmission systems. Mao also inquires about the impact of any unconsolidated investments.

On December 31, 2007, Wayland purchased a 35% ownership interest in a strategic new firm called Optimax for $300,000 cash. The pre-acquisition balance sheets of both firms are found in Exhibit 1.

Exhibit 1: Pre-Acquisition Balance Sheets for Wayland and Optimax

Balance sheets as of Dec. 31, 2007 *in thousands*	**Wayland**	**Optimax**
Assets		
Cash	$710	$100
Marketable securities	2,550	–
Inventory	2,000	400
Accounts receivable	3,000	500
Property, plant, and equipment	2,450	1,000
Total assets	**$10,710**	**$2,000**
Liabilities		
Accounts payable	$3,310	400
Long-term debt	5,000	1,000
Equity	2,400	600
Total liabilities and equity	**$10,710**	**$2,000**

On the acquisition date, all of Optimax's assets and liabilities were stated on its balance sheet at their fair values except for its property, plant, and equipment (PP&E), which had a fair value of $1.2 million. The remaining useful life of the PP&E is ten years with no salvage value. Both firms use the straight-line depreciation method.

For the year ended 2008, Optimax reported net income of $250,000 and paid dividends of $100,000.

During the first quarter of 2009, Optimax sold goods to Wayland and recognized $15,000 of profit from the sale. At the end of the quarter, half of the goods purchased from Optimax remained in Wayland's inventory.

Wayland currently uses the equity method to account for its investment in Optimax. However, given the potential significance of the investment in the

©2011 Kaplan, Inc.

future, Rathbun believes that a proportionate consolidation of Optimax may give a clearer picture of the financial and operating characteristics of Wayland.

Rathbun also notes that Wayland owns shares in Vanry, Inc. (Vanry). Rathbun gathers the data in Exhibit 2 from Wayland's financial statements. The year-end portfolio value is the market value of all Vanry shares held on December 31. All security transactions occurred on July 1, and the transaction price is the price that Wayland actually paid for the shares acquired. Vanry pays a cash dividend of $1 per share at the end of each year. Wayland expects to sell its investment in Vanry in the near term and accounts for it as *held-for-trading*.

Exhibit 2: Share Transaction Data, Vanry, Inc.

Year	Year-End Portfolio Value	Year-End Shares Held	Year-End Share Price	Transaction Price (July 1)
2007	$1,875,000	25,000[a]	$75	$85
2008	$2,280,000	30,000	76	78

[a] Purchased on July 1, 2007.

Wayland owns some publicly traded bonds of the Rotor Corporation that it reports as held-to-maturity securities.

55. The amount of goodwill as a result of Wayland's acquisition of Optimax is *closest* to:
    A. $0.
    B. $20,000.
    C. $50,000.

56. What amount should Wayland report in its balance sheet as a result of its investment in Optimax at the end of 2008?
    A. $352,000.
    B. $345,500.
    C. $380,500.

57. Which of the following *best* describes Wayland's treatment of the intercompany sales transaction for the quarter ended March 31, 2009? Wayland should reduce its equity income by:
    A. $2,625.
    B. $7,500.
    C. $15,000.

58.	Which of the following pairs contain statements regarding the equity method and proportionate consolidation that are both correct?
A.	Proportionate consolidation results in higher net income, AND both methods will result in the same total equity.
B.	Both methods result in the same net income, AND proportionate consolidation will result in higher cost of goods sold.
C.	The equity method will result in a higher net income if the subsidiary is profitable; proportionate consolidation will result in a higher net income if the subsidiary is not profitable; AND proportionate consolidation requires inclusion of minority interest accounts whereas the equity method does not.

59.	Regarding the Rotor Corporation bonds, Wayland would have the option to reclassify them as designated at fair value from held-to-maturity under:
A.	U.S. GAAP only.
B.	IFRS only.
C.	both IFRS and U.S. GAAP.

60.	As a result of its investment in Vanry, what amount should Wayland recognize in its income statement for the year ended 2008?
A.	$35,000 profit.
B.	$45,000 profit.
C.	$55,000 profit.

End of Morning Session

	©2011 Kaplan, Inc.

Exam 2
Afternoon Session

Question	Topic	Minutes (Points)
61 to 66	Alternative Investments	18
67 to 72	Quantitative Methods	18
73 to 78	Financial Reporting and Analysis	18
79 to 84	Financial Reporting and Analysis	18
85 to 90	Portfolio Management	18
91 to 96	Equity Investments	18
97 to 102	Corporate Finance	18
103 to 108	Corporate Finance	18
109 to 114	Derivative Investments	18
115 to 120	Derivative Investments	18

Test Answers

61.	Ⓐ	Ⓑ	Ⓒ		101.	Ⓐ	Ⓑ	Ⓒ
62.	Ⓐ	Ⓑ	Ⓒ		102.	Ⓐ	Ⓑ	Ⓒ
63.	Ⓐ	Ⓑ	Ⓒ		103.	Ⓐ	Ⓑ	Ⓒ
64.	Ⓐ	Ⓑ	Ⓒ		104.	Ⓐ	Ⓑ	Ⓒ
65.	Ⓐ	Ⓑ	Ⓒ		105.	Ⓐ	Ⓑ	Ⓒ
66.	Ⓐ	Ⓑ	Ⓒ		106.	Ⓐ	Ⓑ	Ⓒ
67.	Ⓐ	Ⓑ	Ⓒ		107.	Ⓐ	Ⓑ	Ⓒ
68.	Ⓐ	Ⓑ	Ⓒ		108.	Ⓐ	Ⓑ	Ⓒ
69.	Ⓐ	Ⓑ	Ⓒ		109.	Ⓐ	Ⓑ	Ⓒ
70.	Ⓐ	Ⓑ	Ⓒ		110.	Ⓐ	Ⓑ	Ⓒ
71.	Ⓐ	Ⓑ	Ⓒ		111.	Ⓐ	Ⓑ	Ⓒ
72.	Ⓐ	Ⓑ	Ⓒ		112.	Ⓐ	Ⓑ	Ⓒ
73.	Ⓐ	Ⓑ	Ⓒ		113.	Ⓐ	Ⓑ	Ⓒ
74.	Ⓐ	Ⓑ	Ⓒ		114.	Ⓐ	Ⓑ	Ⓒ
75.	Ⓐ	Ⓑ	Ⓒ		115.	Ⓐ	Ⓑ	Ⓒ
76.	Ⓐ	Ⓑ	Ⓒ		116.	Ⓐ	Ⓑ	Ⓒ
77.	Ⓐ	Ⓑ	Ⓒ		117.	Ⓐ	Ⓑ	Ⓒ
78.	Ⓐ	Ⓑ	Ⓒ		118.	Ⓐ	Ⓑ	Ⓒ
79.	Ⓐ	Ⓑ	Ⓒ		119.	Ⓐ	Ⓑ	Ⓒ
80.	Ⓐ	Ⓑ	Ⓒ		120.	Ⓐ	Ⓑ	Ⓒ
81.	Ⓐ	Ⓑ	Ⓒ
82.	Ⓐ	Ⓑ	Ⓒ
83.	Ⓐ	Ⓑ	Ⓒ
84.	Ⓐ	Ⓑ	Ⓒ
85.	Ⓐ	Ⓑ	Ⓒ
86.	Ⓐ	Ⓑ	Ⓒ
87.	Ⓐ	Ⓑ	Ⓒ
88.	Ⓐ	Ⓑ	Ⓒ
89.	Ⓐ	Ⓑ	Ⓒ
90.	Ⓐ	Ⓑ	Ⓒ
91.	Ⓐ	Ⓑ	Ⓒ
92.	Ⓐ	Ⓑ	Ⓒ
93.	Ⓐ	Ⓑ	Ⓒ
94.	Ⓐ	Ⓑ	Ⓒ
95.	Ⓐ	Ⓑ	Ⓒ
96.	Ⓐ	Ⓑ	Ⓒ
97.	Ⓐ	Ⓑ	Ⓒ
98.	Ⓐ	Ⓑ	Ⓒ
99.	Ⓐ	Ⓑ	Ⓒ
100.	Ⓐ	Ⓑ	Ⓒ

Exam 2
Afternoon Session

Questions 61–66 relate to IGS.

The New York-based Irwin Goldreich Schmidt (IGS) is a mid-sized private equity firm with $300 million capital raised from its investors. Amid a turbulent year, the firm has recently dropped its unsuccessful $100 million bid for a Norwegian media company and is now aggressively searching for new venture or buyout investments in the Eurozone. After several months of intense search, IGS believes it identified two potential investments:

1. Sverig, a rapidly expanding Swedish start-up construction company.

2. L'Offre, a struggling French department store in existence since the late 19th Century.

Following several rounds of successful negotiations, IGS makes a $20 million investment in Sverig and a $100 million leveraged buyout investment in L'Offre, committing to an additional $100 million for possible future capital drawdowns. It retains all of Sverig's managers but replaces L'Offre's management team with experienced IGS managers, many of whom are former company senior executives.

IGS also sets up Sverig-L'Offre Private Equity Fund (SLPEF), a fund to manage both firms. The fund manager's compensation is set at 20% of profits net of fees. IGS also specifies that the manager's profits are calculated on the entire portfolio when portfolio value exceeds invested capital by 30%.

Despite the market's recent turbulence, Sverig's original founders are extremely optimistic and believe the firm could be sold for $400 million in six years. To achieve this, they speculate the firm needs another capital infusion of $40 million in four years in addition to the $20 million capital investment today. Given the high risk of the firm, SLPEF's private equity investors decide that a discount rate of 40% for the first four years and 30% for the last two years is appropriate. The founders of Sverig want to hold 5 million shares.

61. If total proceeds net of fees to SLPEF are worth $180 million upon exit in a year, the fund's general partner (GP) under the total return using invested capital method would receive a compensation of:
   A. $0.
   B. $12 million.
   C. $36 million.

62. An appropriate equity valuation technique for Sverig and L'Offre, respectively, would be the:

Sverig	L'Offre
A. Relative value approach	Venture capital method
B. Venture capital method	DCF method
C. DCF method	Relative value approach

63. Common risk factor(s) faced by both IGS investors and the managers of the private equity firm is(are):
    A. market risk but not agency risk.
    B. agency risk but not market risk.
    C. both market and agency risk.

64. SLPEF's general partner's (GP's) share of fund profits, and management's right to sell their equity interest in the event of an acquisition, respectively, are called:

Profits to the GP	Management's right to sell
A. Carried interest	Ratchet
B. Ratchet	Distribution waterfall
C. Carried interest	Tag-along, drag-along clause

65. Sverig's post-money valuation at the first round of financing, using the NPV venture capital method, is *closest* to:
    A. $61.61 million.
    B. $50.08 million.
    C. $51.20 million.

66. The appropriate stock price after the first-round of financing for Sverig's first-round investors is *closest* to:
    A. $6.24.
    B. $8.32.
    C. $6.02.

©2011 Kaplan, Inc.

Questions 67–72 relate to Joan Fisher and Kim Weatherford.

Joan Fisher and Kim Weatherford are economists responsible for modeling security returns for Quincy Portfolio Managers, which is located in the southwestern United States. Fisher is the firm's chief economist and Weatherford is her assistant.

Fisher has been busy over the past week modeling the macroeconomic data of an emerging market. The data for the past 24 months is shown in Exhibit 1.

Exhibit 1: Time Series of Emerging Markets Data

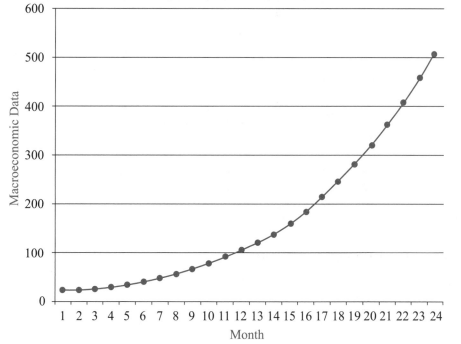

Fisher ponders how she can run a regression that will model the data for this country in the most appropriate way. She decides to regress the macroeconomic values against a time variable. The resulting plot of the residuals is shown in Exhibit 2.

Exhibit 2: Residual Plot from Emerging Markets Data

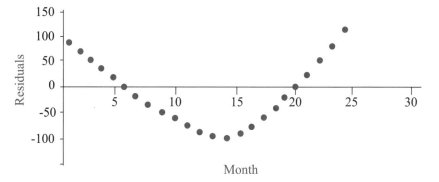

In addition to financial assets, Quincy Portfolio Managers also recommends the use of commodities as a portfolio diversifier. Weatherford has been examining price indices for silver in an attempt to determine whether silver returns are predictable. As an initial step, she uses an autoregressive first-order regression model on daily price data for silver over the past two years. The plot of the raw data and the results of the regression are shown in Exhibits 3 and 4.

Exhibit 3: Time Series of Silver Prices

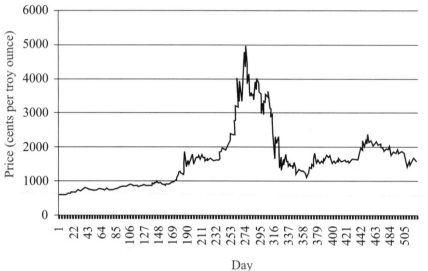

Exhibit 4: Silver Price Regression Results

Regression Statistics	
Multiple R	0.99
R-Square	0.98
Adjusted R-Square	0.98
Standard Error	123.81
Observations	522.00
Durbin-Watson	2.39

©2011 Kaplan, Inc.

Exhibit 4: Silver Price Regression Results (cont.)

ANOVA

	df	SS	MS	F	Significance F
Regression	1.00	365,730,065	365,730,065	23,859.63	0.00
Residual	520.00	7,970,771	15,328		
Total	521.00	373,700,837			

	Coefficients	Standard Error	t-Stat	P-value
Intercept	21.00	11.56	1.82	0.07
Slope	0.99	0.01	154.47	0.00

Fisher and Weatherford later discuss fluctuations in gold prices. Although the arithmetic and geometric mean returns for gold were negative for much of the 1980s and 1990s, Fisher and Weatherford believe that gold should perform better in the future due to higher expected inflation. After appropriate transformation of the data, they use an autoregressive first-order regression model to examine the characteristics of gold returns, the results of which are shown in Exhibit 5.

Exhibit 5: Gold Price Regression Results

Regression Statistics	
Multiple R	0.09
R-Square	0.01
Adjusted R-Square	0.01
Standard Error	123.95
Observations	520.00

ANOVA

	df	SS	MS	F	Significance F
Regression	1.00	66,742	66,742	4.34	0.04
Residual	518.00	7,958,144	15,363		
Total	519.00	8,024,887			

	Coefficients	Standard Error	t-Stat	P-value
Intercept	2.00	5.44	0.37	0.71
Slope	−0.09	0.04	−2.08	0.04

67. In order to *best* model the emerging markets data using linear regression, Fisher should use:
    A. an adjustment for multicollinearity.
    B. the natural log of the dependent variable.
    C. White's correction for the standard errors.

68. The *most likely* problem in Fisher's regression of the emerging market data and the *most appropriate* test for it in the regression are:

Problem	Test
A. Serial correlation	Durbin Watson
B. Serial correlation	Dickey Fuller/Engle Granger
C. Cointegrated variables	Durbin Watson

69. Is the use of the Durbin Watson statistic in Weatherford's silver regression appropriate and, if so, how should it be interpreted?
    A. No.
    B. Yes, and it appears that the error terms are positively correlated.
    C. Yes, and it appears that the error terms are negatively correlated.

70. Which of the following are the *most likely* problem in Weatherford's silver regression and the *most appropriate* test for it?

Problem	Test
A. Multicollinearity	Breusch Pagan
B. Multicollinearity	Dickey Fuller
C. Nonstationary data	Dickey Fuller

71. In order to *best* model the silver price data using an autoregressive first-order regression model, Weatherford should use:
    A. first differences of the data.
    B. the actual silver price levels.
    C. the predicted silver price levels.

72. Using the data for the gold regression, what is the mean reverting level and what is the two-step-ahead forecast if the current value of the independent variable is –0.80?

Mean reverting level	Two-step-ahead forecast
A. 1.830	1.75
B. 1.830	1.81
C. 2.072	1.81

©2011 Kaplan, Inc.

Questions 73–78 relate to Iberia Corporation.

Mark
~~Bryan~~ Stephenson is an equity analyst and is developing a research report on Iberia Corporation at the request of his supervisor. Iberia is a conglomerate entity with significant corporate holdings in various industries. Specifically, Stephenson is interested in the effects of Iberia's investments on its financial performance and has decided to focus on two investments: Midland Incorporated and Odessa Company.

Midland Incorporated

On December 31, 2007, Iberia purchased 5 million common shares of Midland Incorporated for €80 million. Midland has a total of 12.5 million common shares outstanding. The market value of Iberia's investment in Midland was €89 million at the end of 2008, and €85 million at the end of 2009. For the year ended 2008, Midland reported net income of €30 million and paid dividends of €10 million. For the year ended 2009, Midland reported a loss of €5 million and paid dividends of €4 million.

During 2010, Midland sold goods to Iberia and reported 20% gross profit from the sale. Iberia sold all of the goods to a third party in 2010.

Odessa Company

On January 2, 2009, Iberia purchased 1 million common shares of Odessa Company as a long-term investment. The purchase price was €20 per share, and on December 31, 2009, the market price of Odessa was €17 per share. The decline in value was considered temporary. For the year ended 2009, Odessa reported net income of €750 million and paid a dividend of €3 per share. Iberia considers its investment in Odessa as an investment in financial assets.

In addition, Iberia has a number of foreign investments, so Stephenson's supervisor has asked him to draft a report on accounting methods and ratio analysis. The following are statements from Stephenson's research report.

Statement 1: Under U.S. GAAP, firms are required to use proportionate consolidation to account for joint ventures.

Statement 2: In general, if the parent's consolidated net income is positive, the equity method reports a higher net profit margin than the acquisition method.

73. Which of the following is the *most* appropriate classification of Iberia's investment in Odessa Corporation?
    A. Held-to-maturity.
    B. Held-for-trading.
    C. Available-for-sale.

74. What amount should Iberia recognize in its 2009 income statement as a result of its investments in Midland and Odessa?
   A. €1 million profit.
   B. €2 million profit.
   C. €3 million loss.

75. What amount should Iberia report on its balance sheet at the end of 2009 as a result of its investments in Midland and Odessa?
   A. €84.4 million.
   B. €101.4 million.
   C. €102.0 million.

76. What adjustment, if any, must Iberia make to its 2010 income statement as a result of the intercompany transaction with Midland?
   A. Sales and cost of goods sold should be reduced by Iberia's pro-rata ownership interest in the intercompany sale.
   B. Midland's net income should be reduced by 20% of the gross profit from the intercompany sale.
   C. No adjustment is necessary.

77. Is Stephenson's statement regarding proportionate consolidation correct?
   A. Yes.
   B. No, because under U.S. GAAP, proportionate consolidation is allowed only in very limited situations.
   C. No, because under U.S. GAAP, proportionate consolidation is never allowed under any circumstances.

78. Is Stephenson's statement regarding the effect on profit margin correct?
   A. Yes.
   B. No. Net profit margin will be lower using the equity method.
   C. No. Net profit margin will be the same using either the equity method or the acquisition method.

©2011 Kaplan, Inc.

Questions 79–84 relate to Andrew Carson and Samilski Enterprises.

Andrew Carson is an equity analyst employed at Lee, Vincent, and Associates, an investment research firm. In a conversation with his supervisor, Daniel Lau, Carson makes the following two statements about defined contribution plans.

Statement 1:   Employers often face onerous disclosure requirements in their financial reporting.

Statement 2:   Employers often bear all the investment risk.

Carson is responsible for following Samilski Enterprises (Samilski), a publicly traded firm that produces motorcycles and other mechanical parts. It operates exclusively in the United States. At the end of its 2009 fiscal year, Samilski's employee pension plan had a projected benefit obligation (PBO) of $320 million. Also, unrecognized prior service costs were $35 million, the fair value of plan assets was $316 million, and the unrecognized actuarial gain was $21 million.

Carson believes the rate of compensation increase will be 5% as opposed to 4% in the previous year, and the discount rate will be 7% as opposed to 8% in the previous year.

This past year, Samilski began using special purpose entities (SPEs) for various reasons. In preparation for analyzing the SPE disclosures in the footnotes to the financial statements, Carson prepares a memo on SPEs. In the memo, he correctly concludes that the company will be required under new accounting rules to classify them as variable interest entities (VIE) and consolidate the entities on the balance sheet rather than report them using the equity method as in the past.

79.   Is Carson correct with respect to defined contribution plans?
    A. Both statements are incorrect.
    B. Only Statement 1 is incorrect.
    C. Only Statement 2 is incorrect.

80.   Under current U.S. GAAP pension accounting standards, the amount of the pension asset or liability that Samilski should report on its 2009 fiscal year end balance sheet is *closest* to a:
    A. $4 million liability.
    B. $10 million liability.
    C. $14 million liability.

81. Based on Carson's projections of the discount rate, what are the *likely* effects on the projected benefit obligation (PBO) and the pension cost?
    A. Both will increase.
    B. Both will decrease.
    C. One will increase and the other will decrease.

82. Based on Carson's projection of the rate of compensation increase, what are the *likely* effects on the projected benefit obligation (PBO) and the pension cost?
    A. Both will increase.
    B. Both will decrease.
    C. One will increase and the other will decrease.

83. What are the *likely* effects of the required change in accounting for SPEs on Samilski's:

Return on assets?	Return on equity?
A. Decrease	Decrease
B. Decrease	No effect
C. No effect	Decrease

84. Which of the following items, when recognized, will *likely* increase:

PBO?	Pension expense?
A. Actuarial loss	Expected return on plan assets
B. Actuarial loss	Amortization of prior service costs
C. Actuarial gain	Amortization of prior service costs

©2011 Kaplan, Inc.

Questions 85–90 relate to Millennium Investments and Edward Alverson.

Millennium Investments (MI), an investment advisory firm, relies on mean-variance analysis to advise its clients. MI's advisors make asset allocation recommendations by selecting the mix of assets along the capital allocation line that is most appropriate for each client.

One of MI's clients, Edward Alverson, 60 years of age, requests an analysis of four risky mutual funds (Fund W, Fund X, Fund Y, and Fund Z). After examining the four funds, MI finds that all four mutual funds are equally weighted portfolios, and that all of the funds, except Fund Z, are mean-variance efficient. MI also finds that the correlations between all pairs of the mutual funds are less than one.

MI calculates the average variance of returns across all assets within each mutual fund, the average covariance of returns across all pairs of assets within each mutual fund, and each mutual fund's total variance of returns. The results of MI's calculations are reported in Exhibit 1.

Exhibit 1: Mutual Fund Risk Statistics

	Average Asset Variance	Average Covariance	Fund Total Variance
Fund W	0.60	0.24	0.25
Fund X	0.60	0.24	0.36
Fund Y	0.40	0.10	0.16
Fund Z	0.40	0.10	0.25

During his meeting with the MI advisors, Alverson explains that he will retire soon, and, consequently, is highly risk-averse. Alverson agrees with MI's reliance on mean-variance analysis and makes the following statements:

Statement 1:   All portfolios lying on the minimum variance frontier are desirable portfolios.

Statement 2:   Because I am highly risk-averse, I expect that my investment portfolio on the capital allocation line will have risk and return equal to that of the global minimum variance portfolio.

MI operates under the assumption that all investors agree on the forecasts of asset expected returns, variances, and correlations. Based on these assumptions, MI created the Millennium Investments 5000 Fund (MI-5000), which is a market value-weighted portfolio of all assets in the market. MI derives the forecasts for the MI-5000 Fund and for a fund comprising short-term government securities shown in Exhibit 2.

Exhibit 2: Capital Market Forecasts

Asset	Expected Return	Standard Deviation
MI-5000 Fund	0.12	0.20
Government Securities Fund	0.05	0

After assessing Alverson's level of risk aversion, MI's advisors determine that the appropriate standard deviation for Alverson's investment portfolio equals 12%, and that Alverson can achieve his target standard deviation through appropriate allocations to the MI-5000 Fund and to the Government Securities Fund.

85. Of the four mutual funds listed in Exhibit 1, which is *most likely* to include the largest number of assets?
     A. Fund W.
     B. Fund X.
     C. Fund Z.

86. Alverson asks MI to examine the risk-return characteristics for an equal-weighted combination of Funds Y and Z. MI should conclude that the:
     A. expected return on the equal-weighted combination will exceed the arithmetic average of the Fund Y and Fund Z expected returns.
     B. expected return on the equal-weighted combination will be less than the arithmetic average of the Fund Y and Fund Z expected returns.
     C. standard deviation on the equal-weighted combination will be less than the arithmetic average of the Fund Y and Fund Z standard deviations.

87. Are Statements 1 and 2 made by Alverson correct?
     A. Statement 1 is incorrect.
     B. Statement 2 is incorrect.
     C. Both statements are incorrect.

88. According to the capital market forecasts provided in Exhibit 2, the intercept and slope of the capital market line are:

	Intercept	Slope
A.	0.05	0.35
B.	0.05	0.07
C.	0.12	0.07

©2011 Kaplan, Inc.

89.   Given the data in Exhibit 2 and MI's determination that Alverson's
        investment portfolio should have a standard deviation equal to 12%, what
        is the highest possible expected return for Alverson, and what percentage
        should Alverson invest in the MI-5000 fund?

Highest expected return	Percentage invested in MI-5000
A. 7.2%	40%
B. 7.2%	60%
C. 9.2%	60%

90.   Given MI's assumption that all investors have identical expectations of
        expected returns, variances, and correlations, and given the capital market
        forecasts in Exhibit 2, MI should conclude that:
        A. E(R) on Fund W is less than 0.225.
        B. E(R) on Fund Z is less than 0.225.
        C. E(R) on both funds W and Z are less than 0.225.

Questions 91–96 relate to Yi Tang.

Yi Tang updates several economic parameters monthly for use by the analysts and the portfolio managers at her firm. If economic conditions warrant, she will update the parameters even more frequently. As a result of an economic slowdown, she is going through this process now.

The firm has been using an equity risk premium of 5.2%, derived using historical estimates. By comparing the yields on nominal bonds and real bonds, Tang estimates the expected inflation rate to be 2.6%. She expects real domestic growth to be 3.0%. Tang believes that the markets are currently overvalued by 10%. The yield on the market index is 1.7%, and the expected risk-free rate of return is 2.7%.

Elizabeth Trotter, one of the firm's portfolio Managers, asks Tang about the effects of survivorship bias on estimates of the equity risk premium. Trotter asks, "Which method is most susceptible to this bias: historical estimates, Gordon growth model estimates, or survey estimates?"

Tang wishes to estimate the required rate of return for Northeast Electric (NE) using the Capital Asset Pricing Model (CAPM) and the Fama-French model. She uses the following information to accomplish this:

Factor	Risk Premium	Factor Sensitivity
Market	5.2%	0.83 (historical)
Size	3.2%	–0.76
Value	5.4%	–0.04
Liquidity	1.1%	0.20

Trotter has one final question for Tang. Trotter says, "We need to estimate the equity beta for VixPRO, which is a private company that is not publicly traded. We have identified a publicly traded company that has similar operating characteristics to VixPRO, and we have estimated the beta for that company using regression analysis. We used the return on the public company as the dependent variable and the return on the market index as the independent variable. What steps do I need to take to find the beta for VixPRO equity? The companies have different debt/equity ratios. The debt of both companies is very low risk, and I believe I can ignore taxes."

91.   The estimate of the equity risk premium using the Ibbotson-Chen model given the estimates determined by Tang is *closest* to:
        A. 1.5%.
        B. 4.2%.
        C. 4.7%.

©2011 Kaplan, Inc.

92.   The *best* response to Trotter's question about survivorship bias is:
        A. survey estimates.
        B. Gordon model estimates.
        C. historical estimates.

93.   The required rate of return for NE estimated with the CAPM is *closest* to:
        A. 5.7%.
        B. 6.0%.
        C. 7.0%.

94.   The required rate of return for NE estimated with the Fama-French model is *closest* to:
        A. 4.4%.
        B. 4.7%.
        C. 9.0%.

95.   Using the Blume method, the adjusted beta computed by Tang would be *closest* to:
        A. 0.90.
        B. 0.96.
        C. 1.03.

96.   What response should Tang give Trotter about estimating the equity beta for VixPRO?
        A. Estimate the beta for VixPRO by regressing the returns for VixPRO against an index of non-traded equity market securities.
        B. Estimate the VixPRO beta by multiplying the public company beta times the ratio of the equity risk premium of the market to the risk-free rate of return.
        C. Estimate the unlevered beta for the public company based on its debt/equity ratio. Then, use that unlevered beta to estimate the equity beta for VixPRO based on the VixPRO debt/equity ratio.

Questions 97–102 relate to Kazmaier Foods.

The board members for Kazmaier Foods have gathered for their quarterly board of directors meeting. Presiding at the meeting is the Chairman and CEO for Kazmaier, Phil Hinesman. The other eight members of the board are also present, including Allen Kazmaier, the brother of Kazmaier's founder; Elaine Randall, Executive Vice President for Emerald Bank, which Kazmaier uses to obtain short-term financing; and Bill Schram, Kazmaier's President and Chief Operating Officer. Each of the directors was elected to serve on the board for a 4-year term. They were elected two at a time over the past three years. With the exception of Hinesman, Allen Kazmaier, Randall, and Schram, board members had no ties to Kazmaier prior to joining the board and had no personal relationships with management. In addition to the regular board meetings, the five independent board members get together annually, in a meeting separate from the regular board meetings, to discuss the company's operations.

Item 1 on the board meeting agenda is a discussion about the importance of corporate governance and how Kazmaier can improve its corporate governance system. Hinesman begins the discussion by saying, "A strong system of corporate governance is important to our shareholders. Studies have shown that, on average, companies with strong corporate governance systems have higher measures of profitability than companies with weak corporate governance systems." Randall adds her comment to the discussion: "The lack of an effective corporate governance system increases risk for our investors. If we do not have the appropriate checks and balances in place, our investors may be exposed to the risk that information used to make decisions about our firm is misleading or incomplete, as well as the risk that mergers or acquisitions the firm enters into will benefit management at the expense of shareholders."

After a lengthy discussion, the board agrees on five separate recommendations that will enhance its current system of corporate governance. One of these recommendations is to change the function and structure of the board's audit committee. Currently, the audit committee consists of Matthew Bortz, David Smith, and Ann Williams—three independent directors who each have backgrounds in finance and accounting. The board agrees that one more member should be added to the committee and that the committee should expand its list of responsibilities.

Item 2 on the agenda for the board of directors' meeting is a report from Kazmaier's Chief Financial Officer, Doug Layman. The following information

©2011 Kaplan, Inc.

was included in the material that was distributed to each board member before the meeting:

($ Millions)	20X0	20X1*
Net income	$98.50	$112.50
Cash flow from operations	$115.00	$132.00
Capital expenditures (FCInv)	$43.00	$150.00
Net borrowing	$22.00	$75.00
Dividends paid	$42.88	$45.00
Stock repurchases	$42.00	$3.00

*Estimated

Additional information:

Current share price:	$40.00
Shares outstanding:	56,250,000
Target debt-to-equity ratio:	1 to 1
Cost of equity:	8.0%
Constant growth rate:	5.2%

Layman tells the board that his analysis indicates that, based on a constant-growth dividend discount model, the current stable dividend policy would reduce the cost of equity by 1.2% and increase the value of the firm's stock, assuming that earnings, the cost of debt, and the constant growth rate don't change.

Item 3 on the agenda is the sale of Kazmaier's condiment packaging division to Sautter Packaging and Supply Company. Layman believes the sale will net the company $50 million, payable in cash. After discussing the pros and cons of selling the division, the directors agree that the sale is in the best interests of the company and its shareholders. The directors then move to a vote, and the sale of the condiment packaging division is approved unanimously. The committee then moves on to discuss what to do with the proceeds from the sale. Williams suggests that paying out the $50 million to shareholders as a special dividend would continue to give the firm flexibility in how it uses its excess cash. Smith tells the board that a share repurchase can be thought of as an alternative to a cash dividend, and that if the tax treatment between the two alternatives is the same, investors should be indifferent between the two. After debating the merits of special dividends and stock repurchases, Kazmaier's board authorizes the proceeds from the sale of the condiment packaging division to be used for the purchase of $50 million worth of outstanding shares.

An external agency recently included Kazmaier in a review of corporate governance systems to determine whether the structure of the board of directors was consistent with corporate governance best practices. The agency scored companies based on the following criteria:

Criterion 1: Composition of the board of directors.
Criterion 2: Chairman of the board of directors.
Criterion 3: Method of electing the board.
Criterion 4: Frequency of separate sessions for independent directors.

Each of the four criteria was weighted equally, with the firm receiving a positive mark for being in compliance with corporate governance best practice.

A month after the board meeting, the price of Kazmaier stock is still at $40 per share, and the sale of Kazmaier's condiment packaging division does not go through. In order to finance the approved share repurchase, Kazmaier is forced to borrow funds. Schram states, "I am concerned that the cost of the debt used to repurchase shares may cause a reduction in earnings per share."

Jennifer Nagy, a vice president in Kazmaier's finance division, tells Schram not to be concerned about using debt to finance the share repurchase because the rationale behind the repurchase is sound. Nagy then writes down some of the common rationales for share repurchases and hands them to Schram.

Rationale 1: Repurchasing shares can prevent the EPS dilution that comes from the exercise of employee stock options.

Rationale 2: Management can use a share repurchase to alter the company's capital structure by decreasing the percentage of equity.

Rationale 3: Like a dividend increase, a share repurchase is a way to send a signal to investors that Kazmaier's management believes the outlook for the company's future is strong.

97.   Are the comments made by Hinesman and Randall about corporate governance systems correct?
     A. Both comments are correct.
     B. Only Hinesman is correct.
     C. Only Randall is correct.

98. Which of the following pairs of recommendations would be *best* in helping Kazmaier's audit committee comply with corporate governance best practices?
    A. The internal audit staff of the firm should report directly to the audit committee, all of the audit committee members should be independent, and the committee should meet with auditors at least annually without management present.
    B. At least 75% of the audit committee members should be independent, and all of the committee members should have a background in finance and accounting.
    C. All of the audit committee members should be independent and should meet with management at least annually to discuss findings in internal audits.

99. Based on the financial information distributed to the board members, the dividend per share for 20X1 based on a residual dividend approach should be *closest* to:
    A. $0.00.
    B. $0.22.
    C. $0.67.

100. Based on the financial information distributed to the board members, the FCFE coverage ratios for 20X0 and 20X1 are *closest* to:

	20X0	20X1
A.	2.19	1.27
B.	1.11	1.19
C.	1.35	2.75

101. Kazmaier's total score on the corporate governance report is *closest* to:
    A. 25%.
    B. 50%.
    C. 75%.

102. How many of Nagy's rationales for a share repurchase are valid?
    A. One.
    B. Two.
    C. Three.

Questions 103–108 relate to Henke Malfoy.

Henke Malfoy, CFA, is an analyst with a major manufacturing firm. Currently, he is evaluating the replacement of some production equipment. The old machine is still functional and could continue to serve in its current capacity for three more years. If the new equipment is purchased, the old equipment (which is fully depreciated) can be sold for $50,000. The new equipment will cost $400,000, including shipping and installation. If the new equipment is purchased, the company's revenues will increase by $175,000 and costs by $25,000 for each year of the equipment's 3-year life. There is no expected change in net working capital.

The new machine will be depreciated using a 3-year MACRS schedule (note: the 3-year MACRS schedule is 33.0% in the first year, 45% in the second year, 15% in the third year, and 7% in the fourth year). At the end of the life of the new equipment (i.e., in three years), Malfoy expects that it can be sold for $10,000. The firm has a marginal tax rate of 40%, and the cost of capital on this project is 20%. In calculation of tax liabilities, Malfoy assumes that the firm is profitable, so any losses on this project can be offset against profits elsewhere in the firm. Malfoy calculates a project NPV of –$62,574.

103.   The initial outlay for the project is *closest* to:
  A. $350,000.
  B. $370,000.
  C. $400,000.

104.   The after-tax operating cash flow for the first year of operations with the new equipment (excluding the initial outlay) is *closest* to:
  A. $10,800.
  B. $132,000.
  C. $142,800.

105.   What is the effect of taxes on the operating cash flow in year 2?
  A. Decrease by $7,200.
  B. Increase by $7,200.
  C. Increase by $12,000.

106.   The combined after-tax operating cash flow and terminal year after-tax nonoperating cash flow in year 3 is *closest* to:
  A. $131,200.
  B. $151,200.
  C. $152,200.

©2011 Kaplan, Inc.

107.   Suppose for this question only that Malfoy has forgotten to reflect a
        decrease in inventory that will result at the beginning of the project. The
        most likely effect on estimated project NPV of this error:
        A. is to overestimate NPV.
        B. is to underestimate NPV.
        C. depends on whether the inventory is assumed to build back up to its
            previous level at the end of the project or the decrease in inventory is
            permanent.

108.   What is the IRR based on Malfoy's NPV estimate, and should the project
        be accepted or rejected in order to maximize shareholder value?

IRR	Project
A. 8.8%	Accept
B. 8.8%	Reject
C. 21.5%	Accept

Questions 109–114 relate to Shirley Nolte.

Shirley Nolte, CFA, is a portfolio manager for McHugh Investments. Her portfolio includes 5,000 shares of Pioneer common stock (ticker symbol PNER), which is currently trading at $40 per share. Pioneer is an energy and petrochemical business that operates or markets its products in the United States, Canada, Mexico, and over 100 other countries around the world. Pioneer's core business is the exploration, production, and transportation of crude oil and natural gas. Pioneer also manufactures and markets petroleum products, basic petrochemicals, and a variety of specialty products.

Nolte would like to fully hedge her exposure to price fluctuations in Pioneer common stock over the next 90 days. She determines that the continuously compounded risk-free rate is 5%. She also gathers some information on exchange-traded options available on Pioneer stock. This data is shown in Exhibit 1.

Exhibit 1: Exchange-Traded Options on Pioneer Stock

Maturity	Exercise Price	Call Option Price	Call Option Delta	Put Option Price
1-month	$40	$2.84	0.54	$2.67
3-month	$40	$5.00	0.58	$4.50
6-month	$40	$7.14	0.61	$6.15
9-month	$40	$8.81	0.63	$7.34

From this data, she determines that the put option deltas are equal to the following:

- 1-month put option delta = –0.46.
- 3-month put option delta = –0.36.
- 6-month put option delta = –0.29.
- 9-month put option delta = –0.17.

She also concludes that the 9-month put option is mispriced relative to the 9-month call option, and an arbitrage opportunity is possible, but that the 3-month put option is correctly priced relative to its comparable call option. She also estimates the gamma of the 3-month call option to be 0.023.

In an unrelated transaction, Nolte is also considering the purchase of a put option on a futures contract with an exercise price of $22. Both the option and the futures contract expire in six months. The call price is $1, and the futures price today is $20.

©2011 Kaplan, Inc.

109.   Which of the following positions will *best* delta hedge Nolte's long position in Pioneer?
        A. Short 9,259 1-month call options.
        B. Short 8,197 3-month call options.
        C. Short 7,937 6-month call options.

110.   If Nolte hedges the position with the 3-month call options, she:
        A. will have to continuously rebalance the position in order to maintain the delta hedge.
        B. can offset the cost of the hedge and maintain the hedged position by buying an equivalent amount of 3-month put options.
        C. will perfectly hedge the position over the 90-day investment horizon and won't need to rebalance the position only if the stock price of Pioneer remains at $40 for 90 days.

111.   The gamma of the 3-month, $40 call option on Pioneer stock is *most likely*:
        A. greater than the gamma of a 3-month $50 call on Pioneer.
        B. less than the gamma of a 3-month $50 call on Pioneer.
        C. less than the gamma of a 3-month $30 call on Pioneer.

112.   Is Nolte correct in her analysis of the 1-month and 6-month put option deltas?
        A. Nolte is correct on both options.
        B. Nolte is only correct on the 1-month option.
        C. Nolte is only correct on the 6-month option.

113.   Is Nolte correct in her analysis of the relative pricing of the 3-month put option and the 9-month put option?
        A. Nolte is correct on both options.
        B. Nolte is only correct on the 3-month option.
        C. Nolte is only correct on the 9-month option.

114.   The value of the put option on the futures contract is *closest* to:
        A. $2.45.
        B. $2.65.
        C. $2.95.

Questions 115–120 relate to Trent Black.

Trent Black is a government fixed-income portfolio manager, and on January 1, he holds $30 million of fixed-rate, semi-annual pay notes. Black is considering entering into a 2-year, $30 million semi-annual pay interest rate swap as the fixed-rate payer. He must first determine the swap rate. Black notes the following term structure:

Days	Annual Rate (%)	Discount Factor
180	3.25	0.9840
360	3.35	0.9676
540	3.60	0.9488
720	3.85	0.9285

Black is also evaluating receiver and payer swaptions on the same $30 million interest rate swap. The swaptions are European-style swaptions that mature in 240 days. Black anticipates a decline in interest rates and would like to use the swaptions to profit from his interest rate forecast.

Black is also concerned about the potential credit risk inherent in both interest rate swaps and swaptions, so he consults Marcus Coleman, a contract specialist in the legal department. Coleman advises Black that:

Statement 1: The fixed rate payer in any plain vanilla interest rate swap is exposed to potential credit risk at the initiation of the swap, but the floating rate payer is not.

Statement 2: The long position is exposed to potential credit risk in a payer swaption at initiation, but the short position in a payer swaption is not.

On May 1, after 120 days, Black is asked to determine the value of the 2-year, $30 million swap. The term structure after 120 days is:

Days	Annual Rate (%)	Discount Factor
30	3.21	0.9973
60	3.31	0.9945
180	3.66	0.9820
240	3.69	0.9760
360	4.21	0.9596
420	4.42	0.9510
480	4.69	0.9411
540	4.74	0.9336
600	4.89	0.9246
720	5.00	0.9091

 ©2011 Kaplan, Inc.

115. The annualized fixed rate for the $30 million swap on January 1 is *closest* to:
   A. 3.73%.
   B. 3.80%.
   C. 3.91%.

116. Ignore your answer to Question 115 and assume the annualized fixed rate on the swap is 3.80%. The amount of the first fixed payment due on this swap is *closest* to:
   A. $285,000.
   B. $570,000.
   C. $1,140,000.

117. One hundred twenty days after issue, the value of a 2-year, semi-annual fixed rate bond and the value of a 2-year, semi-annual floating rate note (based on $1 of notional principal), assuming the annualized fixed rate is 3.80%, are *closest* to:
   A. $0.98190 fixed and $0.99970 floating.
   B. $0.99000 fixed and $1.01000 floating.
   C. $0.99768 fixed and $1.01066 floating.

118. Ignore your answer to Question 117 for this question. Based on the notional principal, and assuming the value of the fixed-rate bond and floating-rate note are 0.99000 and 1.01000 (per $1 of notional principal), respectively, what is the payment required to terminate the swap, and which party will make the payment?
   A. $600,000 paid by the floating-rate payer.
   B. $1,200,000 paid by the fixed-rate payer.
   C. $600,000 paid by the floating-rate payer, and $1,200,000 paid by the fixed-rate payer.

119. Which position (long or short) should Black take in the payer and receiver swaptions based on his interest rate forecast?

	Payer swaption	Receiver swaption
A.	Short	Short
B.	Long	Short
C.	Short	Long

120. Is Coleman correct with respect to the credit risk of swaps and swaptions?
   A. Correct on both statements.
   B. Only correct on Statement 1.
   C. Only correct on Statement 2.

End of Afternoon Session

Exam 3
Morning Session

Question	Topic	Minutes (Points)
1 to 6	Equity Investments	18
7 to 12	Equity Investments	18
13 to 18	Corporate Finance	18
19 to 24	Equity Investments	18
25 to 30	Equity Investments	18
31 to 36	Derivative Investments	18
37 to 42	Derivative Investments	18
43 to 48	Portfolio Management	18
49 to 54	Portfolio Management	18
55 to 60	Ethics	18

Test Answers

1.	Ⓐ	Ⓑ	Ⓒ		41.	Ⓐ	Ⓑ	Ⓒ
2.	Ⓐ	Ⓑ	Ⓒ		42.	Ⓐ	Ⓑ	Ⓒ
3.	Ⓐ	Ⓑ	Ⓒ		43.	Ⓐ	Ⓑ	Ⓒ
4.	Ⓐ	Ⓑ	Ⓒ		44.	Ⓐ	Ⓑ	Ⓒ
5.	Ⓐ	Ⓑ	Ⓒ		45.	Ⓐ	Ⓑ	Ⓒ
6.	Ⓐ	Ⓑ	Ⓒ		46.	Ⓐ	Ⓑ	Ⓒ
7.	Ⓐ	Ⓑ	Ⓒ		47.	Ⓐ	Ⓑ	Ⓒ
8.	Ⓐ	Ⓑ	Ⓒ		48.	Ⓐ	Ⓑ	Ⓒ
9.	Ⓐ	Ⓑ	Ⓒ		49.	Ⓐ	Ⓑ	Ⓒ
10.	Ⓐ	Ⓑ	Ⓒ		50.	Ⓐ	Ⓑ	Ⓒ
11.	Ⓐ	Ⓑ	Ⓒ		51.	Ⓐ	Ⓑ	Ⓒ
12.	Ⓐ	Ⓑ	Ⓒ		52.	Ⓐ	Ⓑ	Ⓒ
13.	Ⓐ	Ⓑ	Ⓒ		53.	Ⓐ	Ⓑ	Ⓒ
14.	Ⓐ	Ⓑ	Ⓒ		54.	Ⓐ	Ⓑ	Ⓒ
15.	Ⓐ	Ⓑ	Ⓒ		55.	Ⓐ	Ⓑ	Ⓒ
16.	Ⓐ	Ⓑ	Ⓒ		56.	Ⓐ	Ⓑ	Ⓒ
17.	Ⓐ	Ⓑ	Ⓒ		57.	Ⓐ	Ⓑ	Ⓒ
18.	Ⓐ	Ⓑ	Ⓒ		58.	Ⓐ	Ⓑ	Ⓒ
19.	Ⓐ	Ⓑ	Ⓒ		59.	Ⓐ	Ⓑ	Ⓒ
20.	Ⓐ	Ⓑ	Ⓒ		60.	Ⓐ	Ⓑ	Ⓒ
21.	Ⓐ	Ⓑ	Ⓒ					
22.	Ⓐ	Ⓑ	Ⓒ					
23.	Ⓐ	Ⓑ	Ⓒ					
24.	Ⓐ	Ⓑ	Ⓒ					
25.	Ⓐ	Ⓑ	Ⓒ					
26.	Ⓐ	Ⓑ	Ⓒ					
27.	Ⓐ	Ⓑ	Ⓒ					
28.	Ⓐ	Ⓑ	Ⓒ					
29.	Ⓐ	Ⓑ	Ⓒ					
30.	Ⓐ	Ⓑ	Ⓒ					
31.	Ⓐ	Ⓑ	Ⓒ					
32.	Ⓐ	Ⓑ	Ⓒ					
33.	Ⓐ	Ⓑ	Ⓒ					
34.	Ⓐ	Ⓑ	Ⓒ					
35.	Ⓐ	Ⓑ	Ⓒ					
36.	Ⓐ	Ⓑ	Ⓒ					
37.	Ⓐ	Ⓑ	Ⓒ					
38.	Ⓐ	Ⓑ	Ⓒ					
39.	Ⓐ	Ⓑ	Ⓒ					
40.	Ⓐ	Ⓑ	Ⓒ					

Exam 3
Morning Session

Questions 1–6 relate to Pacific Computer Components (PCC).

General Investments is considering the purchase of a significant stake in Pacific Computer Components (PCC). Although PCC has stable production output, the company is located in a developing country with an uncertain economic environment. Since the monetary environment is particularly worrisome, General has decided to approach the valuation of PCC from a free cash flow model using real growth rates. In real rate analysis, General uses a modified build-up method for calculating the required real return, specifically:

required real return = country real rate + industry adjustment + company adjustment

Elias Sando, CFA, an analyst with General, estimates the following information for PCC:

Domestic inflation rate = 8.738%
Nominal growth rate = 12.000%
Real country return = 3.000%
Industry adjustment = 3.000%
Company adjustment = 2.000%

Additionally, Exhibit 1 reports information from PCC's financial statements for the year just ended (stated in LC).

Exhibit 1: Selected Financial Statement Information for PCC

Investment in fixed capital	LC3,200,000
Investment in working capital	LC400,000
New borrowing	LC2,400,000
Debt repayment	LC2,000,000
Depreciation	LC3,500,000
Interest expense	LC5,000,000
Net income	LC7,000,000
Tax rate	34%
Dividends	LC0

PCC generally maintains relatively constant proportions of equity and debt financing and is expected to do so going forward.

Sando has gathered information on earnings before interest, taxes, depreciation, and amortization (EBITDA) and is contemplating its direct use in another cash flow approach aimed at valuing PCC. Consider the following two statements regarding EBITDA:

Statement 1: EBITDA is not a good proxy for free cash flow to the firm (FCFF) because it does not incorporate the importance of the depreciation tax shield, nor does it reflect the investment in working capital or in fixed capital.

Statement 2: EBITDA is also a poor proxy for FCFE.

1. Free cash flow to equity (FCFE) is *closest* to:
   A. LC7,300,000.
   B. LC8,400,000.
   C. LC10,200,000.

2. Free cash flow to the firm (FCFF) for PCC is *closest* to:
   A. LC7,300,000.
   B. LC8,100,000.
   C. LC10,200,000.

3. The current value of PCC equity using a FCFE model is *closest* to:
   A. LC150,380,000.
   B. LC173,420,000.
   C. LC215,150,000.

4. Suppose that PCC initiates a cash dividend, with a target payout ratio of 25% of net income. What is the *likely* magnitude of the effect of the new cash dividend and the net change in the outstanding debt on future FCFE, all else equal?
   A. The dividend has a large effect, and the debt change has a small effect.
   B. The dividend has a large effect, and the debt change has no effect.
   C. The dividend has no effect, and the debt change has a small effect.

5. Under the assumption that PCC maintains relatively constant proportions of equity and debt financing, the *most appropriate* valuation model is the:
   A. FCFF approach.
   B. FCFE approach.
   C. residual income approach.

6. Are the statements concerning EBITDA correct or incorrect?
   A. Only Statement 1 is correct.
   B. Only Statement 2 is correct.
   C. Both statements are correct.

©2011 Kaplan, Inc.

Questions 7–12 relate to Global Drug World.

Carl Warner, CFA, has been asked to review the financial information of Global Drug World (GDW) in preparation for a possible takeover bid by rival competitor Consolidated Drugstores International (Consolidated). GDW has produced impressive results since going public via an initial public offering in 1998. Through a program of aggressive growth by acquisition, GDW is currently seen as a major player and a threat to Consolidated's own plans for growth and profitability. In preparation for his analysis, Warner has gathered the following financial data from GDW's year-end statements:

GDW Statement of Income for Year ended May 31, 2008

Sales	4,052,173
Expenses	
Cost of goods sold, general and operating expenses	3,735,397
Noncash charges	56,293
Interest on long-term debt	20,265
Other interest	5,223
	3,817,178
Income before income taxes	234,995
Income taxes	70,499
Net income	164,497
Earnings per share	0.72

Partial GDW Balance Sheet on May 31, 2008

Assets	
Current assets (excluding cash)	
Accounts receivable	284,762
Inventories	490,755
Prepaid expenses	23,743
Total current assets (excluding cash)	799,260
Property, plant, and equipment	687,890
Other assets	236,417
	1,723,567
Liabilities	
Current liabilities (excluding notes payable)	
Accounts payable and accrued liabilities	296,564
Other	100,039
Total current liabilities (excluding notes payable)	396,603
Long-term debt	262,981
Other liabilities	15,484

Additional Information	
Risk-free rate	4.5%
WACC	7.5%
2008 working capital investment	$7,325
2008 dividends	$82,248
Beta	1.10
Investment in fixed capital in 2008	$143,579
Market risk premium	5%
Total equity May 31, 2007	$1,019,869
Principal repayment of long-term debt in 2008	$33,275
Notes payable issued in 2008	$5,866
2008 change in liabilities	− $27,409
Tax rate	30%

As part of his analysis, Warner needs to forecast the free cash flow to the firm (FCFF) for 2009. The best information he has points to an increase in sales of 6%. The earnings before interest and tax (EBIT) margin is not expected to change from the rate of 6.4% achieved in 2008. Additional fixed capital spending is expected to be $36,470. Investment in net working capital is expected to be $24,313. Moreover, Warner notes that the only noncash charge is depreciation, which he estimates will be $60,000.

Warner has been asked to analyze the effect each of the following corporate events, if taken during 2009, would have on GDW's free cash flow to equity (FCFE):

- 20% increase in dividends per share.
- Repurchase of 25% of the firm's outstanding shares using cash.
- New common share offering that would increase shares outstanding by 30%.
- New issue of convertible bonds that are not callable for five years and would increase the level of debt by 10%.

7. The 2008 free cash flow to the firm (FCFF) for Global Drug World (GDW) in dollars is *closest* to:
    A. $87,728.
    B. $95,374.
    C. $102,378.

©2011 Kaplan, Inc.

8.   By how much (in dollars) does GDW's FCFF exceed its free cash flow to
      equity (FCFE) in 2008?
      A. $9,567.
      B. $45,251.
      C. $52,897.

9.   The cost of equity and the sustainable growth rate (using beginning equity)
      are *closest* to:

	Cost of equity	Sustainable growth rate
A.	6%	8%
B.	10%	8%
C.	10%	16%

10.   The 2009 estimate of FCFF is *closest* to:
      A. $191,646.
      B. $210,329.
      C. $215,329.

11.   Warner determines that on a per-share basis, the FCFE for GDW in 2008
      is $0.19. Further analysis suggests that FCFE per share will grow by $0.02
      in each of the next two years before leveling off to a long-term growth rate
      of 5%. The current value of one share of GDW's equity is *closest* to:
      A. $4.37.
      B. $7.15.
      C. $13.49.

12.   Which corporate event that Warner is analyzing is *likely* to have the largest
      effect on FCFE in 2009?
      A. Share repurchase.
      B. Share offering.
      C. Convertible bond issue.

Questions 13–18 relate to Dan Andrews.

Dan Andrews, CFA is the equity analyst for a large pension fund. One of the fund's holdings is Debian Corporation. After a period of rapid growth, Debian has underperformed its peers over the past two years. Debian's management has announced a change in ownership structure for part of its business, or possibly a disposal of part of the business. Several options are under consideration: a spin-off, a carve-out, or an asset sale. Andrews decides to research each of these options to understand the impact on Debian's business and their shareholders. He has read the following comments regarding the various methods:

Statement 1: Involves shares being issued to the general public.

Statement 2: Shareholders have a choice of holding onto the new shares automatically issued to them or disposing of the shares on the open market.

Statement 3: Shareholders will be more easily able to link executive compensation to the performance of the business involved.

Statement 4: The firm separates a portion of its operations from the parent company.

Statement 5: A new independent entity will be created that is completely distinct from the parent; the parent will lose all control of the business.

Debian's management announced in the last conference call that a potential buyer, Fedora, Inc., is interested in buying Ubuntu, one of Debian's divisions. Fedora has offered to pay $90 million cash to buy Ubuntu. Relevant information is provided in Exhibit 1.

Exhibit 1

Value of Ubuntu as a stand-alone business	$78 million
Value of Ubuntu to Debian	$85 million
Value of Fedora (5 million shares, $10 par)	$132 million
Value of Fedora and Ubuntu as a combined entity (post cash acquisition of Ubuntu)	$135 million

Alternatively, Fedora is prepared to offer to buy Ubuntu by directly issuing to the shareholders of Debian a total of 3 million $1 par value shares that will rank equally with its existing shares.

Andrews frequents continuing education seminars offered by his local CFA society. During one of these seminars, Andrews meets Jason Arnold, a corporate governance specialist. Andrews agrees with Arnold that a

                    ©2011 Kaplan, Inc.

comprehensive equity analysis should include an analysis of corporate governance. Andrews, however, is unsure of the core attributes of an effective corporate governance system. Arnold states that he could recall two specific attributes:

Attribute 1: Description of rights and responsibilities of shareholders and other stakeholders.

Attribute 2: Fairness and equitable treatment in all dealings between managers, directors, and shareholders.

Among other companies that Andrews is researching, he has identified a potential acquisition target, Mandriva, Inc. Mandriva has enjoyed good growth over the past few years and is expected to continue to do so in the near future. Andrews wants to value Mandriva using both the comparable company method and the comparable transaction approach. Andrews obtains data on recent acquisitions of similar companies. Exhibit 2 summarizes this data:

Exhibit 2

- The mean price-to-book ratio of comparable firms is estimated to be 2 times, and the mean price-to-earnings ratio of the same comparable firms is 25 times.
- The mean acquisition price-to-book ratio of recent targets is estimated to be 2.80 times, and the mean price-to-earnings ratio of the same firms is 30 times.
- Mandriva's book value per share is $18, and EPS is $1.50.
- The mean takeover premium of recent acquisitions in the same industry as Mandriva is estimated to be 30%.

36   37.5
50.4

---

13. Which of the statements correctly reflect aspects of a carve-out?
     A. Statements 1, 4, and 5 only.
     B. Statements 1, 3, and 4 only.
     C. Statements 2, 3, and 4 only.

14. If Fedora pays $90 million cash for the purchase of Ubuntu from Debian, what will be the gain to Debian's and Fedora's shareholders?

	Debian's S/H	Fedora's S/H
A.	$5 million	$3 million
B.	$12 million	$5 million
C.	$12 million	$7 million

15. If Debian shareholders accept the stock offer by Fedora, the economic impact on them would be *closest* to:
   A. a gain of $630,000.
   B. a loss of $630,000.
   C. a loss of $1,612,500.

16. Under Fedora's stock offer, the economic impact on the current shareholders of Fedora is *closest* to:
   A. a loss of $7.5 million.
   B. a gain of $8.6 million.
   C. a gain of $1.6 million.

17. Are Arnold's attributes 1 and 2 of an effective corporate governance system correct?
   A. Both of these attributes are incorrect.
   B. Only one of these attributes is correct.
   C. Both of these attributes are correct.

18. Using the data collected by Andrews, the target takeover price per share of Mandriva under the comparable company analysis and under the comparable transaction analysis is *closest* to:

	Comparable company	Comparable transaction
A.	$24	$48
B.	$24	$50
C.	$48	$48

©2011 Kaplan, Inc.

Questions 19–24 relate to JS Investments.

Bryan Galloway is a strategist for JS Investments, a small money management firm. His goal is to analyze industries to determine whether there is justification for over- or under-weighting. His supervisor, Robyn Black, CFA, has asked that he document the process he uses to make his recommendations. However, just to be sure that Galloway understands industry analysis, Black asks him to provide examples of supply and demand analysis. Galloway makes the following two statements to prove that he understands the issue:

Statement 1:   In analyzing supply in the tire and rubber industry, it is clear that the sale of each additional automobile will result in the sale of approximately two winter tires.

Statement 2:   In analyzing demand for services in the healthcare industry, for every 100 new hospital beds required, 20 additional doctors are needed.

Black is not entirely confident in Galloway's abilities to analyze various industries, but decides to allow him to continue with his analysis.

Four of the largest holdings for JS Investments are a tobacco company, a soda drink company, an oil company, and a cable TV company. Black is worried that government intervention will have a serious impact on future growth for these companies and asks Galloway to further research each of the industries involved. However, just to make sure Galloway can handle this project, Black first asks him to review the basics of industry analysis.

In reviewing the factors affecting pricing considerations, Galloway concludes that all of the following are of direct importance:

Factor 1:   Price changes in key supply inputs.

Factor 2:   Product segmentation.

Factor 3:   Ease of entry into the industry.

Factor 4:   Degree of industry concentration.

Galloway also makes the following statements about the characteristics of the phases of the industrial life cycle:

Characteristic 1: Participants compete for market share in a stable industry.

Characteristic 2: Changing tastes have an important impact on the industry.

Characteristic 3: It is not clear that a product will be accepted in the industry.

Characteristic 4: Proper execution of strategy is critical.

Each of the phases is represented by one characteristic.

19. Which of the following choices *best* describes all the elements that Galloway should consider in doing an analysis of external factors in an industry analysis?
    A. Technology; government; social; demographic; foreign.
    B. Social; demographic; foreign; pricing; degree of concentration.
    C. Government; technology; end users; degree of concentration; ease of entry.

20. Excluding external factors, industry analysis is *best* described as including:
    A. industry classification; profitability analysis; innovation turnover.
    B. industry classification; demand analysis; supply analysis; profitability analysis.
    C. profitability analysis; competition analysis; innovation turnover; industry classification.

21. Are the two statements regarding supply and demand analysis correct or incorrect?
    A. Both statements are correct.
    B. Only one of the statements is correct.
    C. Both statements are incorrect.

22. For which of the following global industries would U.S. government involvement *most likely* represent an example of a negative external influence?
    A. The oil industry.
    B. The tobacco industry.
    C. The cable TV industry.

©2011 Kaplan, Inc.

23. Did Galloway correctly identify the factors that directly affect pricing considerations?
    A. Yes.
    B. No, changing tastes do not have a direct impact on pricing.
    C. No, competition for market share in a stable industry is not a pricing consideration.

24. What life cycle phase *most appropriately* reflects Characteristic 1 and Characteristic 3?
    A. Mature and pioneer.
    B. Mature and growth.
    C. Decline and growth.

Questions 25–30 relate to Amie Lear.

Amie Lear, CFA, is a quantitative analyst employed by a brokerage firm. She has been assigned by her supervisor to cover a number of different equity and debt investments. One of the investments is Taylor, Inc. (Taylor), a manufacturer of a wide range of children's toys. Based on her extensive analysis, she determines that her expected return on the stock, given Taylor's risks, is 10%. In applying the capital asset pricing model (CAPM), the result is a 12% rate of return.

For her analysis of the returns of Devon, Inc. (Devon), a manufacturer of high-end sports apparel, Lear intends to use the Fama-French model (FFM). Devon is a small-cap growth stock that has traded at a low market-to-book value in recent years. Lear's analysis has provided a wealth of quantitative information to consider. The return on a value-weighted market index minus the risk-free rate is 5.5%, the small-cap return premium is 3.1%, the value return premium is 2.2%, and the liquidity premium is 3.3%. The risk-free rate is 3.4%. The market, size, relative value, and liquidity betas for Devon are 0.7, –0.3, 1.4, and 1.2, respectively. In estimating the appropriate equity risk premium, Lear has chosen to use the Gordon growth model.

Lear's assistant, Doug Saunders, presents her with a report on macroeconomic multifactor models that includes the following two statements:

Statement 1:   Business cycle risk represents the unexpected change in the difference between the return of risky corporate bonds and government bonds.

Statement 2:   Confidence risk represents the unexpected change in the level of real business activity.

Lear is also attempting to determine the most appropriate method for determining the required return for Densmore, Inc. (Densmore), a closely held company that is considering a debt issue within the next year. The company has not previously issued debt securities to the public, relying instead on bank financing. She realizes that there are a number of models to consider, including the CAPM, multifactor models, and build-up models.

25.   Based on Lear's analysis, Taylor's stock is *most likely* to be:
   A. correctly valued.
   B. overvalued.
   C. undervalued.

©2011 Kaplan, Inc.

26. According to the FFM, the estimate of the required return for Devon is *closest* to:
    A. 9.4%.
    B. 11.8%.
    C. 13.4%.

27. Lear's choice of the Gordon growth model is an example of which of the following types of estimates of the equity risk premium?
    A. Historical estimate.
    B. Forward-looking estimate.
    C. Macroeconomic model estimate.

28. Which of the following approaches/methods is *most appropriate* for Lear to consider in determining the required return for Densmore?
    A. Build-up method.
    B. Risk premium approach.
    C. Bond-yield plus risk premium method.

29. Are Saunders's statements regarding the macroeconomic multifactor models correct?
    A. Both statements are incorrect.
    B. Only Statement 1 is correct.
    C. Only Statement 2 is correct.

30. Which of the following statements regarding the models used to estimate the required return is *most accurate*?
    A. A strength of the capital asset pricing model (CAPM) is that it usually has high explanatory power.
    B. A strength of multifactor models is their relative simplicity and ease of calculation.
    C. A weakness of build-up models is that they typically use historical values as estimates that may not be relevant to current market conditions.

Questions 31–36 relate to Erich Reichmann.

Erich Reichmann, CFA, is a fixed-income portfolio manager with Global Investment Management. A recent increase in interest rate volatility has caused Reichmann and his assistant, Mel O'Shea, to begin investigating methods of hedging interest rate risk in his fixed income portfolio.

Reichmann would like to hedge the interest rate risk of one of his bonds, a floating-rate bond (indexed to LIBOR). O'Shea recommends taking a short position in a Eurodollar futures contract because the Eurodollar contract is a more effective hedging instrument than a Treasury bill futures contract.

Reichmann is also analyzing the possibility of using interest rate caps and floors, as well as interest rate options and options on fixed income securities, to hedge the interest rate risk of his overall portfolio.

Reichmann uses a binomial interest rate model to value 1-year and 2-year 6% floors on 1-year LIBOR, both based on $30 million principal value with annual payments. He values the 1-year floor at $90,000 and the 2-year floor at $285,000.

Reichmann has also heard about using interest rate collars to hedge interest rate risk, but is unsure how to construct a collar.

Finally, Reichmann is interested in using swaptions to hedge certain investments. He evaluates the following comments about swaptions.

- If a firm anticipates floating rate exposure from issuing floating rate bonds at some future date, a payer swaption would *lock in* a fixed rate and provide floating-rate payments for the loan. It would be exercised if the yield curve shifted down.
- Swaptions can be used to speculate on changes in interest rates. The investor would buy a receiver swaption if he expects rates to fall.

31. To *most* effectively hedge his long position in the floating rate bond against declining rates, Reichmann should:
    A. take O'Shea's advice.
    B. go long in a Eurodollar futures contract.
    C. go long in a Treasury bill futures contract.

32. To *most* effectively hedge against an increase in interest rates that would reduce the value of his fixed-income portfolio, what position should Reichmann take?
    A. Long an interest rate cap or long a European call on interest rates.
    B. Short an interest rate cap or short a European call on interest rates.
    C. Long an interest rate cap and short a European call on interest rates.

33.   If LIBOR for Year 2 is 5.8%, the payoff on the 2-year, 6%, $30 million
       interest rate floor at the end of Year 2 is *closest* to:
       A. $56,711.
       B. $60,000.
       C. $63,480.

34.   Based on the results from Reichmann's binomial interest rate model, the
       value of a 2-year, $30 million European put option on LIBOR with a floor
       strike of 6% is *closest* to:
       A. $185,000.
       B. $195,000.
       C. $270,000.

35.   What would be the *most appropriate* way for Reichmann to construct an
       interest rate collar to hedge the fixed-rate portion of the portfolio using the
       2-year 6% floor and a 2-year 12% cap?
       A. Buy the floor and buy the cap.
       B. Buy the floor and sell the cap.
       C. Sell the floor and buy the cap.

36.   Are the comments about swaptions correct?
       A. No, because a payer swaption should be used if the investor anticipates
           a fixed rate exposure at some point in the future.
       B. No, because a payer swaption would be exercised if the yield curve
           shifted up.
       C. No, because an investor would buy a receiver swaption if he expects
           rates to rise.

Questions 37–42 relate to Stan Loper.

Stan Loper is unfamiliar with the Black-Scholes-Merton (BSM) option pricing model and plans to use a two-period binomial model to value some call options. The stock of Arbor Industries pays no dividends and currently trades for $45. The up-move factor for the stock is 1.15, and the risk-free rate is 4%. He is considering buying two-period European style options on Arbor Industries with a strike price of $40. The delta of these options over the first period is 0.83.

Loper is curious about the effect of time on the value of the calls in the binomial model, so he also calculates the value of a one-period European style call option with a strike price of 40.

Loper is also interested in using the BSM model to price European and American call and put options. He is concerned, however, whether the assumptions necessary to derive the model are realistic. The assumptions he is particularly concerned about are:

- The volatility of the option value is known and constant.
- Stock prices are lognormally distributed.
- The continuous risk-free rate is known and constant.

Loper would also like to value options on Rapid Repair, Inc., common stock, but Rapid pays dividends, so Loper is uncertain what the effect will be on the value of the options. Loper uses the two-period model to value long positions in the Rapid Repair call and put options without accounting for the fact that Rapid Repair pays common dividends.

37. The value of a two-period 40 call on Arbor Industries stock is *closest* to:
    A. $6.65.
    B. $8.86.
    C. $9.21.

38. The position in calls necessary to hedge a long position in 1,000 shares of stock over the first period is *closest* to:
    A. short 830 calls.
    B. short 1,150 calls.
    C. short 1,205 calls.

39. The value of the one-period European style call option is *closest* to:
    A. $6.65.
    B. $6.86.
    C. $7.15.

©2011 Kaplan, Inc.

40. The difference in value between the European 40 calls and otherwise identical American 40 calls is *closest* to:
    A. –$1.43.
    B. $0.00.
    C. $1.92.

41. Are the BSM assumptions listed correctly?
    A. No, because stock prices are assumed to be normally distributed.
    B. No, because the expected return on the stock is assumed to be known and constant.
    C. No, because the volatility of the return on the underlying stock is assumed to be known and constant.

42. When Loper failed to account for Rapid Repair dividends, did he *likely* overvalue the calls or the puts?
    A. The calls and the puts are overvalued.
    B. Only the calls are overvalued.
    C. Only the puts are overvalued.

Questions 43–48 relate to Ryan Hendricks.

Ryan Hendricks serves as a security analyst for Investment Management, Inc. (IMI), which employs the Treynor-Black model to evaluate securities and to make portfolio recommendations. IMI uses the capital asset pricing model (CAPM) to determine the degree to which securities may be mispriced relative to IMI's forecasts.

Hendricks evaluates the common shares of Computer Software Associates (CSA), a small company specializing in a unique computer software market niche. Hendricks obtains the following market model results for CSA, using monthly returns for the past 60 months:

$$R_{CSA} = -0.02 + 1.75 R_{S\&P500} + \varepsilon_{CSA} \qquad (1)$$

where:
R_{CSA} = the return on the CSA stock
$R_{S\&P500}$ = the return on the S&P500 stock market index
ε_{CSA} = random regression error term

Hendricks uses the adjusted beta method to derive his forecasts for companies' future betas. In deriving his forecast for any company beta, Hendricks uses the following first-order autoregressive formula:

$$\text{forecast beta} = 0.33 + 0.67 \times (\text{historical beta}) \qquad (2)$$

Hendricks derives required returns for individual securities using the CAPM after making appropriate adjustments using his adjusted beta formula in equation (2).

IMI provides Hendricks with the following capital market forecasts to use as inputs for the CAPM.

Exhibit 1: Capital Market Forecasts

Economic Variable	Expected Return
S&P 500	12%
1-year Treasury bill	4%

IMI asks Hendricks to make decisions to take long and short positions in individual securities for IMI's actively managed portfolio, IMI-Active. Specifically, Hendricks is asked to examine CSA and Millennium Drilling (MD), an oil and gas drilling company specializing in deep sea drilling. After a thorough

©2011 Kaplan, Inc.

examination of the prospects for each company, Hendricks derives the following alpha forecasts for CSA and MD.

Exhibit 2: Alpha Forecasts

Company	Alpha
CSA	0.04
MD	0.08

Hendricks forecasts that the unsystematic variance (the variance of the market model regression error) for MD will be more than double that of CSA.

After determining the appropriate allocations across securities within the IMI-Active portfolio, Hendricks derives the portfolio predictions shown in Exhibit 3.

Exhibit 3: Forecasts for the IMI-Active Portfolio

Forecast Variable	Forecast Value
Alpha, α	5.33%
Beta, β	1.35%
Total standard deviation, σ	40.00%
Unsystematic standard deviation, $\sigma(\varepsilon)$	30.00%

IMI forecasts that the total standard deviation for the S&P500 returns will equal 20%. After examining the historical forecasting abilities of Hendricks, IMI determines that Hendricks has demonstrated perfect forecasting ability in regards to CSA stock, but imperfect forecasting abilities in regards to MD stock. IMI finds that the correlation between the realized alphas for MD and the forecast MD alphas provided by Hendricks equals 0.50.

Referring to the Treynor-Black model, Hendricks makes the following statements:

Statement 1: All else equal, the Treynor-Black model increases the weight to the active portfolio as its unsystematic risk increases.

Statement 2: The Treynor-Black model is based on the premise that only a limited number of stocks should be included in the actively managed portfolio.

43. Hendricks's forecasts for the CSA beta and future return are *closest* to:
    A. 1.17 beta and 12% return.
    B. 1.33 beta and 16% return.
    C. 1.50 beta and 20% return.

44. Using the Treynor-Black model along with the alpha and unsystematic variance information for CSA and MD, should CSA or MD receive a larger weight within the IMI-Active portfolio?
    A. CSA should receive a larger weight.
    B. MD should receive a larger weight.
    C. They should be weighted equally.

45. Using the Treynor-Black model, IMI must select optimal combinations of the S&P500 market index and the IMI-Active portfolio. The optimal combination is expected to lie along a capital allocation line with intercept and slope:
    A. equal to 4% and 40%, respectively.
    B. equal to 4% and greater than 40%, respectively.
    C. greater than 4% and greater than 40%, respectively.

46. The information ratio for the IMI-Active portfolio is *closest* to:
    A. 0.06.
    B. 0.12.
    C. 0.18.

47. To adjust for Hendricks's forecasting record, what alpha forecasts should IMI use for CSA and MD?
    A. 0.06 for CSA and 0.04 for MD.
    B. 0.04 for CSA and 0.04 for MD.
    C. 0.04 for CSA and 0.02 for MD.

48. Are Statements 1 and 2 made by Hendricks correct or incorrect?
    A. Both statements are correct.
    B. Only Statement 1 is correct.
    C. Only Statement 2 is correct.

©2011 Kaplan, Inc.

Questions 49–54 relate to Sara Robinson and Marvin Gardner.

Sara Robinson and Marvin Gardner are considering an opportunity to start their own money management firm. Their conversation leads them to a discussion on establishing a portfolio management process and investment policy statements. Robinson makes the following statements:

Statement 1: Our only real objective as portfolio managers is to maximize the returns to our clients.

Statement 2: If we are managing only a fraction of a client's total wealth, it is the client's responsibility, not ours, to determine how their investments are allocated among asset classes.

Statement 3: When developing a client's strategic asset allocation, portfolio managers have to consider capital market expectations.

In response, Gardner makes the following statements:

Statement 4: While return maximization is important for a given level of risk, we also need to consider the client's tolerance for risk.

Statement 5: We'll let our clients worry about the tax implications of their investments; our time is better spent on finding undervalued assets.

Statement 6: Since we expect our investor's objectives to be constantly changing, we will need to evaluate their investment policy statements on an annual basis at a minimum.

Robinson wants to focus on younger clientele with the expectation that the new firm will be able to retain the clients for a long time and create long-term profitable relationships. While Gardner felt it was important to develop long-term relationships, he wants to go after older, high-net-worth clients.

49. Are Statements 1 and 4 consistent with the appropriate method of developing portfolio objectives?
    A. Both statements are correct.
    B. Only Statement 1 is correct.
    C. Only Statement 4 is correct.

50. Which one of the following factors is the *least likely* to affect the individual investor's ability to accept risk?
    A. Required spending needs.
    B. Financial strength.
    C. Behavioral factors.

51. Are Statements 2 and 3 correct when considering asset allocation?
    A. Both statements are correct.
    B. Only Statement 2 is correct.
    C. Only Statement 3 is correct.

52. Robinson is uncomfortable with Gardner's position on taxes but she can't specifically identify the source of the discomfort. Which of the following statements *least accurately* reflects proper consideration of tax effects on the investment process?
    A. Because investors are ultimately concerned with after-tax returns, it is important that investors consider their own marginal tax rates and the security's tax status when making any investment decision.
    B. Pensions and endowment funds are typically tax-exempt investors and, therefore, are less concerned with tax considerations.
    C. Investors should rely on accountants or other advisors for tax advice; portfolio managers should focus on finding undervalued investments and not be distracted by tax considerations.

53. The *least* important portfolio constraints for individuals are:
    A. legal and regulatory constraints.
    B. investment horizon constraints.
    C. unique needs.

54. In addition to Statement 6, an appropriately developed investment policy statement is *least likely* to address which of the following elements?
    A. Transportability so as to minimize any disruptions if new managers assume responsibility for the portfolio.
    B. Assurances of minimum returns so clients will be better able to ensure their financial goals are met over the long run.
    C. Barriers to short-term strategy shifts driven by panic or overconfidence stemming from portfolio performance or changes in market environments.

©2011 Kaplan, Inc.

Questions 55–60 relate to Carol Blackwell.

Carol Blackwell, CFA, has been hired to manage trust assets for Blanchard Investments. Blanchard's trust manager, Thaddeus Baldwin, CFA, has worked in the securities business for more than 50 years. On Blackwell's first day at the office, Baldwin gives her several instructions.

Instruction 1: Limit risk by avoiding stock options.

Instruction 2: Above all, ensure that our clients' capital is kept safe.

Instruction 3: We take pride in our low cost structure, so avoid unnecessary transactions.

Instruction 4: Remember that every investment must have the quality to stand on its own.

Baldwin realizes that many of the firm's practices and policies would benefit from a compliance check. Because Blackwell recently received her CFA charter, Baldwin tells her she is the "perfect person to work with the compliance officer to update the policy on proxy voting and the procedures to comply with Standard VI(B) Priority of Transactions." Baldwin also wants Blackwell to evaluate whether the firm wants to, or can, claim compliance with the soft dollar standards. Baldwin hands Blackwell a handwritten outline he created, which includes the following statements:

Statement 1: CFA Institute's soft-dollar rules are not mandatory. In any case, client brokerage can be used to pay for a portion of mixed-use research.

Statement 2: Investment firms can use client brokerage to purchase research that does not immediately benefit the client. Commissions generated by outside trades are considered soft dollars, but commissions from internal trading desks are not.

During a local society luncheon, Blackwell is seated next to CFA candidate Lucas Walters, who has been assigned the task of creating a compliance manual for Borchard & Sons, a small brokerage firm. Walters asks for her advice.

When Walters returns to work, he is apprised of the following situation: Borchard & Sons purchased 25,000 shares of CBX Corp. for equity manager Quintux Quantitative just minutes before the money manager called back and said it meant to buy 25,000 shares of CDX Corp. Borchard then purchased CDX shares for Quintux, but not before shares of CBX Corp. declined by 1.5%. The broker is holding the CBX shares in its own inventory.

Borchard proposes three methods for dealing with the trading error.

Method 1:   Quintux directs additional trades to Borchard worth a dollar value equal to the amount of the trading loss.

Method 2:   Borchard receives investment research from Quintux in exchange for Borchard covering the costs of the trading error.

Method 3:   Borchard transfers the ordered CBX shares in its inventory to Quintux, which allocates them to all of its clients on a pro-rata basis.

55.   Which of Baldwin's first-day instructions to Blackwell is consistent with the New Prudent Investor Rule?
A. Instruction 1.
B. Instruction 2.
C. Instruction 3.

56.   When updating the proxy-voting policy to conform to CFA Institute recommendations, which of the following recommendations is *least appropriate* for Blanchard to adopt?
A. Determine the economic impact of non-routine proxy votes.
B. Follow the same proxy-voting procedures regardless of the nature of the proposal.
C. If the proxy voter's preference differs from the preference of a client who has delegated his voting powers, go with the client's preference.

57.   A CFA charterholder who wishes to follow Standard VI(B) Priority of Transactions must:
A. maintain loyalty to pension-plan beneficiaries.
B. limit IPO investments in client and personal accounts.
C. give both clients and employers preference over the charterholder's own accounts.

58.   Are Thaddeus Baldwin's statements on the soft dollar standards correct?
A. Both statements are correct.
B. Only Statement 1 is correct.
C. Only Statement 2 is correct.

    ©2011 Kaplan, Inc.

59. If Walters wants the manual to satisfy the requirements and recommendations of the Code and Standards, which of the following instructions is *least appropriate* to include in the section on fair dealing?
    A. Whenever possible, disseminate investment recommendations to all clients at the same time.
    B. Execute all clients' requested trades promptly and without comment, regardless of the company's opinion on the stock being traded.
    C. Members of the investment-policy committee should not discuss possible changes in investment recommendations with anyone else in the firm until after an official decision has been made.

60. Which method for dealing with the trading error is *most* consistent with the Code and Standards?
    A. Method 1.
    B. Method 2.
    C. Method 3.

End of Morning Session

Exam 3
Afternoon Session

Question	Topic	Minutes (Points)
61 to 66	Ethics	18
67 to 72	Economics	18
73 to 78	Financial Reporting and Analysis	18
79 to 84	Corporate Finance	18
85 to 90	Fixed Income Investments	18
91 to 96	Alternative Investments	18
97 to 102	Quantitative Methods	18
103 to 108	Financial Reporting and Analysis	18
109 to 114	Financial Reporting and Analysis	18
115 to 120	Financial Reporting and Analysis	18

61.	(A)	(B)	(C)		101.	(A)	(B)	(C)
62.	(A)	(B)	(C)		102.	(A)	(B)	(C)
63.	(A)	(B)	(C)		103.	(A)	(B)	(C)
64.	(A)	(B)	(C)		104.	(A)	(B)	(C)
65.	(A)	(B)	(C)		105.	(A)	(B)	(C)
66.	(A)	(B)	(C)		106.	(A)	(B)	(C)
67.	(A)	(B)	(C)		107.	(A)	(B)	(C)
68.	(A)	(B)	(C)		108.	(A)	(B)	(C)
69.	(A)	(B)	(C)		109.	(A)	(B)	(C)
70.	(A)	(B)	(C)		110.	(A)	(B)	(C)
71.	(A)	(B)	(C)		111.	(A)	(B)	(C)
72.	(A)	(B)	(C)		112.	(A)	(B)	(C)
73.	(A)	(B)	(C)		113.	(A)	(B)	(C)
74.	(A)	(B)	(C)		114.	(A)	(B)	(C)
75.	(A)	(B)	(C)		115.	(A)	(B)	(C)
76.	(A)	(B)	(C)		116.	(A)	(B)	(C)
77.	(A)	(B)	(C)		117.	(A)	(B)	(C)
78.	(A)	(B)	(C)		118.	(A)	(B)	(C)
79.	(A)	(B)	(C)		119.	(A)	(B)	(C)
80.	(A)	(B)	(C)		120.	(A)	(B)	(C)
81.	(A)	(B)	(C)					
82.	(A)	(B)	(C)					
83.	(A)	(B)	(C)					
84.	(A)	(B)	(C)					
85.	(A)	(B)	(C)					
86.	(A)	(B)	(C)					
87.	(A)	(B)	(C)					
88.	(A)	(B)	(C)					
89.	(A)	(B)	(C)					
90.	(A)	(B)	(C)					
91.	(A)	(B)	(C)					
92.	(A)	(B)	(C)					
93.	(A)	(B)	(C)					
94.	(A)	(B)	(C)					
95.	(A)	(B)	(C)					
96.	(A)	(B)	(C)					
97.	(A)	(B)	(C)					
98.	(A)	(B)	(C)					
99.	(A)	(B)	(C)					
100.	(A)	(B)	(C)					

Exam 3
Afternoon Session

Questions 61–66 relate to Connor Burton.

Connor Burton, CFA, is the managing partner for United Partners, a small investment advisory firm that employs three investment professionals and currently has approximately $250 million of assets under management. The client base of United Partners is varied, and accounts range in size from small retirement accounts to a $30 million private school endowment. In addition to Burton's administrative responsibilities as the managing partner at United, he also serves as an investment advisor to several clients. Because United Partners is a small firm, the company does not employ any research analysts but instead obtains its investment research products and services from two national brokerage firms, which in turn execute all client trades for United Partners. The arrangement with the two brokers has enabled United to assure its clients that the firm will always seek the best execution for them by having both brokers competitively bid for United's business.

A prospective client, Harold Crossley, has approached Burton about shifting some of his personal assets under management from MoneyCorp to United Partners. Burton provides Crossley with a packet of marketing information that Burton developed himself. The packet contains five years of historical performance data for the private school endowment, United's largest client. Burton states that the composite's management style and performance results are representative of the management style and returns that United can be expected to achieve for Crossley. Also included in the information packet are brief bios on each of United's three investment professionals. Crossley notices that all three of United's investment professionals are described as "CFA charterholders," but he is not familiar with the designation. In response to Crossley's inquiry, Burton explains the significance of the program by stating that the designation, which is only awarded after passing three rigorous exams and obtaining the requisite years of work experience, represents a commitment to the highest standards of ethical and professional conduct.

As a condition of moving his account to United Partners, Crossley insists that all of his trades be executed through his brother-in-law, a broker for Security Bank. Security Bank is a large, New York-based broker/dealer but is not one of the two brokerage firms with which United currently does business. Burton contacts Crossley's brother-in-law and determines that Security Bank's trade execution is competitive, but Crossley's account alone would not generate enough volume to warrant any soft dollar arrangement for research materials.

However, Crossley's brother-in-law does offer for Security Bank to pay a referral fee to Burton for directing any of United's clients to Security Bank's retail banking division. To bring Crossley on as a client, Burton agrees to the arrangement. Going forward, Burton will use Security Bank to execute all of Crossley's trades but will use research materials provided by the other two brokers to assist in the management of Crossley's account.

Several months later, Burton is invited to a road show for an initial public offering (IPO) for SolutionWare, a software company. Security Bank is serving as lead underwriter on SolutionWare's IPO. Burton attends the meeting, which is led by two investment bankers and one software industry research analyst from Security Bank who covers SolutionWare. Burton notes that the bankers from Security Bank have included detailed financial statements for SolutionWare in the offering prospectus and also disclosed that Security Bank provides a warehouse line of credit to SolutionWare. After the meeting, Burton calls Crossley to recommend the purchase of SolutionWare equity. Crossley heeds Burton's advice and tells him to purchase 5,000 shares. Before placing Crossley's order, Burton reads the SolutionWare marketing materials and performs a detailed analysis of expected future earnings and other key factors for the investment decision. Burton determines that the offering would be a suitable investment for his own retirement portfolio in addition to Crossley's portfolio. United Partners, being a small firm, has no formal written policy regarding trade allocation, employee participation in equity offerings, or established blackout periods for employee trading. Burton adds his order to Crossley's order and places a purchase order for the combined number of shares with Security Bank. Burton is later notified that the offering was oversubscribed, and United Partners was only able to obtain roughly 75% of the desired number of shares. To be fair, Burton allocates the shares on a pro-rata basis between Crossley's account and his own retirement account. When Burton notifies Crossley of the situation, Crossley is nonetheless pleased to have a position, though smaller than requested, in such a "hot" offering.

61. Did the marketing materials presented to Crossley by Burton violate Standard III(D) Performance Presentation or Standard VII(B) Reference to CFA Institute, the CFA Designation, and the CFA Program?
    A. Standard III(D) only.
    B. Standard VII(B) only.
    C. Both Standard III(D) and Standard VII(B) are violated.

©2011 Kaplan, Inc.

62. The trading arrangement between Burton and Security Bank is *most likely* to be a violation of the CFA Institute Soft Dollar Standards because:
    A. the practice of directed brokerage violates the member's or candidate's duty of loyalty to the client.
    B. although Security Bank's execution is competitive, Burton will not be able to always obtain the best execution for his client.
    C. the other clients' brokerage will be used to pay for research that will be utilized in the management of Crossley's account.

63. According to CFA Institute Standards of Professional Conduct, which of the following statements *best* describes the circumstances under which Burton may enter into the referral agreement with Security Bank? Burton may enter into the agreement:
    A. under no circumstances.
    B. only after receiving written permission from clients.
    C. only after fully disclosing the referral arrangement to clients and prospective clients.

64. With respect to the road show meeting regarding the initial public offering of SolutionWare, did Security Bank comply with the requirements and recommendations of the CFA Institute Research Objectivity Standards?
    A. No, because it publicly revealed that it also provides corporate finance services for SolutionWare.
    B. No, because it failed to provide Burton with adequate information to make an investment decision.
    C. No, because it allowed an analyst to participate in a marketing road show for a company that he covers.

65. According to CFA Institute Standards of Professional Conduct, Burton's recommendation to Crossley that he purchase shares of the SolutionWare initial public offering is *most likely*:
    A. in violation of Standard III(C) Suitability for not determining the appropriateness of the investment for the portfolio and Standard I(B) Independence and Objectivity for not making the investment recommendation to all of his clients at the same time.
    B. in violation of Standard V(A) Diligence and Reasonable Basis for not thoroughly analyzing the investment before making a recommendation and in violation of Standard III(C) Suitability for not determining the appropriateness of the investment for the portfolio.
    C. in violation of Standard V(A) Diligence and Reasonable Basis for not thoroughly analyzing the investment before making a recommendation and in violation of Standard I(B) Independence and Objectivity for not making the investment recommendation to all of his clients at the same time.

66. According to CFA Standards of Professional Conduct, Burton's participation in the SolutionWare offering *most likely*:
   A. is in violation of the Standards because his actions adversely affected the interests of Crossley.
   B. is in violation of the Standards because he did not disclose his participation in the offering to Security Bank.
   C. is not in violation of the Standards since the shares obtained in the IPO were distributed equitably on a pro-rata basis.

©2011 Kaplan, Inc.

Questions 67–72 relate to Frank Hoskins and Paul Lanning.

Frank Hoskins and Paul Lanning are economists for a large U.S. investment advisory firm, Platinum Advisors. Hoskins and Lanning use their independent research on U.S. stocks and international stocks to provide advice for the firm's network of advisors. As the senior economist at Platinum, Hoskins is a partner in the firm and is Lanning's supervisor. Lanning has worked for Platinum for the past four years. At a lunch meeting, the two economists discuss the usefulness of economic theory, economic data, and the resulting forecasts of the global economic and stock market activity.

Hoskins is investigating the growth prospects of the country of Maldavia. Maldavia is a formerly communist country with a population of 3 million located in Eastern Europe. The Maldavian government had been aggressive in instituting political reform and encouraging the growth of financial markets. However, due to a recent insider trading scandal and resulting stock market volatility, the Maldavian government is considering restrictions on further stock market growth and the establishment of a national securities regulator. Hoskins states that these developments are not encouraging for future economic growth.

Lanning is examining the country of Petra. Petra is a country of 25 million located in South America and rich with natural resources, including oil. The recently elected president of Petra, Carlos Basile, has announced that he would like to diversify the country's economy away from natural resources while nationalizing the oil industry. Lanning states that these changes would not be beneficial for the future growth of the Petrian economy.

One of the many items they study when examining an economy or stock market is the economic information released by governments and private organizations. Hoskins and Lanning use this information to determine the effects on economic growth and the appropriate portfolio allocations to the bond and stock markets. Examining information for Maldavia, Hoskins has learned that the Maldavian private sector has embarked on an ambitious plan to increase labor productivity by purchasing more machinery for its factories. The private sector feels compelled to do this because Maldavia has historically relied too heavily on labor as the main input into production. Plotting the productivity curve for Maldavia, Hoskins states that labor productivity should increase because the productivity curve will shift upward and to the right.

Lanning is examining the historical record of economic growth in Petra. He has gathered the data in Exhibit 1 to determine potential economic growth.

Exhibit 1: Economic Data for Petra from 2001 to 2007 (in U.S. $)

Real GDP per labor hour in 2001	$20.00
Capital per labor hour in 2001	$35.00
Average increase in fiscal spending 2001–2007	4.20%
Average growth in taxes 2001–2007	3.20%
Real GDP per labor hour in 2007	$21.50
Capital per labor hour in 2007	$36.80

Hoskins is also examining data for the country of Semeria. Semeria is an emerging country that has benefited from recent changes in the political environment as well as technological advances. Its economy is growing rapidly, and changes in the Semerian economy and society have resulted in more opportunities for women. The Semerian economy has experienced 17 consecutive quarters of positive growth in GDP, which is unprecedented in Semerian history. Interest rates have increased over time because businesses have been borrowing heavily to invest in new machinery and technologies. Most economists are forecasting further increases in interest rates in Semeria.

Using the economic theory he was taught in college, Hoskins takes a contrarian view. He concludes that real interest rates should actually start to decline because the future returns to business investment will decline. He further states that although more women are entering the workforce and having fewer children, the population is actually holding steady because the increased wealth in Semeria has improved healthcare and people are living longer.

It has long been Platinum's policy that its economists use long-term economic growth trends to forecast future economic growth, stock returns, and dividends in a country. Lanning is examining the economy of Tiberia. Tiberia has a population of 11 million and is located in northern Africa. Its economy is diversified, and its main exports are agricultural products and heavy machinery. The country's economy has been growing at an annual rate of 6.2% for the past ten years, in part because of technological advances in the manufacture of heavy equipment. These advances involve the use of computer-operated welding machines that have made the manufacture of heavy equipment less expensive. Lanning is worried, however, that the 6.2% GDP growth rate may not be sustainable and is considering advising Platinum's portfolio managers to decrease their portfolio allocations in the country. Before doing so, he will consult with Hoskins.

©2011 Kaplan, Inc.

67. Are the statements made by Hoskins and Lanning regarding the future growth of the Maldavian and Petrian economies *likely* to be correct or incorrect?
   A. Both are correct.
   B. Only Hoskins is correct.
   C. Only Lanning is correct.

68. Hoskins's statement on Maldavian labor productivity and its productivity curve is:
   A. incorrect, because labor productivity is not affected in this scenario.
   B. incorrect, because labor productivity will decrease as a result of the low skilled labor force.
   C. incorrect, because although labor productivity will increase, the increase will result from a movement along the productivity curve.

69. Which of the following choices is *closest* to Petra's growth in real labor productivity from 2001 to 2007 and the portion that is due to technology?

Growth in real labor productivity	Portion due to technology
A. 5.14%	1.71%
B. 5.14%	3.43%
C. 7.50%	5.79%

70. Regarding Hoskins assessment of the Semerian economy and the effect of women in the workforce, he is *most likely* utilizing the:
   A. new growth theory.
   B. endogenous growth theory.
   C. neoclassical growth theory.

71. The classical growth theory is *most likely* to predict that Tiberia's long-run future GDP per capita will:
   A. decline due to a diminishing marginal productivity of capital.
   B. settle at subsistence level due to adjustments in the population.
   C. remain unchanged from the current growth rate unless the government increases the budget deficit.

72. The new growth theory is *most likely* to predict that the Tiberian dividend growth rate:
   A. will settle at a long-run steady state because of a diminishing marginal productivity of capital.
   B. can continue to increase because technological advances will be shared by many sectors of the economy.
   C. will decline because the current GDP growth rate is not sustainable, and as it falls, so will the dividend growth rate.

Questions 73–78 relate to Tobin Yoakam.

Tobin Yoakam, CFA, is analyzing the financial performance of Konker Industries, a U.S. company which is publicly traded under the ticker KONK. Yoakam is particularly concerned about the quality of Konker's financial statements and its choices of accounting methodologies.

Below is a summary of Konker's financial statements prepared by Yoakam.

Konker Industries				
Income Statement	**20X8**	**Balance Sheet**		**20X8**
($ in thousands)		*($ in thousands)*		
Gross sales	55,435	Cash and equivalents		457
Sales discounts, returns, and allowances	1,352	Short term marketable securities		927
Net sales	54,083	Accounts receivable (net)		47,740
Cost of goods sold	26,500	Inventories		20,963
SG&A expenses	15,625	PP&E (net of depreciation)		25,371
Depreciation expense	1,082	Total assets		95,458
Earnings before interest and taxes	10,876			
Interest expense	693	Accounts payable		24,994
Earnings before taxes	10,183	Other current liabilities		1,209
Taxes (tax rate 40%)	4,073	Long term debt		21,770
Net income	6,110	Total liabilities		47,973
		Common stock		40,314
Dividends	5,046	Retained earnings		7,171
Net addition to retained earnings	1,064	Total liabilities and shareholders equity		95,458

Konker has an operating lease for several of its large machining tools. The lease term expires in five years, and the annual lease payments are $2 million. The applicable interest rate on the operating lease is 9%. Yoakam believes that the operating lease should be capitalized and treated as a finance lease. For purposes of adjusting the financial statements, Yoakam believes that the machining tools should be depreciated using straight-line depreciation with a salvage value of $3 million.

©2011 Kaplan, Inc.

At the beginning of 20X8, Konker formed a qualified special purposes entity (QSPE) and sold a portion of its accounts receivables to the QSPE. The total amount of accounts receivables sold to the QSPE was $13.5 million. Yoakam has noted in his research that the Financial Accounting Standards Board (FASB) is considering the elimination of qualified special purposes entities.

Konker has three major operating divisions: Konker Industrial, Konker Defense, and Konker Capital. Yoakam has computed the EBIT margin for each division over the last three years, as well as the ratio of the percentage of total capital expenditures to the percentage of total assets for each division.

	EBIT / Assets			CapEx % / Assets %		
	20X8	**20X7**	**20X6**	**20X8**	**20X7**	**20X6**
Konker Industrial	6.2%	7.5%	6.7%	1.5	1.3	1.2
Konker Defense	6.7%	7.2%	6.9%	0.5	0.6	0.7
Konker Capital	10.1%	12.1%	11.1%	0.7	0.6	0.5

Since Yoakam is concerned about the quality of Konker's earnings, he decides to analyze the accrual ratios using the balance sheet approach. The table below contains the last three years of accrual ratios for Konker and the industry average.

Balance Sheet Accrual Ratios	**20X8**	**20X7**	**20X6**
Konker	4.5%	15.0%	7.0%
Industry average	4.8%	4.4%	5.2%

73. With respect to the balance sheet accrual ratio, which of the following, other things equal, would *most likely* lead to an increase in the ratio for a growing company?
    A. Extending the time the firm takes to pay its suppliers.
    B. A significant build-up of cash.
    C. A build-up of inventory.

74. If Yoakam capitalizes Konker's operating lease in his analysis, the Konker's adjusted interest coverage ratio for 20X8 would be *closest* to:
    A. 7.12.
    B. 8.56.
    C. 15.69.

75. If the FASB were to retroactively eliminate the allowance of QSPEs created for the securitization of receivables, the *most likely* impact on Konker's financial statements would be:
    A. an increase in equity and an increase in interest expense.
    B. no change in assets but an increase in financial leverage ratios.
    C. an increase in financial leverage ratios and a decrease in the interest coverage ratio.

76. An analyst is considering the effects of income reported under the equity method on certain financial ratios. For a firm that reports equity income as non-operating income (not included in EBIT), removing equity income from the financial statements would *most likely* result in:
    A. an increase in the tax burden term in the extended Du Pont decomposition of ROE.
    B. an increase in the asset turnover ratio.
    C. a decrease in the interest coverage ratio.

77. Regarding the three operating divisions of Konker, Yoakam should be *most* concerned that:
    A. Konker is growing the Industrial division over time.
    B. the operating ROA of the Capital division has fallen over the last year.
    C. the ratio of the Capex percent change to the asset percentage is significantly less than one for the Defense division.

78. Based on the balance sheet accruals ratios, Yoakam would *most likely* conclude which of the following regarding the earnings of Konker?
    A. The volatile accruals ratios are indicators that Konker may be manipulating earnings.
    B. Konker's earnings quality was lower than its peer group in 20X8 but higher in 20X6 and 20X7.
    C. Konker's earnings quality worsened from 20X6 to 20X8 but was superior to its peer group over the 3-year period.

©2011 Kaplan, Inc.

Questions 79–84 relate to Cummings Enterprises, Inc.

Cummings Enterprises, Inc. (CEI), is a U.S. conglomerate that operates in a variety of markets. One of CEI's divisions manufactures small fiberglass products, such as bird baths and outdoor storage lockers. CEI is currently considering the expansion of its fiberglass product line to include booms and buckets for aerial lift trucks (often called cherry pickers), which are used for applications such as high voltage power line maintenance. The addition of this new product line is expected to increase CEI's sales by $750,000 per year.

Cal Holbrook, CEI's manager of fiberglass operations, is deciding whether to purchase a robotic system to produce cherry picker booms and buckets. The price of the robotic system will be $700,000, plus an additional $100,000 for shipping, site preparation, and installation. The new equipment will require a $50,000 increase in inventory and a $20,000 increase in accounts payable. The company uses MACRS to calculate depreciation for tax purposes and the straight-line method for financial reporting. The project has an expected life of four years, at which time the robot is expected to be sold for $75,000. The project will be funded with the debt/equity mix reflected by the company's current capital structure. CEI's pretax cost of new debt is 7%. Assume a WACC of 8%. Some of the relevant end-of-year cash flows for the robotic project are presented in Exhibit 1.

Exhibit 1: Relevant Cash Flows for Robotics Project

	Year 1	*Year 2*	*Year 3*	*Year 4*
Sales	$750,000	$750,000	$750,000	$750,000
Variable costs	$225,000	$225,000	$225,000	$225,000
Fixed expense	$75,000	$75,000	$75,000	$75,000
Depreciation	$264,000	$360,000	$120,000	$56,000
Earnings before tax (EBT)	$186,000	$90,000	$330,000	$394,000
Total after-tax cash flow	**$375,600**	**$414,000**	**$318,000**	?

Holbrook calculates the NPV of the robotic project and presents his findings to his supervisor, Geoffrey Mans. After reviewing the report, Mans makes the following recommendations:

1. "You forgot to include the $100,000 we have spent so far on consultants and project engineers and who knows what else to evaluate the project's feasibility. Rerun the numbers including that amount and get the revised calculations to me this afternoon."

2. "Rerun the analysis assuming straight-line depreciation for tax purposes. The NPV will be higher, and we'll be more likely to get the project funded."

Cummings has two other projects under consideration that would affect the production of storage lockers. Project 1 relates to changing the production process, and Project 2 relates to expanding the distribution facility. Holbrook estimates the NPV of the expected cash flows for Project 1 at negative $7 million. An additional investment of $3 million would allow management to more rapidly adjust to the demand for a certain type of locker. The value of this flexibility is estimated at $9 million. He estimates that the NPV of the expected cash flows for Project 2 at $3 million. An expansion option would require an additional investment of $2 million. At this time, Cummings does not have any capital rationing restrictions.

Holbrook e-mails the lead analyst for the budgeting group and indicates that he cannot make a decision on Project 2 without knowing the value the expansion option will provide.

Holbrook calls a capital budgeting meeting with CEI's production and quality control manager. Holbrook opens the meeting by stating: "I think we should accept this project based solely on the fact that it provides great operating margins. Nevertheless, I think we should conduct net present value (NPV) analysis to confirm my opinion." Holbrook then receives the following comments:

Comment 1: It is important that interest is included in the discounted cash flows used with NPV analysis because interest is a real and very significant expense.

Comment 2: If applied correctly, the NPV of this project will be higher if we discount economic profits instead of net after-tax operating cash flows in our analysis. I suggest we calculate economic profit as net operating profit after tax minus the dollar cost of capital.

79. Which of the following choices is *closest* to the Year 4 total cash flow for the robotics project in Exhibit 1?
    A. $292,400.
    B. $345,400.
    C. $367,400.

80. Are Mans's recommendations regarding the robotic project correct or incorrect?
    A. Both recommendations are correct.
    B. Only one of the recommendations is correct.
    C. Both recommendations are incorrect.

©2011 Kaplan, Inc.

81. For this question only, assume that the investment in net working capital of $30,000 at the project inception is an inflow and that the amount nets to zero with the outflow that will occur at the end of the project. However, Holbrook does not include a cash flow for net working capital at the beginning or the end of the project. Assuming he correctly analyzes all the other components of the project, has Holbrook correctly estimated the project's net present value?
    A. Yes.
    B. No, he underestimated the project's NPV by approximately $7,950.
    C. No, he underestimated the project's NPV by approximately $2,222.

82. Which of the following choices is *closest* to the overall NPV for Project 1, and is Holbrook correct to wait for more information before deciding on Project 2?
    A. The overall NPV is –$1 million, and Holbrook is correct.
    B. The overall NPV is –$1 million, and Holbrook is incorrect.
    C. The overall NPV is $13 million, and Holbrook is incorrect.

83. The economic income for Year 3 for the robotics project from Exhibit 1 is *closest* to:
    A. $19,400.
    B. $48,700.
    C. $49,400.

84. Are the comments made by the CEI's production and quality assurance manager correct or incorrect?
    A. Both comments are correct.
    B. Only one of the comments is correct.
    C. Both comments are incorrect.

Questions 85–90 relate to Langsford Investments.

Kylie Autumn, CFA, is a consultant with Tri-Vision Group. Robert Lullum, Senior Vice President at Langsford Investments, has asked for assistance with the evaluation of mortgage-backed and collateralized mortgage obligation (CMO) derivative securities for potential inclusion in several client portfolios. Langsford Investments mainly deals with equity investments and REITs, but the company recently purchased a small firm that invests mainly in fixed-income securities.

Lullum has done some research on the appropriate spread measures and option valuation models for fixed-income securities and wants to clarify some points. He wants to know if the following statements are correct:

Statement 1:   The proper spread measure for option-free corporate bonds is the nominal spread.

Statement 2:   Callable corporate bonds and mortgage-backed securities should be measured using the option-added spread.

Statement 3:   The Z-spread is appropriate for credit card ABS and auto loan ABS.

While Lullum meets with Autumn, Janet Van Ark, CFA charterholder and equity-income portfolio manager for Langsford, is attempting to purchase bonds that may also provide her with equity exposure in the future. She has decided to analyze an 8% annual coupon bond with exactly 20 years to maturity. The bonds are convertible into 10 common shares for each $1,000 of par (face) value. The bond's market price is $920, and the common stock has a market price of $40. VanArk estimates that the stock will increase in value to $70 within the next two years. The stock's annual dividend is $0.40 per share, and the market yield on comparable non-convertible bonds is 9.5%.

Carl Leighton, a Langsford analyst and Level II CFA candidate, works with mortgage-backed and other asset-based securities. He provides Lullum with a list of credit enhancements for asset-backed securities, which includes letters of credit, excess servicing spread funds, overcollateralization, and bond insurance. Lullum then asks him for a status report of the firm's exposure to paythrough securities. He also asks Leighton to calculate the single-monthly mortality rate (SMM) and estimate the prepayment for the month for a seasoned mortgage pool with a $500,000 principal balance remaining. The scheduled monthly principal payment is $150 and the conditional prepayment rate (CPR) is 7%.

©2011 Kaplan, Inc.

85. Autumn should tell Lullum that the *most appropriate* models for valuing the option on mortgage-backed securities (MBS) and credit card asset-backed securities (ABS) are:
   A. Monte Carlo for both the MBS and the ABS.
   B. Monte Carlo or binomial for the MBS, but binomial only for the ABS.
   C. Monte Carlo for the MBS. No model is needed for the ABS.

86. How many of the three statements on appropriate spread measures and valuation models are correct?
   A. Only two statements are correct.
   B. Only one statement is correct.
   C. None of the three statements are correct.

87. Van Ark computes the convertible bond's market conversion premium per share (MCPPS) using only the information given, and then wants to know how a sudden increase in the stock price of $2 would impact the bond price. Which of the following choices is *most* correct?
   A. The original MCPPS is $60 per share.
   B. The sudden $2 increase would have a small effect.
   C. The sudden $2 increase would have a large effect.

88. Which of the following statements about interest-only (IO) and principal-only (PO) strips is *least accurate*?
   A. The IO price is positively related to interest rates, and at low current rates, POs exhibit some negative convexity.
   B. IO cash flows start out large and diminish over time. As a result, IO investors are most concerned with extension risk.
   C. In general, the volatility of the combined IO and PO strips equals the price volatility of the source passthrough.

89. Which of the following pairs correctly identifies the two external credit enhancements in Leighton's list?
   A. Letters of credit and excess servicing spread funds.
   B. Excess servicing spread funds and bond insurance.
   C. Letters of credit and bond insurance.

90. The estimated prepayment for each month for the $500,000 mortgage pool is *closest* to:
   A. $3,014.
   B. $3,028.
   C. $3,051.

Questions 91–96 relate to Riviera Terrace.

Russell Larson, CFA, is an investment analyst for Sentry Properties, Inc., a group of wealthy investors that is currently interested in purchasing Riviera Terrace, a 60-unit apartment complex in Southeastern Florida. The current owners of Riviera Terrace have agreed to sell the property for $40,000,000. Larson estimates that Riviera Terrace's net operating income for the first year after the sale is finalized will be $4,200,000, and it is expected to maintain its historic annual growth rate of 5%.

At Sentry's request, Larson will evaluate the investment in Riviera Terrace over a 5-year horizon using selling prices of $45,000,000 and $60,000,000.

During the due diligence process, Larson has determined that the average selling price for apartment complexes similar to Riviera Terrace is $1,250,000 per unit, with annual net operating income equal to $135,000 per unit. Larson has also determined that net operating income is typically 80% of gross income.

Larson has collected the following information to aid in his evaluation of Riviera Terrace.

- The property will be fully depreciated at a rate of $1,250,000 per year over 32 years.
- Rental contracts are expected to be reissued on the date the sale is completed.
- Sentry has arranged to finance the investment with a 30-year, 7% interest-only loan, with monthly payments and a face value equal to 80% of the initial investment.
- Selling expenses will be 7% of the gross selling price.
- The capital gains tax rate is 15%, the tax on recaptured depreciation is 28%, and the tax rate on ordinary income is 40%.
- Sentry Properties' required return on equity is 20%.
- The interest rate on U.S. government bonds after adjustments for real estate based tax savings = 5.0%.
- The premium investors require for the illiquidity of real estate investments = 2.5%.
- The average real estate return net of appreciation = 1.25%.
- The real estate investment risk premium = 3.0%.
- The average internal rate of return for properties that are comparable to Riviera Terrace is 22%.

As part of the diligence process, Larson deems it to be appropriate to estimate the market value of Riviera Terrace using capitalization rates based on the market extraction and built-up methods. One of the partners in Sentry Properties has also asked Larson to estimate the market value of Riviera Terrace using: (1) the direct income capitalization approach and (2) the gross income multiplier approach.

©2011 Kaplan, Inc.

There are several indicators that the Florida real estate market may take a downward turn over the next five years. With this in mind, Larson determines that there is a reasonable chance that Sentry will have to terminate its investment in Riviera Terrace at the end of Year 3 at the initial purchase price of $40,000,000. Under this scenario, he estimates the equity reversion after tax (ERAT) in Year 3 to be $4,934,000. Cash flow after tax in years 1 and 2 are $1,676,000 and $1,802,000, respectively.

91.   The highest estimated capitalization rate for Riviera Terrace, comparing the market extraction method and the built-up method, is *closest* to:
A. 10.50%.
B. 10.80%.
C. 11.75%.

92.   Larson values Riviera Terrace using the direct income capitalization approach. His estimate is *closest* to:
A. $31,111,111.
B. $38,888,889.
C. $48,611,111.

93.   In the scenario in which Sentry will sell Riviera Terrace for $60,000,000 at the end of the investment horizon, the total tax liability is *closest* to:
A. $1,750,000.
B. $2,370,000.
C. $4,120,000.

94.   In the scenario in which Sentry will sell Riviera Terrace for $45,000,000 at the end of the investment horizon, the equity reversion after tax is *closest* to:
A. $2,027,500.
B. $4,983,334.
C. $7,822,500.

95.   The cash flow after tax (CFAT) for Riviera Terrace in Year 3 is *closest* to:
A. $1,934,300.
B. $2,073,215.
C. $2,219,076.

96.   Under Larson's early termination scenario, and based on the internal rate of return (IRR) method of analysis, should he recommend that Sentry Properties invest in Riviera Terrace, assuming his estimate of ERAT is correct?
A. No, because the IRR for the investment is 11%, which is less than Sentry Properties' required return of 20%.
B. No, because the IRR for the investment is 11%, which is less than the real estate capitalization rate of 15%.
C. No, because the IRR for the investment is 12%, which is less than the IRR of 22% for properties that are comparable to Riviera Terrace.

Questions 97–102 relate to Ernie Smith.

Ernie Smith and Jamal Sims are analysts with the firm of Madison Consultants. Madison provides statistical modeling and advice to portfolio managers throughout the United States and Canada.

In an effort to estimate future cash flows and value the Canadian stock market, Smith has been examining the country's aggregate retail sales. He runs two autoregressive regression models in an attempt to determine whether there are any patterns in the data, utilizing nine years of unadjusted monthly retail sales data. One model uses a lag one variable and the other adds a lag twelve variable. The results of both regressions are shown in Exhibits 1 and 2.

Exhibit 1: Canadian Autoregressive Model with Lag 1

Multiple R	0.91
R-Square	0.83
Adjusted R-Square	0.83
Standard Error	17,252.76
Observations	108.00

ANOVA

	df	SS	MS	F	Significance F
Regression	1.00	150,813,197,793	150,813,197,793	506.67	0.00
Residual	106.00	31,551,711,544	297,657,656		
Total	107.00	182,364,909,338			

	Coefficients	Standard Error	T-stat	P-value
Intercept	21,750.16	10,379.77	2.10	0.04
Lag 1	0.92	0.04	22.51	0.00

©2011 Kaplan, Inc.

Exhibit 2: Canadian Autoregressive Model with Lag 1 and Lag 12

Regression Statistics for 2nd Regression	
Multiple R	0.96
R-Square	0.93
Adjusted R-Square	0.92
Standard Error	11,336.27
Observations	108.00

ANOVA

	df	SS	MS	F	Significance F
Regression	2.00	168,871,246,751	84,435,623,375	657.03	<0.01
Residual	105.00	13,493,662,586	128,511,072		
Total	107.00	182,364,909,338			

	Coefficients	Standard Error	T-stat	P-value
Intercept	–24,861.28	7,872.56	–3.16	<0.01
Lag 1	0.30	0.06	5.22	<0.01
Lag 12	0.84	0.07	11.85	<0.01

Sims has been assigned the task of valuing the U.S. stock market and uses data similar to the data that Smith uses for Canada. He decides, however, that the data should be transformed. He takes the natural log of the data and uses it in the following model:

$$\Delta \ln \text{sales}_t = b_0 + b_1 \Delta \ln \text{sales}_{t-1}$$

Parameter estimates for the autoregressive model and the actual data for the two most recent months are shown in Exhibit 3.

Exhibit 3: U.S. Autoregressive Model

Intercept	0.052
Lag 1 coefficient	0.684
Actual sales one month ago (–1)	6,270
Actual sales two months ago (–2)	6,184

Smith and Sims are concerned that the data for Canadian retail sales may be more appropriately modeled with an ARCH process. Smith states, that in order to find out, he would take the residuals from the original autoregressive model for Canadian retail sales and then square them.

Sims states that these residuals would then be regressed against the Canadian retail sales data using the following equation: $e_t = b_0 + b_1 X_t$, where e represents the residual terms from the original regression and X represents the Canadian retail sales data. If b_1 is statistically different from zero, then the regression model contains an ARCH process.

Smith also examines the quarterly inflation data for an emerging market over the past nine years. He models the data using an autoregressive model with a lag one independent variable, which he finds is statistically different from zero. He wonders whether he should also include lag two and lag four terms, given the magnitude of the autocorrelations of the residuals shown in Exhibit 4, assuming a 5% significance level. The critical t-values, assuming a 5% significance level and 35 degrees of freedom, are 2.03 for a two-tail test and 1.69 for a one-tail test.

Exhibit 4: Emerging Market Autoregressive Model

Lag	Autocorrelation
1	0.0829
2	0.1293
3	0.0227
4	0.1882

Sims is investigating the performance of 5-year European and British bonds based on the actions of the U.S. Federal Reserve. He uses the U.S. Federal Funds rate. The two regressions he uses are:

$$BY_{E,t} = b_0 + b_1 FF_{US,t}$$

$$BY_{B,t} = b_0 + b_1 FF_{US,t}$$

where: FF is the Federal Funds rate in the United States (US), and BY is the bond yield in the European Union (E) and Great Britain (B).

Before he runs this regression, he investigates the characteristics of the dependent and independent variables. He finds that the Federal Funds rate in the United States and the bond yield in Great Britain have a unit root but that the bond yield in the European Union does not. Furthermore, the Federal Funds rate in the United States and the bond yield in Great Britain are cointegrated, but the Federal Funds rate in the United States and the bond yield in the European Union are not.

©2011 Kaplan, Inc.

97. Which of the following models would be the *best* formulation for the Canadian retail sales data?
    A. $X_t = b_0 + b_1 X_{t-1}$.
    B. $X_t = b_1 X_{t-1} + b_2 X_{t-12}$.
    C. $X_t = b_0 + b_1 X_{t-1} + b_2 X_{t-12}$.

98. The estimate of forecasted sales for the United States this month, using Sims's model, is *closest* to:
    A. $6,329.
    B. $6,453.
    C. $6,667.

99. Are the comments of Smith and Sims on the construction of an ARCH model correct?
    A. Both comments are correct.
    B. Only Smith is correct.
    C. Only Sims is correct.

100. Regarding Smith's emerging market regression, should lag two and lag four terms be included in the regression?
    A. Neither Lag should be included.
    B. Only Lag 2 should be included.
    C. Only Lag 4 should be included.

101. Will Sims's regressions of European and British bond yields on the U.S. Federal Funds rate produce valid results?
    A. Neither Regression is valid.
    B. Only Regression 1 is valid.
    C. Only Regression 2 is valid.

102. Which of the following is the *appropriate* test for cointegration?
    A. Breusch-Pagan.
    B. Durbin-Watson.
    C. Dickey-Fuller/Engle-Granger.

Questions 103–108 relate to Galena Petrovich.

Galena Petrovich, CFA, is an analyst in the New York office of TRS Investment Management, Inc. Petrovich is an expert in the industrial electrical equipment sector and is analyzing Fisher Global. Fisher is a global market leader in designing, manufacturing, marketing, and servicing electrical systems and components, including fluid power systems and automotive engine air management systems.

Fisher has generated double-digit growth over the past ten years, primarily as the result of acquisitions, and has reported positive net income in each year. Fisher reports its financial results using International Financial Reporting Standards (IFRS).

Petrovich is particularly interested in a transaction that occurred seven years ago, before the change in accounting standards, in which Fisher used the pooling method to account for a large acquisition of Dartmouth Industries, an industry competitor. She would like to determine the effect of using the purchase method instead of the pooling method on the financial statements of Fisher. Fisher exchanged common stock for all of the outstanding shares of Dartmouth.

Fisher also has a 50% ownership interest in a joint venture with its major distributor, a U.S. company called Hydro Distribution. She determines that Fisher has reported its ownership interest under the proportioned consolidation method, and that the joint venture has been profitable since it was established three years ago. She decides to adjust the financial statements to show how the financial statements would be affected if Fisher had reported its ownership under the equity method. Fisher is also considering acquiring 80% to 100% of Brown and Sons Company. Petrovich must consider the effect of such an acquisition on Fisher's financial statements.

Petrovich determines from the financial statement footnotes that Fisher reported an unrealized gain in its most recent income statement related to debt securities that are designated at fair value. Competitor firms following U.S. GAAP classify similar debt securities as available-for-sale.

Finally, Petrovich finds a reference in Fisher's footnotes regarding a special purpose entity (SPE). Fisher has reported its investment in the SPE using the equity method, but Petrovich believes that the consolidation method more accurately reflects Fisher's true financial position, so she makes the appropriate adjustments to the financial statements.

©2011 Kaplan, Inc.

103. Regarding the prior purchase that was accounted for under the pooling of interests method, had Fisher Global reported this purchase under the acquisition method:
   A. the assets and liabilities of the purchased firm would not be included on Fisher's balance sheet.
   B. balance sheet assets and liabilities of the purchased firm would have been reported at fair value.
   C. reported goodwill could be less depending on the fair value of the identifiable assets and liabilities compared to their book values.

104. Had Fisher Global reported its investment in the joint venture under the equity method rather than under the proportionate consolidation method, it is *most likely* that:
   A. reported revenue would have been the same.
   B. reported expenses would have been higher.
   C. Fisher's net income would not have been affected.

105. Regarding any potential goodwill on the acquisition of Brown and Sons being considered by Fisher Global, which of the following statements is correct?
   A. It is equal to the excess of the purchase price over the fair value of the identifiable assets and liabilities and must be amortized over no longer than 30 years.
   B. It will be reported as an asset, not amortized, and must be reviewed for impairment at least annually, with same test for impairment under IFRS and U.S. GAAP.
   C. It will be reported as an asset, not amortized, and must be reviewed for impairment at least annually, with different test for impairment under IFRS and U.S. GAAP.

106. If Fisher Global decides to purchase only 80% of Brown and Sons, under IFRS they will have the option to:
   A. report the acquisition as either a business combination or as an acquisition.
   B. value the identifiable assets and liabilities of Brown and Sons at their current book values or at fair market value.
   C. report more or less goodwill depending on the accounting method they choose.

107. For comparison purposes, Petrovich decides to reclassify Fisher Global's debt securities as available-for-sale. Ignoring any effect on income taxes, which of the following *best* describes the effects of the necessary adjustments?
   A. Net income is lower and asset turnover is higher.
   B. Return on assets is lower and debt-to-equity is lower.
   C. Return on equity is lower and debt-to-total capital is not affected.

108. What are the *likely* effects on return on assets (ROA) and net profit margin (ignoring any tax effects) of correctly adjusting for Fisher Global's investment in the SPE using the acquisition method?

	ROA	Net profit margin
A.	No change	Decrease
B.	Decrease	No change
C.	Decrease	Decrease

 ©2011 Kaplan, Inc.

Questions 109–114 relate to Wayward Distributing, Inc.

Jenna Stuart is a financial analyst for Deuce Hardware Company, a U.S. company that reports its results in U.S. dollars. Wayward Distributing, Inc., is a foreign subsidiary of Deuce Hardware, which began operations on January 1, 2007. Wayward is located in a foreign country and reports its results in the local currency called the Rho. Selected balance sheet information for Wayward is shown in the following table.

Selected Balance Sheet Accounts Wayward Distributing Inc. (in Rho)

	12/31/07	12/31/08
Cash and accounts receivable	5,000	5,200
Inventory	3,800	4,900
Net fixed assets	6,200	7,400
Total assets	15,000	17,500
Current liabilities	2,000	2,000
Long-term debt	9,000	9,500
Shareholders' equity	4,000	6,000

Stuart has been asked to analyze how the reported financial results of Wayward will be affected by the choice of the current rate or temporal methods of accounting for foreign operations. She has gathered the following exchange rate information on the $/Rho exchange rate:

- Spot rate on 1/01/08: $0.35 per Rho
- Spot rate on 12/31/08: $0.45 per Rho
- Average spot rate during 2008: $0.42 per Rho

109. Will the current rate method report a translation gain or loss for 2008, and will that gain or loss be reported on Deuce's income statement or the balance sheet?
   A. Gain on the balance sheet.
   B. Gain on the income statement.
   C. Loss on the balance sheet and a gain on the income statement.

110. Will the temporal method report a translation gain or loss for 2008, and will that gain or loss be reported on Deuce's income statement or the balance sheet?
   A. Gain on the balance sheet.
   B. Loss on the income statement.
   C. Gain on the balance sheet and a loss on the income statement.

111. Will total asset turnover (calculated using end-of-period balance sheet figures) *likely* be larger when calculated from the Rho financial statements or the financial statements translated into the reporting currency (U.S.$) using the current rate method?
    A. Larger on US$ statements.
    B. Larger on Rho statements.
    C. No difference.

112. Will fixed asset turnover (calculated using end-of-period balance sheet figures) *likely* be lower when calculated using the current rate method or remeasured using the temporal method?
    A. Lower under the temporal method.
    B. Lower under the current rate method.
    C. The same under either method.

113. Suppose for this question only that Stuart has determined that (1) the operating, financing, and investing decisions related to Wayward's operations are typically made by Wayward's local management located in the foreign country; and (2) some of Wayward's accounts receivable are denominated in a different foreign currency called the Del (Dl). Which method is the *best* to use to translate the Del receivables into Rho, according to U.S. GAAP?
    A. The current rate method.
    B. The temporal method.
    C. The method will depend on inflation.

114. Suppose for this question only that Stuart decides to use the current rate method to translate Wayward's results into U.S. dollars. Is it *likely* that the quick ratio and the interest coverage ratio will be the same or different in Rho before translation and in U.S. dollars after translation?
    A. Neither the quick ratio nor the interest coverage ratio will change.
    B. Only the interest coverage ratio will change.
    C. Only the quick ratio will change.

©2011 Kaplan, Inc.

Questions 115–120 relate to Monica Garza.

Monica Garza, CFA is a sell-side analyst for Schubert Brokerage Services. Garza is analyzing the financial statements of Project Depot, a home improvement retailer based in the United States that also has operations outside the United States. Garza is particularly concerned with evaluating Project Depot's inventory and long-lived assets.

Project Depot reports under U.S. GAAP and uses the last-in, first-out (LIFO) method to account for inventory. Garza investigates the notes accompanying Project Depot's financial statements. The notes indicate that the prices of new inventory have been steadily rising and that the inventory balance has grown over the last few years.

Garza has collected the following information from Project Depot's financial statements:

Exhibit 1: Selected Financial Information

	($ millions)	
	20X0	*20X1*
Revenues	41,322	45,737
Cost of goods sold	28,687	30,757
Depreciation	1,588	1,614
Interest expense	121	139
Taxes	2,312	2,811
Inventory	8,209	8,249
Gross plant and equipment	30,858	32,268
Accumulated depreciation	8,155	9,769
Working capital	15,132	16,299
LIFO reserve	3,250	5,750

Garza also has been comparing the operating margins of Project Depot to a close competitor, Fine Depot. While analyzing Fine Depot's financial statements, Garza notices that Fine Depot had a major LIFO liquidation in 20X1.

To begin her analysis of Project Depot's long-lived assets, Garza reviews the notes to the financial statements to determine the depreciation method Project Depot uses. The notes indicate that Project Depot currently utilizes a straight-line method of depreciation but is contemplating using the double-declining balance method of depreciation. Garza is concerned about the impact this will have on the financial statements if the change is made.

After determining the depreciation method, Garza wants to analyze the age of the long-lived assets to determine when Project Depot will require major investments.

Continuing her analysis of Project Depot's long-lived assets, Garza reads in a major news publication that Project Depot had assets in Louisiana revalued by a professional appraisal to test for impairment. The fair value of the assets was determined in a professional appraisal to be $350 million. The assets are currently in use and are valued on the balance sheet at $300 million. The current balance sheet value reflects previously recognized impairment losses of $43 million. The original cost of the assets was $525 million.

115. Based on the information collected by Garza, by using last-in, first-out (LIFO) instead of first-in, first-out (FIFO), Project Depot has higher:
   A. cash flows.
   B. net income.
   C. working capital.

116. Based solely on the LIFO liquidation, Fine Depot's financial statements for 20X1 would have reported:
   A. lower earnings.
   B. higher earnings.
   C. an increase in inventory.

117. If Garza adjusts Project Depot's inventory from last-in, first-out (LIFO) to first-in, first-out (FIFO), the COGS for 201X would be ($ millions):
   A. $2,540.
   B. $25,007.
   C. $28,257.

118. If Project Depot switches depreciation methods, which of the following statements is the *most accurate*?
   A. Return on Investment going forward will increase over the life of an asset.
   B. Asset turnover ratio going forward will decrease over the life of an asset.
   C. Current ratio going forward will increase over the life of an asset.

119. Based on the information collected by Garza, the average remaining useful life of Project Depot's plant and equipment is:
   A. 6.05 years.
   B. 13.94 years.
   C. 20.00 years.

120. Based on the new appraised value of the assets in Lousiana, Garza can *most likely* expect:
   A. no change to Project Depot's financial statements.
   B. a $50 million gain in other comprehensive income.
   C. a $43 million gain on the income statement and a $7 million gain in other comprehensive income.

End of Afternoon Session

©2011 Kaplan, Inc.

Exam 1
Morning Session Answers

To get valuable feedback on how your score compares to those of other Level II candidates, use your Username and Password to gain Online Access at schweser.com and choose the left-hand menu item "Practice Exams Vol. 1."

1. B	21. A	41. B
2. C	22. B	42. B
3. A	23. A	43. C
4. C	24. C	44. C
5. A	25. A	45. A
6. C	26. A	46. B
7. C	27. B	47. B
8. B	28. C	48. B
9. C	29. C	49. A
10. C	30. B	50. C
11. C	31. A	51. A
12. C	32. C	52. A
13. B	33. C	53. C
14. B	34. C	54. C
15. A	35. B	55. A
16. A	36. B	56. B
17. C	37. B	57. A
18. B	38. C	58. B
19. A	39. C	59. C
20. A	40. A	60. B

EXAM 1
MORNING SESSION ANSWERS

1. **B**   The bond will be called in the lower node if the interest rate is 5.0% because the present value of the remaining cash flows ($100.95) is greater than the call price ($99.50). The bond will not be called if rates increase to 7.5% in the upper node because the value of the bond ($98.60) is less than the call price ($99.50). The value of the callable bond according to the model is 101.01:

$$V_0 = \frac{1}{2} \times \left[\frac{98.60 + 6.00}{1.04} + \frac{99.50 + 6.00}{1.04} \right] = 101.01$$

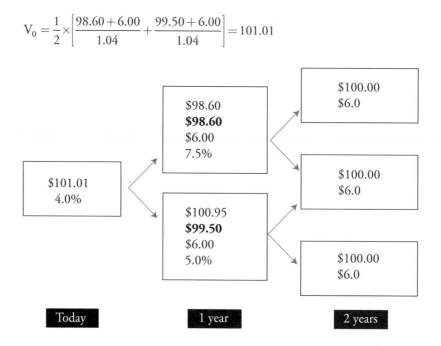

(Study Session 14, LOS 50.d)

2. **C**   The value of a putable bond is equal to the value of an otherwise equivalent option-free bond plus the value of the embedded put option. The value of the embedded put option will decrease if yield volatility decreases. The value of the option-free bond will not be affected by changes in yield volatility, so the value of the putable bond will also decrease. Evermore is incorrect in her analysis of both effects. (Study Session 14, LOS 50.e,f)

3. **A**   Evermore creates the interest rate tree that she uses to compute option-adjusted spreads using Treasuries as a benchmark because she first develops the tree so that it correctly prices Treasury issues. (Study Session 14, LOS 50.g)

©2011 Kaplan, Inc.

4. **C** The benchmark securities used to create the tree are Treasury securities, so the OAS for each callable corporate bond reflects additional credit risk and liquidity risk relative to the benchmark. The bonds are overvalued if their OAS are smaller than the required OAS and undervalued if their OAS are larger than the required OAS. The required OAS for both bonds is the *Z*-spread over Treasuries on comparably-rated securities with no embedded options. That required spread is not provided in the vignette.

    The BB-rated issue is overvalued because its OAS is less than zero, which means it must be less than the required OAS. Therefore, Evermore is correct in her analysis of the BB-rated issue.

    The AA-rated issue has a positive OAS relative to the Treasury benchmark, but we don't know the required OAS on similar bonds, so we can't determine whether or not the AA-rated issue is over or undervalued based on the information given. Therefore, Evermore is incorrect to conclude that the issue is undervalued. (Study Session 14, LOS 50.a)

5. **A** Davenport has correctly outlined the appropriate methodology for using a binomial model to estimate effective duration and effective convexity. Evermore fails to adjust for the OAS and, instead, simply adds 100 basis points to every rate on the tree rather than shifting the yield curve upward and then recreating the entire tree using the same rate volatility assumption from the first step. Even if both use the same rate volatility assumption and the OAS is equal to zero, the two methodologies will generate significantly different duration and convexity estimates. (Study Session 14, LOS 50.h)

6. **C** The value of a callable convertible bond is equal to the value of an option-free bond plus the value of the conversion option on the stock minus the value of the call option on the bond.

    A decrease in the volatility of Highfour's common stock returns will decrease the value of the conversion option on the stock. Consequently the value of the convertible bond will also decrease. Evermore was correct in her analysis, and Davenport was incorrect to disagree with her.

    A decrease in the yield volatility will decrease the value of the embedded call option. The issuer has written the call option, so a decrease in the value of the call option will increase the value of the convertible bond. Evermore is incorrect in her analysis, and Davenport was correct to disagree with her. (Study Session 14, LOS 50.f,j)

7. **C** The slope of the market model is the beta. Systematic risk is high for high beta funds. From Exhibit 1, the market beta is lower for CF (0.70) versus EF (1.50). Unsystematic risk is measured by the variance of the market model error (ε). The information provided in the vignette states that the variances are identical for CF and EF. We can determine which fund has larger unsystematic risk by using the market model formula for the variance:

$$\sigma_{CF}^2 = \beta_{CF}^2 \sigma_M^2 + \sigma_{\varepsilon,CF}^2$$

$$\sigma_{EF}^2 = \beta_{EF}^2 \sigma_M^2 + \sigma_{\varepsilon,EF}^2$$

We know $\beta_{CF}^2 \sigma_M^2 < \beta_{EF}^2 \sigma_M^2$ because the beta is smaller for CF versus EF. The vignette states that the variances for CF and EF are identical. Therefore, if the total variances are identical, and if the first component is smaller for CF versus EF, then the second component (unsystematic risk) must be larger for CF versus EF. (Study Session 18, LOS 60.f,g)

8. **B** The equations for the CAPM and a 2-factor APT, respectively, are:

CAPM for EF: $\qquad k = R_F + \beta_{EF}[E(R_M) - R_F]$

2-factor APT for EF: $\qquad k = R_F + \beta_{EF,1}(\lambda_1) + \beta_{EF,2}(\lambda_2)$

where each λ_1 and λ_2 are the expected risk premium associated with the GDP risk factor and the Investor Sentiment risk factor, respectively.

Using the data provided in Exhibits 2 and 3:

CAPM $\qquad k = 0.04 + 0.80(0.08) = 0.104 = 10.4\%$

2-factor APT $\qquad k = 0.04 + 1.5(0.05) + 2(0.02) = 0.155 = 15.5\%$

Note that the beta estimate for EF in Exhibit 1 from the market model is an estimate of the historical beta based on historical data. The question asks you to use the forecast beta from Exhibit 3.

Rodriguez forecasts that the EF fund return will equal 12%, which exceeds the CAPM required return. Therefore, Rodriguez predicts that the EF portfolio return will exceed its CAPM required return (a signal to continue investing in EF). But the forecast EF return (12%) is less than the 2-factor APT model required return of 15.5% (a signal to sell or not continue investing in EF). (Study Session 18, LOS 60.e,l,n)

9. **C** A portfolio that has a factor beta equal to one for one factor and factor betas equal to zero for all other factors is called a "factor portfolio." In contrast, a portfolio that has factor betas equal to the benchmark factor betas is called a "tracking portfolio." Unlike the tracking portfolio, the factor portfolio betas are not identical to the benchmark betas. As a result, factor portfolios have higher active factor risk (which refers to the deviations of a portfolio's factor betas from those of the benchmark). Therefore, Woodson's first statement is not correct.

Her second statement is correct. When markets are in equilibrium, all expected (i.e., forecast) asset returns equal their required returns. An arbitrage opportunity refers to an investment that requires no cost and no risk yet still provides a profit. If markets are in equilibrium, no profits can be earned from a costless, riskless investment. (Study Session 18, LOS 60.j,m)

10. **C** The SML is the graph of the CAPM:

$E(R) = R_F + \beta[E(R_M) - R_F]$

From Exhibit 2 the intercept of the CAPM is the risk-free rate (the Treasury bond yield = 0.04), and the slope equals the market risk premium $[E(R_M) - R_F = 0.08]$. (Study Session 18, LOS 60.f)

11. **C** Macroeconomic factor models assume that asset returns are explained by surprises (or "shocks") in macroeconomic risk factors (e.g., GDP growth and Investor Sentiment). A factor surprise is defined as the difference between the realized value of the factor and its expected value, which is the expected return from the APT model (0.155 from Question 8). Therefore, the intercept must equal the expected return on the portfolio.

©2011 Kaplan, Inc.

The equation for the macroeconomic factor model employed by Factor Analytics Capital Management is:

$$R_{EF} = a_{EF} + b_{EF,1}F_{GDP} + b_{EF,2}F_{IS} + \varepsilon_{EF}$$

where the expected values of both factors are zero, and the expected value of the error term also is zero. Therefore, when markets move as expected:

$$E(R_{EF}) = a_{EF} + 0 + 0 + 0 = 0.155, \text{ so } a_{EF} = 0.155$$

(Study Session 18, LOS 60.j)

12. **C** The information ratio equals active return divided by active risk. Active return equals the average difference between the CF portfolio return and the benchmark return. Active risk equals the standard deviation of the CF minus benchmark returns. From the comments made by Rodriquez about the historical performance of the CF portfolio, we know that the numerator of the information ratio is positive and the denominator is very close to zero. Therefore, the information ratio will be high.

    The fund standard deviation was very close to its benchmark (since its returns were nearly always a constant percentage above the benchmark). The CF fund rose and fell with the benchmark (same risk as the benchmark) but always beat the benchmark (outperformed the benchmark). Therefore, tracking risk (which is also referred to as active risk) is low. (Study Session 18, LOS 60.m)

13. **B** The beta of 1.04 is estimated from the slope coefficient on the independent variable (the return on the market) from the regression.

    From the CAPM: required return on equity = 0.03 + [1.04 (0.07 – 0.03)] = 0.072 = 7.2%. (Study Session 10, LOS 35.c)

14. **B** The value of the stock in early 2009 is the present value of the future dividends. After 2011, dividends are expected to grow at the rate of 4%. The dividend that begins the constantly growing perpetuity is $2.63 × 1.04 = $2.74. You are told to assume the appropriate discount rate is the cost of equity of 7.2% from Question 13. Note that for the third cash flow, we add the third dividend ($2.63) to the present value of the constantly growing perpetuity that begins in the fourth year = $2.74 / (0.072 – 0.04) = $85.63. This is valid since they both occur at the same point in time (i.e., at the end of the third year). Using a financial calculator we can estimate the value of one share of O'Connor stock as follows:

    CFO = 0; C01 = $2.13; C02 = $2.36; C03 = $2.63 + $85.63 = $88.26; I = 7.2; CPT → NPV = $75.68

    (Study Session 11, LOS 39.b)

15. **A** De Jong's estimate of value of $75.68 from Question 14 (based on a high-growth period of three years) is greater than the market's consensus of $70.00, which means the market's consensus high-growth duration must be less than three years, all else equal. (Study Session 11, LOS 39.b)

16. **A** In order for the dividend discount model to produce a reasonable estimate of share price, the investor should have a non-control perspective. For the FCFE model to be appropriate, there should be a link between FCFE and profitability. (Study Session 11, LOS 39.a)

17. **C** The estimate of the required return on equity using the CAPM does not depend on whether the company pays dividends. (Study Session 18, LOS 60.e)

18. **B** She is correct on one count but incorrect on the other. Using adjusted standard errors will change the *t*-statistic and potentially the statistical significance, but not the beta estimate itself. So, she is incorrect with regard to the impact of adjusting the standard errors. The mean-reverting level of the beta is 1. If the historical beta is greater than 1, then the adjusted beta will be less than the historical beta and closer to 1. If the historical beta is less than 1, then the adjusted beta will be greater than the historical beta and closer to 1. The adjusted beta forecast will move toward 1 more quickly for larger values of α_0, so she is correct in regard to this matter. (Study Session 3, LOS 12.i and Study Session 18, LOS 60.h)

19. **A** Increasing invested capital to take advantage of positive NPV projects will increase NOPAT and the dollar cost of capital ($WACC). The increase in NOPAT will be larger than the increase in $WACC, so EVA will increase. (Study Session 8, LOS 30.d and Study Session 12, LOS 42.a)

20. **A** All of the justifications noted by De Jong are appropriate reasons to use the residual income model. (Study Session 12, LOS 42.j)

21. **A** When residual income is expected to persist at its current level forever, the persistence factor is highest. When ROE declines over time to the cost of equity, residual income declines over time to zero, and the persistence factor will have a value between 0 and 1. When residual income falls to zero immediately, the persistence factor has a value of zero. (Study Session 12, LOS 42.h)

22. **B** Residual income = net income − equity charge
Equity charge = equity capital × cost of equity capital
Equity charge = $73,000,000 × 0.08 = $5,840,000
Residual income = $10,035,000 − $5,840,000 = $4,195,000

EVA = NOPAT − (C% × TC)

EVA = $28,517,640 − (0.054 × $324,000,000) = $11,021,640
(Study Session 12, LOS 42.a)

23. **A** We need to solve for *g* in the relationship:

$$V_0 = B_0 + \left(\frac{ROE - r}{r - g}\right)B_0$$

$$\$70.00 = \$4.29 + \left(\frac{0.1184 - 0.08}{0.08 - g}\right)\$4.29$$

Solving for *g*, we get g = 7.75%. (Study Session 12, LOS 42.g)

24. **C** Only Statement 2 is correct. Residual income valuation is related to P/B. When the present value of expected future residual income is negative, the justified P/B based on fundamentals is less than 1. Statement 1 is not correct: residual income models recognize value *earlier* than other valuation models. (Study Session 12, LOS 42.e,i)

25. **A** Cost of finished jewelry = 11.06 + 2.897 × (cost of gold)
$2,000 = 11.06 + 2.897× (cost of gold)
Price of gold = ($2,000 − 11.06) / 2.897 = $686.55

(Study Session 3, LOS 11.h)

26. **A** Singh is correct that a change in the relationship between gold prices and jewelry costs would be an example of parameter instability.

     Hara is correct to fail to reject the null hypothesis that the value of the slope coefficient is equal to 4.0 at the 5% level of significance.

     The critical *t*-value for the slope coefficient with 31 − 2 = 29 df at the 5% level for a two-tailed test is 2.045. The test statistic is (2.897 − 4.000)/0.615 = −1.79. The absolute value (1.79) is less than 2.045, and the correct decision is to fail to reject the null hypothesis that the slope coefficient is equal to 4.0. (Study Session 3, LOS 11.g, LOS 13.h)

27. **B** Biscayne is incorrect in the specification of the formula because the appropriate R^2 to use in calculating a Breusch-Pagan chi-square statistic is not the R^2 of the regression of jewelry prices on gold prices but rather the R^2 of the regression of squared residuals from the original regression on the independent variable(s). (Study Session 3, LOS 12.i)

28. **C** Singh is incorrect because a potential result of misspecifying a regression equation is nonstationarity (not stationarity, which is desirable).

     Biscayne is incorrect because the effect of omitting an important variable in a regression is that the regression coefficients are often biased (not unbiased) and/or inconsistent. (Study Session 3, LOS 12.k)

29. **C** Hara is incorrect because the Durbin-Watson statistic indicates the presence of negative, not positive, autocorrelation (serial correlation). As a practical matter, the DW statistic is so close to four that the answer can be surmised without calculation.

     The DW statistic can range between zero and four. Serial correlation is not a problem if the DW statistic is close to two. Positive serial correction is a potential problem if the DW statistic is significantly less than two, and negative serial correlation is a problem if it is significantly greater than two. Because the DW statistic for this regression is between two and four, negative serial correlation is a potential problem, but positive serial correlation is not. (Study Session 3, LOS 12.i)

30. **B** Biscayne is incorrect because a serial correlation problem can be corrected by using the Hansen method to adjust the coefficient standard errors, not the R^2. (Study Session 3, LOS 12.i)

31. **A** Stale pricing leads to low computed standard deviation values. Mean variance optimization utilizing artificially low standard deviation of hedge funds would lead to higher allocation for hedge funds in the portfolio. Consideration of higher moment risks, in addition to standard deviation, would lead to reduced allocation to hedge funds. Similarly, high traditional market risk exposures would increase correlations between hedge fund returns and traditional asset classes in the portfolio and reduce the diversification benefit of (and hence the allocation to) hedge funds. (Study Session 13, LOS 47.g)

32. **C** Nagoree would prefer a hurdle rate (minimum return on the portfolio before an incentive fee is payable) and a high-water mark provision (so that the manager does not earn an incentive fee on the same dollar of portfolio return more than once). (Study Session 13, LOS 47.a)

33. **C** Returns on hedge fund indices have selection, survivorship, and backfill (or instant history) biases. Funds of funds are individual hedge funds and not indices, and hence their returns are not subject to such biases. (Study Session 13, LOS 47.c)

34. **C**   Equity market neutral strategies hedge market risk, but size, industry, and value risk may remain. (Study Session 13, LOS 47.b)

35. **B**   Merger arbitrage strategy is compared to selling insurance; the investor makes a small profit if the merger is successful, but may incur a large loss if it fails. (Study session 13, LOS 47.b)

36. **B**   Hedge fund return distributions are non-normal and generally exhibit negative skewness and positive excess kurtosis. (Study Session 13, LOS 47.e)

37. **B**   While the Treynor-Black model can be modified to include analyst forecast accuracy in the calculation of active portfolio weights, this is not part of the model itself. The unsystematic risk of securities in the active portfolio is an important input into the information ratio and active portfolio weights. A change in the risk-free rate can be expected to change an investor's allocation between the risk-free asset and the optimal risky portfolio and will change the estimates of abnormal returns (alpha) for active portfolio stocks and, thereby, their portfolio weights. (Study Session 18, LOS 63.b)

38. **C**   Active portfolio management (generally) and separation theorem (specifically) supports the conclusion that all investors should hold a combination of the risk-free asset and the market portfolio. This allows the portfolio manager to identify the optimal risky portfolio, independent to the investor's risk aversion. The optimal portfolio for an individual investor is a combination of the risk-free asset and the optimal risky asset portfolio that does depend on the investor's degree of risk aversion. (Study Session 18, LOS 63.a)

39. **C**   A tracking portfolio is designed to have the same systematic risk as the benchmark. Hence, any difference in portfolio versus benchmark returns comes from security selection. (Study Session 18, LOS 60.m)

40. **A**   The Sharpe ratio for the optimal risky asset portfolio (a combination of the passive market index portfolio and the optimal active security selection portfolio) is its excess return (risk premium) divided by its standard deviation, so we have $0.45 = (10 - 3) / \sigma_{port}$, and the standard deviation of the optimal risky portfolio = $7 / 0.45 = 15.55\%$. With a 70% allocation to the risk-free asset, the investor's optimal portfolio will have a standard deviation of $(1 - 0.7) 15.55 = 4.67\%$. (Study Session 18, LOS 60.f)

41. **B**   In the Treynor-Black model, the weightings for securities in the actively managed portfolio are computed as:

$$w_i = \frac{\text{alpha}_i}{\text{unsystematic risk}_i} \Bigg/ \sum_{j=1}^{n} \frac{\text{alpha}_j}{\text{unsystematic risk}_j}$$

where:
n = number of assets in actively managed portfolio

The weight of a security in the active portfolio is positively related to its own alpha and negatively related to its unsystematic risk and to the alpha of other securities in the active portfolio. (Study Session 18, LOS 63.b)

©2011 Kaplan, Inc.

42. **B** An analyst's forecasting ability can be judged based on past performance. The Treynor-Black weightings within actively managed portfolios can be adjusted based on an analyst's prior forecasting ability. The process is to:
    - Collect the time-series alpha forecasts for the analyst.
    - Calculate the correlation between the alpha forecasts and the realized alphas.
    - Square the correlation to derive the R^2.
    - Adjust (shrink) a forecast alpha by multiplying it by the analyst's R^2.

    (Study Session 18, LOS 63.c)

43. **C** The present value of the next coupon payment (per $100 face value) is

    $$\frac{2.50}{1.04^{\left(\frac{182}{365}\right)}} = 2.4516.$$

    The no-arbitrage forward price is $(98.25 - 2.4516) \times 1.04^{\left(\frac{270}{365}\right)} = 98.62.$

    (Study Session 16, LOS 54.c)

44. **C** PV of the coupon is now $\dfrac{2.50}{1.04^{\left(\frac{122}{365}\right)}} = 2.4674$, and the value of the forward contract to

    the long is $98.11 - 2.4674 - \dfrac{98.62}{1.04^{\left(\frac{210}{365}\right)}} = -0.77693$ per $100, or –$77,693.

    The value to the short is +$77,693. (Study Session 16, LOS 54.c)

45. **A** Adams used the 90-day rate (0.0352) and the time period (90/360) in the numerator instead of the 150-day rate (0.0392) and the 150-day time period (150/360). The denominator is correct, so two out of the four terms are used correctly. The correct calculation is:

    $$\left[\frac{1 + 0.0392\left(\frac{150}{360}\right)}{1 + 0.0332\left(\frac{60}{360}\right)} - 1\right]\left(\frac{360}{90}\right) = \left[\frac{1.01633}{1.00553} - 1\right](4) = 4.30\%$$

    (Study Session 16, LOS 54.c)

46. **B** $(0.0430 - 0.0414) \times \$10 \text{ million} \times \dfrac{90}{360} = \$4,000$ (expected payoff in 120 days)

    PV of payoff is $\dfrac{\$4,000}{1 + 0.0392\left(\frac{120}{360}\right)} = \$3,948$

    (Study Session 16, LOS 54.c)

47. **B** $1.1854\left(\dfrac{1.03}{1.04}\right) = \$1.174$ (Study Session 16, LOS 54.c)

48. **B** If the spot rate for euros at maturity is greater than the forward contract rate at initiation, the long (euros) position value is positive and the short position value is negative. Because the short owes the long, the long has credit risk. (Study Session 16, LOS 54.d)

49. **A** CMOs are structured so that the prepayment risk (as measured by the average life variability) is lower for the PAC I tranche than the support tranche. The average life of Tranche YY in Exhibit 1 is constant at 5.1 over a relatively large range of prepayment speeds (100 – 300 PSA). Therefore, Tranche YY is the PAC I tranche, and the effective collar of the PAC I tranche (the range of prepayment speeds over which the average life of the tranche is constant) is 100 – 300 PSA. Tranche XX has a much higher average life variability, so it must be the support tranche. (Study Session 15, LOS 51.h,i)

50. **C** Statement 1 is incorrect. The PAC I tranche has less extension risk and less contraction risk than the support tranche. It has less contraction risk because when rates fall and prepayment speeds increase, the average life of the PAC I tranche falls by less than the average life of the support tranche. It has less extension risk because when rates rise and prepayment speeds fall, the average life of the PAC I tranche increases by less than the support tranche's average life.

Statement 2 is correct. If interest rates decrease by 100 basis points, prepayment speeds will increase. The support tranche will absorb most of the unexpected prepayments, however, and its cash flows will be significantly affected, while the PAC I tranche will be minimally affected. (Study Session 15, LOS 51.h,i)

51. **A** None of the three statements is correct.

Statement 3 is incorrect because CDOs are not typically collateralized by home equity bank loans.

Statement 4 is incorrect because the credit risk of the two structures is the same. The difference is that with synthetic CDOs, the bondholders take on the risks of the underlying assets but do not take legal ownership of them.

Statement 5 is incorrect because all CDOs include an equity tranche to reduce the prepayment and credit risk of the senior and mezzanine tranches. (Study Session 15, LOS 52.g)

52. **A** Both statements are accurate, so Wayne is incorrect to disagree with Statement 6. (Study Session 15, LOS 51.c)

53. **C** Wayne is incorrect with respect to the debt service coverage ratio because the higher the ratio, the lower the credit risk. Wayne is correct with respect to the loan-to-value ratio because the higher the ratio, the higher the credit risk. (Study Session 15, LOS 51.l)

54. **C** The Z-spread should not be used for bonds with embedded options (like callable corporate bonds and home equity ABS) because it does not reflect the possibility that the cash flows from the bond may change as interest rates change. Instead OAS should be used for both. The callable corporate should be valued with an OAS from a binomial model because its cash flows are not interest rate path dependent; the home equity ABS should use an OAS from a Monte Carlo model because its cash flows are interest rate path dependent. (Study Session 14, LOS 50.c,g and Study Session 15, LOS 53.b,e)

55. **A** The sum of a portfolio's key rate durations is the effective duration of the portfolio. Each of the portfolios has an effective duration of five, so a parallel shift in the yield curve will have the same effect on each portfolio, and each will experience the same price performance. (Study Session 14, LOS 49.f)

©2011 Kaplan, Inc.

56. **B** The exposure of each portfolio to changes in the 5- and 10-year rates are equal to the sum of the 5- and 10-year key rate durations:

portfolio 1 exposure = 0.20 + 0.15 = 0.35
portfolio 2 exposure = 0.40 + 4.00 = 4.40

Portfolio 2 has the largest exposure, and portfolio 1 has the smallest exposure. If the 5- and 10-year key rates increase, portfolio 1 will fall by the smallest amount and will experience the best price performance (i.e., the smallest decrease in value).

You can confirm this by doing the calculations for a 20 basis point increase:

% change in portfolio 1 = (−0.20 × 0.002 × 100) + (−0.15 × 0.002 × 100)
$\qquad$ = (−0.35 × 0.002 × 100) = −0.07%

% change in portfolio 2 = (−0.40 × 0.002 × 100) + (−4.00 × 0.002 × 100)
$\qquad$ = (−4.40 × 0.002 × 100) = −0.88%

(Study Session 14, LOS 49.f)

57. **A** Swap rates are fixed rates on plain-vanilla interest rate swaps. The swap rate curve (also known as the LIBOR curve) is the series of swap rates quoted by swap dealers over maturities extending from 2 to 30 years. Both of Berg's observations are advantages to using the swap rate curve instead of a government bond curve as a benchmark rate curve. (Study Session 14, LOS 49.d)

58. **B** If the benchmark is Treasuries or a bond sector (with a credit rating higher than the bond we're valuing), any callable corporate bond with an OAS less than or equal to zero is overvalued relative to the benchmark because it must have more credit risk, and most likely more liquidity risk, than the benchmark. If the OAS is positive, the callable bond is undervalued relative to the benchmark only if the OAS is greater than the required OAS. In this question we aren't given the required OAS relative to a Treasury benchmark, so we can't draw any conclusions from the Steigers Corp. callable bond's OAS relative to Treasuries.

If we use an issuer-specific benchmark (assuming relative liquidity risk is zero), the callable bond is undervalued relative to the benchmark if the OAS is positive, fairly valued if the OAS is zero, and overvalued if the OAS is negative. In this question the OAS relative to Steigers' spot rate curve is negative, which means the callable bond is overvalued. (Study Session 14, LOS 50.a,g)

59. **C**   The steps in the process of calculating the effective duration of a callable bond using a binomial tree are as follows:

Step 1: Given assumptions about benchmark interest rates, interest rate volatility, and the call and/or put rule, calculate the OAS for the issue using the binomial model.

Step 2: Impose a small parallel shift in the on-the-run yield curve by an amount equal to $+\Delta y$.

Step 3: Build a new binomial interest rate tree using the new yield curve.

Step 4: Add the OAS to each of the 1-year forward rates in the interest rate tree to get a "modified" tree. (We assume that the OAS does not change when interest rates change.)

Step 5: Compute $BV_{+\Delta y}$ using this modified interest rate tree.

Step 6: Repeat steps 2 through 5 using a parallel rate shift of $-\Delta y$ to estimate a value of $BV_{-\Delta y}$.

There is no restriction on the relationship between the assumed change in the yield (Δy) and the OAS. (Study Session 14, LOS 50.h)

60. **B**   An upward sloping yield curve predicts an increase in short-term rates according to the pure expectations theory but not necessarily the liquidity premium theory.

The liquidity theory says that forward rates are a biased estimate of the market's expectation of future rates because they include a liquidity premium. Therefore, a positive sloping yield curve may indicate either (1) that the market expects future interest rates to rise or (2) that rates are expected to remain constant (or even fall), but the addition of the liquidity premium results in a positive slope. (Study Session 14, LOS 49.e)

©2011 Kaplan, Inc.

Exam 1
Afternoon Session Answers

To get valuable feedback on how your score compares to those of other Level II candidates, use your Username and Password to gain Online Access at schweser.com and choose the left-hand menu item "Practice Exams Vol. 1."

61. A	81. B	101. C
62. C	82. C	102. A
63. A	83. A	103. B
64. C	84. B	104. B
65. B	85. C	105. C
66. B	86. A	106. C
67. C	87. A	107. A
68. C	88. A	108. C
69. A	89. C	109. B
70. B	90. C	110. A
71. C	91. A	111. C
72. A	92. B	112. A
73. A	93. C	113. B
74. B	94. C	114. B
75. C	95. B	115. C
76. B	96. A	116. A
77. A	97. B	117. A
78. C	98. C	118. A
79. A	99. A	119. C
80. A	100. C	120. B

Exam 1
Afternoon Session Answers

61. **A** Item (i) is a likely violation of the Code and Standards. Working as a waitress is not a conflict of interest for an investment analyst, but Cooken's employer can reasonably assume that a 30-hour-a-week side job could be tiring, depriving the company of her skills and ability during her internship, which would violate Standard IV(A) Loyalty (to employer).

    Cooken's description of the CFA exam is accurate, and she takes no liberties with a title. Thus she has not violated Standard VII(B) Reference to CFA Institute, the CFA Designation, and the CFA Program.

    One conviction as a teenager before working as an investment professional is not a violation of Standard I(D) Misconduct. Standard IV(A) Loyalty (to employer) does not hold when illegal activities are involved, and Cooken's willingness to talk to the FBI would most likely not be considered a violation. The Standards do suggest, however, that the member consult with his employer's compliance personnel or outside counsel before disclosing any confidential client information. (Study Session 1, LOS 2.a)

62. **C** While Cooken's tax avoidance may represent a professional-conduct issue, it has no bearing on her ability to write a report on Mocline. While Clarrison may be an expert on Mocline Tobacco, Cooken does not know enough about the stock to write about it without taking the risk of being in violation of Standard V(A) Diligence and Reasonable Basis. Because of Cooken's relationship to the CFO of Mocline and ownership of Mocline stock, her objectivity might be questioned. (Study Session 1, LOS 2.a)

63. **A** Standard IV(A) Loyalty (to employer) requires that members and candidates act for the benefit of their employer and not deprive the employer of their skills and abilities. In addition, members and candidates must not cause harm to their employers. It's safe to say that a bar does not compete with a stock-analysis company, and a 6-hour-a-week part-time job should not interfere with her ability to perform analysis duties. Standard IV(B) Additional Compensation Arrangements relates to additional compensation related to an employee's services to the employer. The moonlighting is not related to her analysis job and, as such, does not violate the standard. There is nothing inherently unethical about working as a bartender, and moonlighting as a barkeeper does not compromise Cooken's professional reputation, integrity, or competence. Thus, Standard I(D) Misconduct has not been violated. (Study Session 1, LOS 2.a)

64. **C** Request 3 is a likely violation. Potential clients are not entitled to performance data beyond what the company chooses to disclose. Providing data, particularly client-specific data, could be a violation of the clients' confidentiality.

    Members and candidates must answer questions asked by CFA Institute's Professional Conduct Program. Members and candidates may report illegal activities (and in some cases may have a legal obligation to report such activities) on the part of clients without fear of violating Standard III(E) Preservation of Confidentiality, so 1 is not likely a violation. And unless the firm's policy requires silence about job openings, answering questions about them is ethical, if not always wise, so 2 is not likely a violation. (Study Session 1, LOS 2.a)

                    ©2011 Kaplan, Inc.

65. **B**   The five general fiduciary standards for a trustee that carry over from the old Prudent Man Rule to the new Prudent Investor Rule are care, caution, impartiality, loyalty, and skill. The ability to delegate investment authority is a new feature of the Prudent Investor rule that was prohibited under the Prudent Man rule. (Study Session 2, LOS 10.c)

66. **B**   According to Standard VI(C) Referral Fees, members and candidates must disclose to their employer, clients, and prospective clients any compensation, consideration, or benefit obtained from or given to other entities in exchange for referrals related to products or services. There is no prohibition on such arrangements as long as they are disclosed so clients and prospects can assess the full cost of services. (Study Session 1, LOS 2.a)

67. **C**   If Montpier uses material, nonpublic information in her research reports and/or recommendations, she will comply with local industry practice and local law but will violate the Code and Standards [Standard I(A) Knowledge of the Law and Standard II(A) Material Nonpublic Information]. Montpier has not used material nonpublic information, however. She has merely observed meetings between investment bankers and the company executives. By assembling this information with the well-known fact that one of the companies in the meetings is actively trying to acquire other companies, the information becomes material. This is the mosaic theory. Montpier has come to a conclusion of a material and nonpublic nature by assembling both public information and nonpublic, non-material information. Therefore she has not violated the Standards. (Study Session 1, LOS 2.a)

68. **C**   Montpier has violated Standard I(A) Knowledge of the Law. It is a good idea for members to meet the compliance officer when starting a new job and periodically thereafter to keep informed about appropriate rules and regulations within the organization and in the regulatory environment that governs the member's job responsibilities. This may be especially important if the member changes job functions or relocates to another location or jurisdiction. Maintaining current files of appropriate statutes, rules, and regulations, as well as internal policies and procedures, is also effective for maintaining compliance. (Study Session 1, LOS 2.a)

69. **A**   Montpier is not in compliance with Standard IV(B) Additional Compensation Arrangements. She has undertaken an independent practice in competition with her employer, World Renowned Advisers, which will result in compensation without obtaining the prior consent of her employer to the terms of the arrangement. Although no compensation has yet been paid to Montpier, she has still violated Standard IV(B). As a practical matter, in her statement to her employer, Montpier should include (1) the types of services to be provided, (2) expected time frame of the services, and (3) compensation to be received. (Study Session 1, LOS 2.a)

70. **B**   According to Standard VII(B), Taylor may reference his participation or candidate status in the CFA program but must not misrepresent the meaning of his participation. Taylor has taken the Level I exam but has not received his results or registered for the next exam. Therefore, he may refer to himself as a Level I candidate but not as a Level II candidate. (Study Session 1, LOS 2.a)

71. **C** Standard I(C) Misrepresentation is violated because Taylor uses research reports from outside the firm without acknowledging or identifying the original author(s) of the reports. Although Taylor added "some general industry information" and indicated a "strong buy" rating, he must still credit the original author(s) for the material that he did not create. A violation of Standard I(C) involving plagiarism also causes a violation of Standard I(A) Knowledge of the Law, which prohibits knowingly violating any laws, rules, or regulations. The unauthorized use of the external research material violates copyright laws, as Taylor did not obtain permission to use information from the research reports. Taylor violated Standard V(A) Diligence and Reasonable Basis because he does not appear to have exercised diligence and thoroughness in making his investment recommendation, nor does he have a reasonable and adequate basis for his recommendation. The fact that Taylor has not researched the companies in his report and uses the research information provided by another analyst indicates that he has not adequately investigated and supported his recommendation. Because Taylor is not recommending the investment to a particular client, his recommendation does not violate Standard III(C) Suitability. If he had been making investment recommendations or taking investment action on the behalf of a client as part of an advisory relationship, he would have needed to establish that the investment was appropriate for the client's portfolio. (Study Session 1, LOS 2.a)

72. **A** Although the information received supplemented Taylor's current research, it was material, nonpublic information. The fact that Taylor obtained the information by participating in a confidential study, and the fact that once the news was eventually released by Next Breakthrough the stock plunged by over 30%, confirms that the information was material and nonpublic. Taylor's sell recommendation to clients based on the information received was a violation of Standard II(A) Material Nonpublic Information, which prohibits trading or causing others to trade on material nonpublic information. (Study Session 1, LOS 2.a)

73. **A** Based on the APT, the appropriate discount rate for Trailblazer is:
$$E\left(R_{Trailblazer}\right) = 3.5\% + (0.81 \times 1.91\%) - (0.45 \times 1.22\%) + (0.24 \times 3.47\%) + (0.74 \times 4.15\%) = 8.4\%$$

Based on the BYPRP method, the required return on Trailblazer's equity = 7.25% + 3% = 10.25%. (Study Session 10, LOS 35.c)

74. **B** The expected holding period return is:

$$r = \frac{D_1}{P_0} + \frac{P_1 - P_0}{P_0} = \frac{\$1.47}{\$32} + \frac{\$35 - \$32}{\$32} = 0.1397 = 13.97\%$$
(Study Session 10, LOS 35.a)

75. **C** All three statements are consistent with the assumptions of the Gordon growth model. Regarding Statement 3, there is nothing to prevent the growth rate from being negative. The model can still be applied in this case. (Study Session 11, LOS 39.d)

76. **B** For a DDM to be appropriate for valuation purposes, dividends must be a reasonably good measure of the cash flow of a firm. Dividends are appropriate for measuring cash flow when a company has a history of dividend payments, when the dividend policy is clear and related to the firm's earnings, and when the perspective is that of a minority shareholder. The two statements relate to the history of dividends and the relationship between dividends and earnings. Statement 4 supports the use of dividends since the history of paying dividends is fairly long and consistent. Statement 5 suggests that the relationship between dividends and earnings is not very strong since the company continues to pay regular dividends regardless of whether losses are incurred or profits are earned. (Study Session 11, LOS 39.a)

                    ©2011 Kaplan, Inc.

77. **A** From a purely theoretical point of view, one cannot say that the APT is better than the CAPM because the CAPM relies on a single risk premium. If anything, due to the greater number of inputs required in APT estimation, input uncertainty is probably a more significant problem for the APT than it is for the CAPM. Thus, Statement 6 is incorrect. Statement 7 is not a reasonable statement as both approaches suffer from model uncertainty. It is not clear in the case of the APT what the appropriate number of factors to use is; for the CAPM, the appropriate proxy for the market is not clear. (Study Session 10, LOS 37.c and Study Session 18, LOS 60.l)

78. **C** required return = 3.5% + (1.2 × 4.5%) = 8.9%

    retention ratio = b = ($4.00 − $2.60)/ $4.00 = 0.35

    payout ratio = (1 − b) = 1 − 0.35 = 0.65

    justified leading P/E = $\frac{1-b}{r-g} = \frac{0.65}{0.089-0.05} = 16.67$

    justified trailing P/E = $\frac{(1-b)\times(1+g)}{(r-g)} = \frac{0.65\times1.05}{0.089-0.05} = 17.50$

    Notice that the current market price is irrelevant for calculating justified P/E ratios. (Study Session 11, LOS 39.f)

79. **A** Both statements are correct. IFRS permits either the partial goodwill or full goodwill method to value goodwill and the noncontrolling interest under the acquisition method. U.S. GAAP requires the full goodwill method. U.S. GAAP requires equity method accounting for joint ventures. Under IFRS, proportionate consolidation is preferred, but the equity method is permitted. (Study Session 6, LOS 22.b)

80. **A** Switching costs are costs incurred by the buyer in switching from one supplier to another. High switching costs act as a disincentive for buyers to switch products and decrease the bargaining power of buyers. From the supplier's perspective, the higher the switching costs, the greater the bargaining power of suppliers. (Study Session 11, LOS 36.a,b)

81. **B** The neoclassical growth theory relates technological change to increases in real GDP, savings, and capital, which in turn lead to increased investment and higher dividends. Note, however, that higher dividend levels do not imply an increase in the long-run growth in dividends, and higher savings do not affect a country's long-run economic growth rate.

    The new growth theory holds that technological advances lead to sustainable economic growth. These advances allow developed countries to realize both higher dividend levels and long-term dividend growth rates through increased savings.

    Multifactor models are used in assessing asset returns and risk exposures through multiple factors such as industry and country. Factor sensitivities are estimated through multiple linear regression. Note that there is no theory called "multifactor model theory." (Study Session 4, LOS 14.d)

82. **C** P/E ratio is likely to be *understated* as the earnings in the denominator are likely to be overstated (due to artificially low depreciation). EV/EBITDA would not be affected by low depreciation expense. Regardless, it still would not mean that the EV/EBITDA multiple would be overstated. (Study Session 11, LOS 38.a)

83. **A** Higher inflation leads to high nominal earnings (due to low nominal depreciation). Reported assets are lower (they are reported at historical costs), leading to high turnover and return on invested capital ratios. Reported leverage is higher due to lower value of reported assets. (Study Session 11, LOS 38.a)

84. **B** For free cash flow to firm models, to account for higher risk, the discount rate can be adjusted by adding a country risk premium to the weighted average cost of capital (WACC) and not to the required return on equity. (Study Session 11, LOS 38.d)

85. **C** Bond covenants can create an incentive to engage in earnings manipulation. If High Plains remains non-compliant, the bondholders can demand immediate repayment of the debt. (Study Session 7, LOS 26.c)

86. **A** Revenue should be recognized when earned and payment is assured. High Plains is recognizing revenue as orders are received. Since High Plains still has an obligation to deliver the goods, revenue is not yet earned. By recognizing revenue too soon, net income is overstated and ending inventory is understated. Understated ending inventory would result in an overstated inventory turnover ratio. (Study Session 7, LOS 26.f)

87. **A** The cash flow accrual ratio increased during 2008 from 15% to 19%. (Study Session 7, LOS 26.d)

in thousands	2008	2007
Net income	$158,177	$121,164
– Cash from operations	12,262	88,692
– Cash from investing	(39,884)	(63,953)
= Accruals	$185,799	$96,425
÷ Net operating assets	$977,890	$642,830
= Cash flow accrual ratio	19%	15%

88. **A** Maintenance and repairs, and advertising and marketing, are discretionary expenses. Both items are declining as the investment in capital assets and sales are increasing (investment in capital assets is increasing because CFI is greater than depreciation expense for the period). The change to the straight-line depreciation method is certainly less conservative. However, measuring earnings quality based on conservative earnings is an inferior measure as most accruals will correct over time.

    Note that the reason answer C is incorrect is that using LIFO as an inventory cost flow assumption during periods of stable or rising prices would cause net earnings to reflect economic (real) earnings, thereby leading to a higher quality of earnings. (Study Session 7, LOS 27.d,f)

89. **C** A finance (capital) lease is reported on the balance sheet as an asset and as a liability. In the income statement, the leased asset is depreciated and interest expense is recognized on the liability. Thus, capitalizing a lease *enhances* earnings quality. An *operating* lease lowers earnings quality.

    The receivable sale, with recourse, lowers earnings quality. The sale is treated as a collection thereby increasing operating cash flow. However, High Plains is still responsible to the buyer in the event the receivables are not ultimately collected. Thus, the receivable sale is a collateralized borrowing arrangement that remains off-balance-sheet. (Study Session 7, LOS 26.d,f)

©2011 Kaplan, Inc.

90. **C** It appears that High Plains manipulated its earnings upward in 2008 to avoid default under its bond covenants. However, the higher earnings are lower quality as measured by the cash flow accrual ratio. Because of the estimates involved, a *lower* weighting should be assigned to the accrual component of High Plains' earnings. Extreme earnings (including revenues) tend to revert to normal levels over time (mean reversion). (Study Session 7, LOS 26.b,e)

91. **A** In a defined contribution plan, pension expense is equal to the amount contributed by the firm. The plan participants bear the shortfall risk. There is no ABO in a defined contribution plan. (Study Session 6, LOS 23.a)

92. **B** At the end of 2008, Global Oilfield reported a net pension asset of €7,222 in accordance with IFRS. Under SFAS No. 158, Global Oilfield's funded status of €2,524 should be reported on the balance sheet. Thus, it is necessary to reduce the net pension asset by €4,698 (€7,222 as reported − €2,524 funded status). In order for the accounting equation to balance, it is also necessary to reduce equity by €4,698. (Study Session 6, LOS 23.d)

93. **C** The assumed discount rate increased from 6.25% in 2007 to 6.75% in 2008 (Exhibit 5). There is an inverse relationship between the discount rate and the present value of a future sum. Thus, the increase in the discount rate resulted in an actuarial gain (lower PBO). An increase in life expectancy would result in an actuarial loss. (Study Session 6, LOS 23.c)

94. **C** A decrease in the compensation growth rate will reduce service cost. Lower service cost will result in lower pension expense and, thus, higher net income. Lowering the compensation growth rate will also reduce the PBO. A lower PBO will increase the funded status of the plan (make the plan appear more funded). The compensation growth rate has no effect on the ABO and plan assets. (Study Session 6, LOS 23.c)

95. **B** For the year-ended 2008, Global Oilfield's reported pension expense was €7,704 (Exhibit 4), and its economic pension expense was €3,410 (€8,298 service cost + €4,128 interest cost − €1,932 actuarial gain − €7,084 actual return). Alternatively, economic pension expense can be calculated as the change in the funded status excluding contributions (€2,524 funded status for 2008 − €934 funded status for 2007 − €5,000 contributions for 2008). (Study Session 6, LOS 23.f)

96. **A** Economic pension expense represents the true cost of the pension. If the firm's contributions exceed its economic pension expense, the difference can be viewed as a reduction in the overall pension obligation similar to an excess principal payment on a loan. Pension contributions are reported as operating activities in the cash flow statement while principal payments are reported as financing activities. Thus, the adjustment involves increasing operating cash flow by €750 (€5,000 employer contributions − €4,250 economic pension expense) and decreasing financing cash flow by the same amount. (Study Session 6, LOS 23.e)

97. **B** Consolidated current assets are equal to $119 million ($96 Valley current assets − $9 cash for investment in Southwest + $32 Southwest current assets). (Study Session 6, LOS 22.a)

98. **C** ROA is calculated as net income / total assets. Both methods result in the same net income, so Statement 1 is incorrect. However, the acquisition method leads to higher reported total assets. Hence, the ROA is greater under the equity method and lower under the acquisition method (Statement 2 is correct). (Study Session 6, LOS 22.b)

99. **A** Proportionate consolidation only considers the proportion of the assets and liabilities owned by the parent firm (Statements 4 and 5 are incorrect). Also, proportionate consolidation is generally not allowed under U.S. GAAP (Statement 3 is incorrect). Proportionate consolidation is the preferred method under IFRS. Therefore, none of the three statements is correct. (Study Session 6, LOS 22.b)

100. **C** See following table for 100 and 101. (Study Session 6, LOS 24.c,d)

101. **C** (Study Session 6, LOS 24.c,d)

The following financial statements reflect the use of the current rate method (functional currency is the CHF) since Mountain is a self-contained company and is less dependent on Valley. The solutions to Questions 100 and 101 pertain to the current rate method.

Income Statement (in $ thousands)

Sales	$5,600	= 0.80 × 7,000
Cost of goods sold	$5,440	= 0.80 × 6,800
Depreciation	80	= 0.80 × 100
Net income	$80	

Balance sheet (in $ thousands)

Cash and accounts receivable	$510	= 0.85 × 600
Inventory	425	= 0.85 × 500
Fixed assets	510	= 0.85 × 600
Total assets	$1,445	
Accounts payable	$170	= 0.85 × 200
Long-term debt	85	= 0.85 × 100
Common stock	1,001	= 0.77 × 1,300
Retained earnings	80	= 0 + 80
FC translation adjustment	109	Calculated
Total liabilities and equity	$1,445	

102. **A** Under U.S. GAAP, the nonmonetary assets and liabilities of the foreign subsidiary are not restated for inflation. Under IFRS, the subsidiary's financial statements are adjusted for inflation, and the net purchasing power gain or loss is recognized in the income statement. Then, the subsidiary is translated into U.S. dollars using the current rate method. If Mountain operates in a highly inflationary environment, the appropriate method is the temporal method. Under the temporal method, the functional currency is considered to be the parent's presentation currency. Thus, Mountain's functional currency is the U.S. dollar. (Study Session 6, LOS 24.f)

103. **B** Ozer's memo states that in an acquisition, Alertron would want to maintain the successful Escarigen brand and operational structure. As a result, the most likely form of integration would be a subsidiary merger in which Escarigen would become a subsidiary of Alertron. Most subsidiary mergers occur when the target has a well-known brand that the acquirer wants to maintain, which is the case here. Note that in a statutory merger, the target company would cease to exist as a separate entity. Since both Alertron and Escarigen are involved in the pharmaceutical industry, the type of merger would be best described as horizontal. The merger would not be vertical as Alertron would not be moving up or down the supply chain. (Study Session 9, LOS 32.a)

©2011 Kaplan, Inc.

104. **B** The potential acquisition of Carideo is described as a stock purchase, which means that Carideo's shareholders would be responsible for paying capital gains taxes on the deal and no taxes would be levied against Carideo at the corporate level. The other answers are incorrect. The potential deal with Escarigen is described as a cash offering. In most cash offerings, the acquirer borrows money to raise cash for the deal, which would increase the acquirer's financial leverage. In the potential deal with BriscoePharm, shareholders generally only approve asset purchases when the purchase is substantial (greater than 50% of firm assets). In this case, shareholder approval would not be required. In a proxy battle for Dillon Biotech, Alertron would try to have shareholders approve new members of the board of directors to try to gain control of the company. Trying to purchase shares from shareholders individually is a tender offer. (Study Session 9, LOS 32.e)

105. **C** The only pair combination that correctly identifies a pre-offer and post-offer defense, respectively, is a supermajority voting provision, which is a pre-offer defense requiring shareholder approval in excess of a simple majority; and a leveraged recapitalization, which is a post-offer defense where a target borrows money to repurchase its own shares. Pre-offer defenses suggested include poison puts, fair price amendments, restricted voting rights, poison pills, and staggered board elections. The only other post-offer defense suggested was greenmail, which was incorrectly categorized. (Study Session 9, LOS 32.f)

106. **C** First, calculate the value of the combined firm after the merger:

Post merger value of the combined firm: $V_{AT} = V_A + V_T + S - C$

V_A = \$9,000
V_T = \$3,120
S = \$600
C = \$0 because no cash is changing hands

The value of the combined firm is therefore V_{AT} = \$9,000 + \$3,120 + \$600 − 0 = \$12,720

Next, to account for the dilution and to find the price per share for the combined firm, P_{AT}, divide the post merger value by the post merger number of shares outstanding. Since we are told that Alertron would exchange 0.75 shares of its stock for each share of Carideo, the number of new shares issued is:

80 million shares × 0.75 = 60 million new shares

So, $P_{AT} = \dfrac{\$12,720}{150 + 60} = \$60.57$

This means the actual value of each share given to Carideo's shareholders is \$60.57 and the actual price paid for Carideo is:

$P_T = (N \times P_{AT}) = (60 \times \$60.57) = \$3,634.20$

Carideo's gain in the merger as the target is:

$Gain_T = TP = P_T - V_T = \$3,634.20 - \$3,120 = \$514.20$

Note that Carideo's gain simply represents the takeover premium in the transaction. (Study Session 9, LOS 32.k)

107. **A** In a cash offer, the acquirer assumes the risk and receives the potential reward from the merger, while the gain to the target shareholders is limited to the takeover premium. In this case, Alertron is comfortable with the estimate of synergies and thinks the estimate may even be conservative. By making a cash offer, the takeover premium realized by Carideo would remain unchanged, with any excess benefit from synergies going to Alertron. Based on its forecasts, Alertron would prefer a cash deal.

However, if the synergies were less than expected, the takeover premium realized by Carideo would still be unchanged with a cash deal, but Alertron's gain may decrease. Since Carideo management believes the estimate of synergies is too high, they would also prefer a cash deal to lock in the gain they realize from the takeover premium. (Study Session 9, LOS 32.l)

108. **C** Pre-merger HHI =
$$\frac{(0.20 \times 100)^2 + (0.18 \times 100)^2 + (0.15 \times 100)^2 + (0.12 \times 100)^2 +}{(0.10 \times 100)^2 + (0.07 \times 100)^2 + \left[(0.03 \times 100)^2 \times 6\right]} = 1,296$$

The post merger market share of the combined firms would be 15% + 10% = 25%.

Post-merger HHI =
$$\frac{(0.25 \times 100)^2 + (0.20 \times 100)^2 + (0.18 \times 100)^2 + (0.12 \times 100)^2 +}{(0.07 \times 100)^2 + \left[(0.03 \times 100)^2 \times 6\right]} = 1,596$$

Change in HHI = 1,596 − 1,296 = 300

A post-merger HHI that is between 1,000 and 1,800 indicates a moderately concentrated industry. With a change in an HHI that is greater than 100, there is certainly the potential for an antitrust challenge by regulators. (Study Session 9, LOS 32.g)

109. **B** The real exchange rate, X, is calculated as follows: S (P_{CAD} / P_{GBP}). S is the spot exchange rate (stated GBP/CAD). Hence, the real exchange rate is 0.4 (1 / 0.3) = 1.33. (Study Session 18, LOS 62.e)

110. **A** The GBP return is equal to the CAD return, plus appreciation of the CAD. The CAD return is 22% [= (P_1 − P_0) / P_0 = (122 − 100) / 100]. Since the real exchange rate remained constant, the change in the nominal rate must be equal to the inflation differential. Since U.K. inflation is 4% and Canadian inflation is 7%, there is an inflation differential of −3%. This means that the C$ is expected to depreciate by 3% or, equivalently, the £ is expected to appreciate by 3%. Hence, the GBP return is 19% (= 22% minus 3% depreciation of the CAD). (Study Session 18, LOS 62.f)

111. **C** The end-of-period real rate is 1.41. Since inflation is perfectly predictable, we can use the real exchange rate formula to solve for the end-of-period spot rate (i.e., the end-of-period nominal rate). The real rate (X) is calculated as X = S (P_{CAD} / P_{GBP}), where S is stated in GBP per CAD. The end-of-period (inflation adjusted), consumption basket price ratio is 1.07 / 0.312 = 3.4295 (P_{CAD} = 1 × 1.07 = 1.07; P_{GBP} = 0.3 × 1.04 = 0.312). Substituting into the real exchange rate equation and solving for S we get:

1.41 = S (3.4295)
S = 0.41114

Now we know that the end-of-period nominal exchange rate is 0.4111 (the £ depreciated when we expected it to appreciate). The CAD appreciation is (S_1 − S_0) / S_0 = (0.41114 − 0.4) / 0.4 = 0.02785 or 2.785%. Now we know both the CAD return on the stock, 22% [= (P_1 − P_0) / P_0 = (122 − 100) / 100] and the CAD appreciation of 2.785%. Therefore, the GBP return must be 24.79% (CAD return plus CAD appreciation). (Study Session 18, LOS 62.f)

©2011 Kaplan, Inc.

112. **A** Since the beginning-of-period $/C$ spot exchange rate is not given directly, we must calculate it from the £/$ and £/C$ quotes. Dividing £/C$ by £/$ gives a rate for the $/C$ exchange rate of 0.5. Next we need to determine whether there was any real change in the exchange rate during the year. Inflation in the United States is 2%, and inflation in Canada is 7% (remember that inflation is perfectly predictable). The 5% inflation differential means that to maintain parity, the C$ must depreciate by 5%. If the C$ depreciates by 5%, the new exchange rate would be 0.5(1 − 0.05) = 0.475. Since the end-of-period rate is less than what was expected given the inflation differential, the real value of the C$ has decreased. Hence, the firm should have a higher value because it is primarily an exporter, and exporters are helped by real domestic currency depreciation. (Study Session 18, LOS 62.e,m)

113. **B** The sensitivity of Slapshot returns to changes in the £/C$ exchange rate is 1.4. The sensitivity is a function of the CAD reaction; specifically, the sensitivity of the currency return is equal to $\gamma(CAD) + 1$ (recall that γ is the sensitivity measure). Since $\gamma = 1.4$, $\gamma(CAD)$ must be 0.4. This means that the CAD value of Slapshot changes by 40% of the amount of the currency change. Hence, if the C$ suddenly depreciates by 10%, the CAD value of the firm falls by 4%. (Study Session 18, LOS 62.l)

114. **B** The ICAPM (with only one foreign currency) is $E(R_i) = R_0 + B_{iw} \times RP_w + \gamma_{i1} \times SRP_1$. All parameters are provided in the problem statement except the foreign currency risk premium (SRP). The SRP is calculated as expected foreign currency appreciation minus the rate differential (domestic-foreign). The problem indicates that Holmes expects the C$ to depreciate by 2% or, equivalently, to appreciate by −2%. Interest rates are 6% in the U.K. and 9% in Canada. Therefore, the SRP is 1% [= −2% appreciation minus −3% interest rate differential, or SRP = −2% − (−3%) = +1%]. Plugging into the model, we get:

$$E(R_i) = R_0 + (B_{iw} \times RPw) + (\gamma_{i1} \times SRP_1) = 6\% + 1.2\,(6\%) + 1.4(1\%) = 14.6\%$$

(Study Session 18, LOS 62.i,j)

115. **C** The behavior of foreign buyers in ceasing their monitoring operations is a creative response known as the feedback effect. Under the feedback effect, the buyers become less concerned about abusive practices in the carpet manufacturing industry in Bundovia. (Study Session 4, LOS 15.b)

116. **A** Williams is correct in his assessment of the effects of a tariff and a quota. Both would benefit Bundovian Semiconductors. The company would be more competitive in the domestic market because imports would fall and domestic production would rise. (Study Session 4, LOS 16.b)

117. **A** In the short term, higher economic growth (and higher incomes in Bundovia) should lead to increased demand for imports to Bundovia, and consequently depreciation of the BU (higher BU/USD). (Study Session 4, LOS 18.d))

118. **A** The bid rate in GBP/SFr is the rate a trader can convert SFr into GBP (remember "up-the-bid"). To do this indirectly through USD, convert SFr into USD at the bid rate of 0.8550 ("up-the-bid") and then convert USD to GBP at the ask rate of 2.0020 ("down-the-ask"). To arrive at GBP/SFr, divide the USD/SFr bid rate by the USD/GDP ask rate. The cross bid rate in GBP/SFr would be:

$$\frac{USD0.8550}{SFr} \bigg/ \frac{USD2.0020}{GBP} = \frac{GBP0.4271}{SFr}$$

The ask rate in GBP/SFr is the rate a trader can convert GBP into SFr ("down-the-ask"). To do this indirectly through USD, convert GBP into USD at the bid rate of 2.0010 ("up-the-bid") and then convert USD to SFr at the ask rate of 0.8560 ("down-the-ask"). To arrive at GBP/SFr, divide the USD/SFr ask rate by the USD/GDP bid rate. The cross ask rate in GBP/SFr would be:

$$\frac{USD0.8560}{SFr} \bigg/ \frac{USD2.0010}{GBP} = \frac{GBP0.4278}{SFr}$$

The GBP/SFr quote would be: GBP/SFr = 0.4271 – 78

(Study Session 4, LOS 17.c)

119. **C** Use the mid-points of the spot and forward bid-ask spreads (2.0015 and 2.0050, respectively) to calculate the premium or discount. Notice that the quotes are in USD/GBP with GBP as the reference currency, so to calculate the 30-day forward premium or discount on the USD, take the reciprocal of each mid-point.

$$\frac{\dfrac{1}{2.0050} - \dfrac{1}{2.0015}}{\dfrac{1}{2.0015}} \times \frac{360}{30} = -0.021 = 2.1\% \text{ discount}$$

(Study Session 4, LOS 17.g)

120. **B** Interest rate parity requires that $\dfrac{F}{S} = \dfrac{(1+R_\$)}{(1+R_{BU})}$

$$\frac{F}{S} = \frac{2.10}{2.00} = 1.05$$

$$\frac{(1+R_\$)}{(1+R_{BU})} = \frac{(1+0.05)}{(1+0.03)} = 1.019$$

BU should appreciate by 1.9% per year. However, in the forward market, BU is trading at a premium of 5%. Therefore the appropriate arbitrage strategy is to sell BU in the forward market as below:

1. Borrow $1,000 at 5%. At the end of one year, Williams will be obligated to repay $1,000(1.05) = $1,050.

2. Convert the $1,000 to BU at the spot rate, which yields $1,000/($2/BU) = BU500.

3. Simultaneously enter into a 1-year forward contract to convert BU to USD at the forward rate of $2.1000/BU.

4. Invest BU500 at 3%. In one year, Williams will receive proceeds of BU500(1.03) = BU515.

5. Convert the BU515 back to USD at the forward rate, which was locked in at the beginning of the year and yields BU515($2.1/BU) = $1,081.50.

6. Arbitrage profits = $1,081.50 – $1,050 = $31.50.

(Study Session 4, LOS 17.h)

©2011 Kaplan, Inc.

Exam 2
Morning Session Answers

To get valuable feedback on how your score compares to those of other Level II candidates, use your Username and Password to gain Online Access at schweser.com and choose the left-hand menu item "Practice Exams Vol. 1."

1. B	21. A	41. C
2. C	22. A	42. B
3. C	23. B	43. C
4. B	24. A	44. B
5. B	25. A	45. A
6. C	26. A	46. B
7. C	27. B	47. B
8. C	28. A	48. A
9. C	29. B	49. A
10. C	30. A	50. B
11. A	31. C	51. B
12. C	32. C	52. B
13. C	33. B	53. A
14. A	34. B	54. C
15. B	35. A	55. B
16. B	36. B	56. B
17. A	37. A	57. A
18. C	38. A	58. B
19. B	39. A	59. A
20. C	40. B	60. B

Exam 2
Morning Session Answers

1. **B** Topel recommended the stock to his superiors, but they chose not to buy it. While Topel should not buy the stock in advance of his recommendation, he is not prohibited from purchasing it for himself should the company choose not to act. Kennedy's research may have been thorough, and there is no evidence that she violated the reasonable-basis Standard. However, the loyalty Standard requires that Kennedy put Samson Securities' interest before her own and not deprive her employer of her skills and abilities. Since Kennedy spent five days of company time researching Koral Koatings, the company has a right to benefit from her research. (Study Session 1, LOS 2.a)

2. **C** The Koons's gift does not violate Standard I(B). According to the standard, gifts from clients are different from gifts from other parties because the potential for obtaining influence to the detriment of other clients is not as great. Therefore, according to the standard, Garvey may accept the Koons's gift as long as she discloses it to her employer, which she did. See Example 7 on pages 22 and 23 of the *Standards of Practice Handbook, 9th edition*, for an example of how the standard was applied in a similar situation.

    The Jones's gift is a bonus from a job that does not compete with Garvey's work for Samson, and as such, does not violate the Standard. The fact that Jones is a Samson client is irrelevant in terms of this gift, as there is no information in the vignette about Garvey providing investment-related services for Jones. (Study Session 1, LOS 2.a)

3. **C** Topel's purchases of Vallo do not violate Standard II(A) because it was not based on material nonpublic information, and he has no duty to keep the information to himself. Therefore, Garvey's purchase of Vallo for her own account is also consistent with Standard II(A).

    The brokers discussing Metrona mentioned that their star analyst came out with a report with a "buy" recommendation that morning, which suggests that the information has already been made public. Therefore, Garvey's purchase of Metrona for her own account is consistent with Standard II(A). (Study Session 1, LOS 2.a)

4. **B** Garvey's idea for a growth estimate is interesting, but a number of factors affect the growth rate of a beverage company, many arguably more so than GDP growth. In addition, it is not sufficient to use two years worth of quarterly data (eight observations) to estimate a regression model and forecast growth over the following three years. The research was not thorough enough to satisfy Standard V(A).

    Standard I(C) as it deals with plagiarism was not violated because the consensus GDP estimates were derived from a recognized reporting service. (Study Session 1, LOS 2.a)

 ©2011 Kaplan, Inc.

5. **B** The impartiality standard requires prudent handling of different interests, such as those of different beneficiaries. This standard changed very little with the adoption of the Prudent Investor Rule. All of the other statements reflect provisions of the Prudent Investor Rule that would not have been permitted under the old Prudent Man Rule. Under the old Prudent Man Rule:
    - The trustee was not allowed to delegate any duties to others.
    - The preservation of the principal and purchasing power by earning a return sufficient to offset inflation was required. Under the new Prudent Investor Rule, growth in the real value of the principal (returns in excess of inflation) is permissible.

    (Study Session 2, LOS 10.c)

6. **C** In the first statement, Garvey accurately calls herself a CFA Level III candidate, but she is not permitted to project when she will receive the charter, as she must still meet the work and eligibility restrictions and pass the Level III exam. Therefore, the first statement violates Standard VII(B).

    In the second statement, the use of the CFA mark as a noun also violates the Standard VII(B). (Study Session 1, LOS 2.a)

7. **C** Standard I(B) Professionalism: Independence and Objectivity prohibits members and candidates from accepting any gift that reasonably could be expected to compromise their independence and objectivity. The purpose of the gift appears to be to ensure that Islandwide continues to do business with Quadrangle and can be seen, therefore, as a clear attempt to influence her choice of brokers in the future.
    (Study Session 1, LOS 2.a)

8. **C** Standard II(A) Integrity of Capital Markets: Material Nonpublic Information prohibits members and candidates who possess material nonpublic information to act on or cause others to act on that information. Information disclosed to a select group of analysts is not made "public" by that fact. (Study Session 1, LOS 2.a)

9. **C** Standard I(B) Professionalism: Independence and Objectivity indicates that gifts from clients are seen to less likely affect a member's independence and objectivity, and only disclosure is required. The offer from Baker is based on future performance and is seen to carry greater risk of affecting objectivity because preferential treatment for one client could be detrimental to others. Thus, according to Standard IV(B) Duties to Employer: Additional Compensation Arrangements, Harris must disclose the offer to her employer (in writing) and receive the employer's permission before accepting the offer from Baker. (Study Session 1, LOS 2.a)

10. **C** Michaels has not violated Standard II(B) Integrity of Capital Markets: Market Manipulation by either of these actions. In neither case is there the intent to mislead market participants. A large buy program may well increase the price of a stock. The trading desk has informed market participants that they will create additional liquidity for a period of 90 days after the offering and created no expectation that the liquidity of the stock will permanently remain at that level. (Study Session 1, LOS 2.a)

11. **A** According to Standard IV Duties to Employers, Swamy must secure written permission before undertaking the investment advisory work for the symphony because this work competes with her employer and could create a conflict of interest, as she is receiving compensation in the form of season tickets. Her service on her brother-in-law's board may be subject to employer rules about outside employment but is not covered by the Standard because there is no likely competition or potential conflict with her employer. The question says *most likely*, so it is important to focus on the key difference between the two outside activities. Both are compensated; the fact that one is cash and the other tickets is irrelevant. The key difference is that for the symphony, Swamy is acting as an investment advisor for a large endowment, which clearly competes with her employer's business. (Study Session 1, LOS 2.a)

12. **C** Standard III(B) Fair Dealing requires that shares of an oversubscribed IPO be prorated fairly to all subscribers. Arbitrarily increasing the allocation to the "problem client" is a violation, as is the resulting underallocation to the remainder of the firm's clients. (Study Session 1, LOS 2.a)

13. **C** Subsidiaries whose operations are well integrated with the parent will use the parent's currency as the functional currency. When the functional currency is the same as the parent's presentation currency (reporting currency), as it is in this case, the temporal method is used. Therefore, Statement 1 is incorrect.

    Self-contained, independent subsidiaries whose operating, investing, and financing activities are primarily located in the local market will use the local currency as the functional currency. When the functional currency is not the same as the parent's presentation currency (reporting currency), as in this case, the current rate method is used. Therefore, Statement 2 is incorrect. (Study Session 6, LOS 24.c)

14. **A** Sales will be lower after translation because of the depreciating U.S. dollar. (Study Session 6, LOS 24.d)

15. **B** Depreciation expense and COGS are remeasured at the historical rate under the temporal method. Under the current rate method, depreciation and COGS are translated at the average rate. Because the U.S. dollar is depreciating, depreciation expense and COGS are lower under the current rate method. (Study Session 6, LOS 24.d)

16. **B** Since the subsidiary's operations are highly integrated with the parent, the temporal method is used. Accordingly, a loss of CAD 31,200 is recognized in the parent's income statement (see balance sheet and income statement worksheet). However, no calculations are actually necessary to answer this question. The parent has a net monetary asset position in the subsidiary (monetary assets > monetary liabilities). Holding net monetary assets when the foreign currency is depreciating will result in a loss. Under the temporal method, the loss is reported in the income statement. Only choice B satisfies this logic. (Study Session 6, LOS 24.d)

Use the following to answer Question 16.

The Canadian dollar is the functional currency because the subsidiary is highly integrated with the parent. Therefore, the temporal method applies.

©2011 Kaplan, Inc.

Step 1: Remeasure the balance sheet using the temporal method.

	2008 (USD)	Rate	2008 (CAD)
Cash and account receivables	775,000	1.32	1,023,000
Inventory (given in Item 9)	600,000	Given	810,000
PP&E (net)	730,000	1.50	1,095,000
Total assets	2,105,000		2,928,000
Accounts payable	125,000	1.32	165,000
Long-term debt	400,000	1.32	528,000
Common stock	535,000	1.50	802,500
Retained earnings	1,045,000	(a)	1,432,500
Total liabilities and shareholders' equity	2,105,000		2,928,000

(a) Retained earnings is a plug figure that makes the accounting equation balance CAD
2,928,000 assets – CAD 165,000 accounts payable – CAD 528,000 long-term debt
– CAD 802,500 common stock = CAD 1,432,500.

Step 2: Derive net income from the beginning and ending balances of retained earnings and
dividends paid as follows:

	CAD	
Beginning retained earnings	1,550,000	Given Item 6
Net income	(83,250)	Calculate
Dividends paid in the year	(34,250)	(25,000 × 1.37 historical rate)
Ending retained earnings	1,432,500	From Step 1

Step 3: Remeasure the income statement using the temporal method.

	2008 (USD)	Rate	2008 (CAD)
Sales	1,352,000	1.35	1,825,200
Cost of goods sold (given Item 11)	(1,205,000)	Given	(1,667,250)
Depreciation expense	(140,000)	1.50	(210,000)
Remeasurement loss		(b)	(31,200)
Net income	7,000	From Step 2	(83,250)

(b) The remeasurement loss is a plug that is equal to the difference in net income of
–CAD 83,250 and income before remeasurement of –CAD 52,050 (CAD 1,825,200
sales – CAD 1,667,250 COGS – CAD 210,000 depreciation).

17. **A** The local currency (the USD) is depreciating, so the historical rate will be higher than the current rate. Fixed asset turnover (sales divided by net PP&E) will be higher under the current rate method. Net PP&E will be translated at the lower current rate, and because sales are the same under both methods, the ratio will be higher.

    If you want to do the calculations, net PP&E under the current rate method is USD730,000 × 1.32CAD/USD = CAD 963,600, and fixed asset turnover is CAD 1,825,200/CAD 963,600 = 1.9 times. Fixed asset turnover under the temporal method is CAD 1,825,200/CAD 1,095,000 = 1.7 times. (Study Session 6, LOS 24.d)

18. **C** Return on assets prior to translation will be different than the ratio after translation because the numerator (net income) is translated at the average rate, and the denominator (assets) is translated at the current rate using the current rate method.

    Net profit margin will be the same because both the numerator (net income) and the denominator (sales) are translated at the average rate using the current rate method. (Study Session 6, LOS 24.d)

19. **B** Residual income models are appropriate when expected free cash flows are negative for the foreseeable future.

    Residual income models are applicable even when dividends are volatile. (Study Session 12, LOS 42.k)

20. **C** A high persistence factor will be associated with low dividend payments, which is exactly the case with Schubert.

    A low persistence factor will be associated with significant levels of nonrecurring items. However, Schubert has very few nonrecurring items (which would suggest a high persistence factor). (Study Session 12, LOS 42.h)

21. **A**

Beginning book value (B_{t-1})	$32.16 ($4,181,000 / 130,000)
Earnings per share forecast (E_t)	$4.50 (given)
Dividend forecast ($D_t = E_t \times$ payout ratio)	$0.23 ($4.50 × 5%)
Forecast book value per share ($B_{t-1} + E_t - D_t$)	$36.43
Equity charge per share ($r \times B_{t-1}$)	$4.12 (0.128 × $32.16)
Per share RI_t $[(E_t - (r \times B_{t-1})]$	$0.38 ($4.50 − $4.12)

    (Study Session 12, LOS 42.c)

22. **A** Economic value added (EVA) is calculated as follows:

    $WACC = WACC × invested capital

    Note that invested capital = net working capital + net fixed assets OR book value of long-term debt + book value of equity

    = 0.119 × ($6,211,000 + $2,100,000 + $2,081,000) = $1,236,648

    EVA = NOPAT − $WACC
       = EBIT(1 − t) − $WACC
       = $1,868,000(1 − 0.30) − $1,236,648
       = $70,952

©2011 Kaplan, Inc.

market value of the company = market value of the equity + market value of the debt

= ($36 × 130,000) + (0.95 × 6,211,000)
= $10,580,450

market value added (MVA) = market value – invested capital

= $10,580,450 – ($6,211,000 + $2,100,000 + $2,081,000) = $188,450

(Study Session 12, LOS 42.a)

23. **B** $g = r - \dfrac{\left[B_0 \times (ROE - r)\right]}{V_0 - B_0}$

$B_0 = [(2,100,000 + 2,081,000)] / 130,000 = \$32.16$

r = cost of equity = 12.8%

$g = 0.128 - \dfrac{[32.16 \times (0.14 - 0.128)]}{36 - 32.16}$

$= 0.0275 = 2.75\%$

(Study Session 12, LOS 42.g)

24. **A**   The clean surplus relationship (i.e., ending book value = beginning book value + net income – dividends) may not hold when items bypass the income statement and affect equity directly. Foreign currency gains and losses under the current rate method bypass income statement and are reported under shareholders equity as CTA. Changes in the market value of trading securities are included in net income and do not violate the clean surplus relationship. Changes in working capital do not bypass the income statement. [Usually, changes in working capital do not affect the income statement. When they do (e.g., inventory writeoffs, bad debts, etc.), the income statement will not be bypassed.] (Study Session 12, LOS 42.l)

25. **A**   According to the H-model:

$$V_0 = \frac{D_0(1 + g_L)}{r - g_L} + \frac{D_0 H(g_S - g_L)}{r - g_L} = \frac{\$1 \times (1 + 0.04)}{0.12 - 0.04} + \frac{\$1 \times 3 \times (0.08 - 0.04)}{0.12 - 0.04} = \$14.50$$

(Study Session 11, LOS 39.l)

26. **A**   The key assumption underlying the H-model is that the dividend growth rate declines linearly from a high rate in the first stage to a long-term level growth rate. (Study Session 11, LOS 39.i)

27. **B**   The relationship we need to evaluate is $V_0 = \dfrac{E_1}{r} + PVGO$.

This expression can be rewritten as $PVGO = V_0 - \dfrac{E_1}{r} = \$18 - \dfrac{\$0.90}{0.12} = \$10.50$.

(Study Session 11, LOS 39.e)

28. **A**   The P/E ratio can become unreliable for ranking purposes when earnings are close to zero. When this happens, the P/E will be unrealistically large and its reciprocal, the earnings yield (E/P), will instead approach zero. Therefore, Statement 1 is correct. A high E/P suggests an underpriced security, and a low (or negative) E/P suggests an overpriced security. Therefore, Statement 2 is incorrect. (Study Session 12, LOS 41.d)

29. **B**   Earnings must be adjusted to reflect the nonrecurring extraordinary item restructuring costs and asset write downs.
    Adjusted 2008 earnings before tax = $30,400,000 + $189,100,000 = $219,500,000.
    Adjusted 2008 after-tax earnings = $219,500,000 × (1 − 0.34) = $144,870,000.
    2008 underlying EPS = $144,870,000 / 106,530,610 = $1.36

    (Study Session 12, LOS 41.c)

30. **A**   FDS has a price-to-sales ratio in 2008 of: $\dfrac{\$18}{\left(\dfrac{\$6,435,900,000}{106,530,610}\right)} = \dfrac{\$18}{\$60.41} = 0.30.$

    Because its price-to-sales ratio is less than the industry average of 0.50, FDS is relatively underpriced. (Study Session 12, LOS 41.h,k)

31. **C**   Notice that in this case, $g_S = g_L$ and, accordingly, the H-model simplifies to the Gordon growth model. We can then solve for the unknown rate:

    $$r = \dfrac{D_0\left(1+g_L\right)}{V_0} + g_L = \dfrac{\$1.25 \times \left(1+0.06\right)}{\$25} + 0.06 = 0.113 = 11.3\%$$

    (Study Session 11, LOS 39.m)

32. **C**   Among the choices given, the only drawback to the P/S ratio is that it is susceptible to manipulation if management should choose to act aggressively with respect to the recognition of revenue. (Study Session 12, LOS 41.c)

33. **B**   UHS trailing P/E = $25 / $0.82 = 30.49

    UHS trailing PEG = 30.49 / 6% = 5.08

    Trailing industry P/E = 22.50

    Trailing industry PEG = 22.50 / 10% = 2.25

    The PEG ratio for UHS exceeds that of the industry. This implies that UHS's growth rate is relatively more expensive than is the industry's growth rate. We can therefore conclude that on the basis of the PEG ratio, UHS stock is overvalued.

    UHS P/S = $25 / ($7,400,100,000 / 95,366,000) = 0.32

    Industry P/S = 0.50

    Relative to the industry, the P/S ratio for UHS stock is low, and it would therefore be considered as undervalued.

    Conflicting results between different ratios is common in practice. When this occurs, an analyst must look deeper to arrive at a reliable conclusion. An important consideration in this case is whether or not there has been any manipulation of sales and/or earnings. The estimation of the dividend growth rate is also an important factor. (Study Session 12, LOS 41.h,i)

34. **B** Average ROE $= \dfrac{0.032 + 0.040 + 0.045 + 0.039}{4} = 0.039$

   $\text{BVPS}_{2008} = \$25.58$

   Normalized EPS $= \overline{\text{ROE}} \times \text{BVPS}_{2008} = 0.039 \times \$25.58 = \$1.00$

   (Study Session 12, LOS 41.e)

35. **A** Beta = 0.8
   4-year average ROE = 3.9% (Question 34)
   5-year growth forecast = 6%
   Predicted P/E = 5 – (10 × 0.8) + (3 × 3.9%) + (2 × 6%) = 20.7
   (Study Session 12, LOS 41.i)

36. **B** The belief that there are patterns of persistence or reversals in returns provides the rationale for valuation using relative strength indicators. There has been a considerable amount of empirical research in this area. Research suggests that the investment horizon is also an important determining factor in the appearance of these patterns.
   (Study Session 12, LOS 41.p)

37. **A** We must start by calculating the JPY/EUR spot rate. This is a simple algebra problem. We know that the JPY/USD spot rate is 120 and the EUR/USD spot rate is 0.7224. Dividing JPY/USD by EUR/USD leaves us with JPY/EUR. Plugging in the numbers, we get a JPY/EUR spot rate of 166 (= 120 / 0.7224). Next, we estimate the JPY/EUR spot rate two years from now using the relative PPP formula (for two years):

   $E(S_1) = S_0 \left[(1 + i_{JPY})^2 / (1 + i_{EUR})^2 \right] = 166 \left[(1)^2 / (1.05)^2 \right] = 150.57$

   (Study Session 4, LOS 18.g,h)

38. **A** Using the international Fisher relation, we can solve for the inflation forecasts in Japan and Europe, given interest rate differentials and the U.S. inflation forecast:

   $\dfrac{1 + 0.0388}{1 + i_{jpy}} = \dfrac{1 + 0.07}{1 + 0.03} \Rightarrow i_{jpy} = 0\%$

   $\dfrac{1 + 0.0908}{1 + i_{eur}} = \dfrac{1 + 0.07}{1 + 0.03} \Rightarrow i_{eur} = 5\%$

   Both implied inflation rates are consistent with the forecasts from the econometrics department. (Study Session 4, LOS 18.i,j)

39. **A** The forward premium/discount is approximated by the interest rate differential: $r_{JPY} - r_{US}$. The interest rate differential is –3.12% (= 3.88% – 7%). Is this a discount or a premium? Since Japanese interest rates are lower than U.S. interest rates, interest rate parity (IRP) tells us that the forward price of the JPY must be greater than the USD. Hence, it takes more USD to buy JPY forward, so the JPY should be trading at a premium to the USD. (Study Session 4, LOS 17.g,h,i)

40. **B** Wilson's expected future spot rate $[E(S_1)]$ is 2% below the current spot ($120 \times 0.98 = 117.6$), so the JPY is expected to appreciate by approximately 2% (it takes less JPY to buy 1 USD). You can confirm that by converting the quotes to USD/JPY and calculating the percent change:

$$\%\Delta JPY = \frac{\left(\dfrac{1}{117.60}\right) - \left(\dfrac{1}{120.00}\right)}{\dfrac{1}{120.00}} = 2.04\% \approx 2\%$$

The USD is the DC and the JPY is the FC. Hence, the FCRP is:

FCRP = 2% − (7% − 3.88%) = −1.12%

$$= \%\Delta JPY - (r_{USD} - r_{JPY})$$

$$= \%\Delta FC - (r_{DC} - r_{FC})$$

Another way to look at this is to think of the expected change in the spot rate (2%) as the unhedged expected return, and the interest rate differential (3.12%) as the hedged return. The "extra" expected return from remaining unhedged is unhedged minus hedged, or 2 − 3.12% = −1.12%. (Study Session 18, LOS 62.h)

41. **C** This question requires you to look at deviations from international parity conditions and then determine whether those deviations will tend to work to the advantage of the customer. In this problem, you are given the necessary information to examine parity conditions using relative purchasing power parity (RPPP). For the JPY, RPPP tells us that, since the spot rate one year ago was 116, the spot rate today should be (JPY is considered the foreign currency):

$$s_{today(assuming\ RPPP\ held)} = s_{last\ year}\left[\frac{1 + i_{JPY}}{1 + i_{USD}}\right] = 116\left[\frac{1.00}{1.03}\right] = 112.62$$

Since the expected spot rate today, based on RPPP (i.e., 112.62), is not equal to the actual spot rate today (i.e., 120), RPPP did not hold over the past year. Since the actual rate is higher than the rate forecast by RPPP, the long-term trend based on deviations from international parity conditions will be for the rate to fall and the JPY to appreciate. Hence, using deviations from parity conditions as indicators of future currency movements, the bank should recommend that the JPY exposure be left unhedged.

Using the same RPPP process for the EUR exposure, we can calculate an RPPP spot rate today of 0.7340 (given that the rate was 0.72 one year ago).

$$s_{today(assuming\ RPPP\ held)} = s_{last\ year}\left[\frac{1 + i_{EUR}}{1 + i_{USD}}\right] = 0.72\left[\frac{1.05}{1.03}\right] = 0.7340$$

Again, RPPP did not hold (i.e., the actual rate today, 0.7224, is not equal to the RPPP rate that should exist today given the inflation rates). However, for the EUR case, the RPPP expected spot is higher than the actual spot, indicating that the EUR may be currently overvalued and, thus, more likely to depreciate in the future. EUR exposure should be hedged. (Study Session 4, LOS 18.g,h)

  ©2011 Kaplan, Inc.

42. **B** If there were an unexpected decline in the growth rate of the money supply, real interest rates would rise, causing an appreciation of the dollar. (Study Session 4, LOS 18.e)

43. **C** Statement 1 is correct. If the volatility of interest rates decreases, the call option is less valuable, which increases the value of the callable bond. Recall that $V_{callable}$ = $V_{noncallable} - V_{call}$. Statement 3 is also correct. The value of the noncallable bond increases by more than the callable bond because as yield falls, the value of the call goes up. As the call value increases, the callable value (noncall value – call option value) goes up by less than the noncall value. (Study Session 14, LOS 50.e,f)

44. **B** Statement 2 is incorrect because the noncallable bond value *will be affected* by a change in the *level* of interest rates.

    Statement 4 is correct because higher interest rate volatility will increase the value of the embedded put option and increase the value of the puttable bond. (Study Session 14, LOS 50.f)

45. **A** The answer is 1.56 and is found by taking the difference between the value of the callable and the noncallable bonds: Call option value = 99.77 − 98.21 = 1.56. *Note: This is an example of a basic question that you should get right! Don't give up these points or lose time by starting a complicated calculation. The question might be as easy as it seems.* (Study Session 14, LOS 50.e)

46. **B** In this case, the bond is callable and putable at the same price (100). Because Walters states that the embedded options (the issuer's call option and the holder's put option) will be exercised if the option has value (i.e., is in-the-money), the value of the bond must be 100 (plus the interest) at all times. Why? If rates fall and the computed value goes above 100, the company will call the issue at 100. Conversely, if rates increase and the computed value goes below 100, the bondholder will "put" the bond back to the issuer for 100.

    The OAS is a constant spread added to every interest rate in the tree so that the model price of the bond is equal to the market price of the bond. In this case, using the interest rate lattice, the model price of the callable bond is greater than the market price. Hence, a positive spread must be added to every interest rate in the lattice. When a constant spread is added to all the rates such that the model price is equal to the market price, you have found the OAS. The OAS will be positive for the callable bond. (Study Session 14, LOS 50.g)

47. **B** The answer is 93.26. This value of the non-callable bond at node A is computed as follows:

$$\text{value} = \frac{\left[0.5 \times \left(V_{up} + \frac{coupon}{2}\right)\right] + \left[0.5 \times \left(V_{down} + \frac{coupon}{2}\right)\right]}{\left(1 + \frac{interest\ rate}{2}\right)}$$

$$= \frac{\left[0.5 \times \left(91.73 + \frac{6}{2}\right)\right] + \left[0.5 \times \left(96.17 + \frac{6}{2}\right)\right]}{\left(1 + \frac{0.0791}{2}\right)} = 93.26$$

(Study Session 14, LOS 50.d)

48. **A** The correct value is 100.00. The computed value of the callable bond at node A is obtained as follows:

$$\text{value} = \frac{\left[0.5 \times \left(100 + \frac{6}{2}\right)\right] + \left[0.5 \times \left(100 + \frac{6}{2}\right)\right]}{\left(1 + \frac{0.0315}{2}\right)} = 101.4$$

However, when working with a callable bond, you have to remember that the value of the bond at any node is the lesser of (1) the bonds computed value or (2) the call price. So, we have:

$$\text{value} = \text{Min}\left[100 \, , \, \frac{\left[0.5 \times \left(100 + \frac{6}{2}\right)\right] + \left[0.5 \times \left(100 + \frac{6}{2}\right)\right]}{\left(1 + \frac{0.0315}{2}\right)}\right] = 100$$

In this case, since the computed value (101.4) is greater than the call price (100), the nodal value is $100. (Study Session 14, LOS 50.d)

49. **A** Both the 2008 EBITDA/interest and the EBIT/interest ratios for Marietta are greater than their comparable industry medians of 5.5 and 3.2, respectively.

$$\frac{\text{EBITDA}}{\text{interest expense}} = \frac{2,450}{380} = 6.45$$

$$\frac{\text{EBIT}}{\text{interest expense}} = \frac{1,650}{380} = 4.34$$

(Study Session 14, LOS 48.c)

50. **B** Marietta's free CFO-to-LT obligations ratio of 3.9% is between the BBB median (5.7%) and the BB median (3.4%).

$$\text{free CFO-to-LT obligations} = \frac{189}{3,100 + 1,800} = 0.039 = 3.9\%$$

(Study Session 14, LOS 48.c)

51. **B** Marietta's long-term obligations-to-capitalization ratio of 59.4% is between the BBB median (56.3%) and the BB median (68.5%).

$$\text{LT obligations-to-capitalization} = \frac{3,100 + 1,800}{3,100 + 1,800 + 3,350} = 0.594 = 59.4\%$$

(Study Session 14, LOS 48.c)

©2011 Kaplan, Inc.

52. **B** First, compare Marietta's ratios to the median ratios:

Marietta's EBIT/interest (4.34) is between the A median (5.9) and the BBB median (3.2).

Marietta's EBITDA/interest (6.45) is between the A median (8.8) and the BBB median (5.5).

Marietta's EBIT-to-sales ratio of 18.3% is between the A median (18.8%) and the BBB median (15.7%).

Marietta's free CFO-to-LT obligations ratio of 3.9% is between the BBB median (5.7%) and the BB median (3.4%).

Marietta's long-term obligations-to-capitalization ratio of 59.4% is between the BBB median (56.3%) and the BB median (68.5%).

Next, compare Marietta's yield spread to 20-year yield spreads by bond rating:

Marietta's yield spread of 1.55% is comparable to the average for A-rated bonds.

Therefore, Sanders should recommend selling the Marietta bonds because the spread is comparable to A-rated bonds, but the ratios are more consistent with a BBB rating. (Study Session 14, LOS 48.d)

53. **A** Both of Yan's statements are correct. The two most important factors in an analysis of a corporate issuer are the capacity to pay (particularly a cash flow analysis) and the corporate governance structure. This requires an analysis of the issuer's business and operating risks (e.g., profitability, solvency, and leverage).

However, there are no business or operating risks to assess with an ABS. Instead, the emphasis is on the quality of the collateral that backs the ABS, particularly the collateral's capacity to generate cash flow to meet the repayment obligations of each tranche under various scenarios of default and delinquency experience.

The analysis of municipal tax-backed and revenue bonds is similar to that of corporate issuers. The only important difference in the analysis of municipal bonds is that the rate covenants and priority-of-revenue claims clause are unique to the trust indenture of municipal revenue bonds, so they require an additional level of analysis not necessary with corporate bonds. (Study Session 14, LOS 48.g,h,j)

54. **C** Choice C is most likely to best complement the other three factors Petrovich already mentioned. Choice A sounds reasonable, but it is very similar to factor (1) because both measure the municipality's debt burden, which means she already identified it. Covenants (as suggested in choice B) are important in the analysis of revenue bonds, not necessarily in the analysis of tax-backed bonds. (Study Session 14, LOS 48.h)

55. **B** The excess of purchase price over the pro-rata share of the book value of Optimax is allocated to PP&E. The remainder is goodwill.

Purchase price (in thousands)	$300
Less: Pro-rata share of Optimax	210 [$600 Optimax book value × 35%]
Excess of purchase price	90
Less: Excess allocated to PPE	70 [($1,200 fair value − $1,000 book value) × 35%]
Acquisition goodwill	$20

(Study Session 6, LOS 22.c)

56. **B** Under the equity method, Wayland recognizes its pro-rata share of Optimax's net income less the additional depreciation that resulted from the increase in fair value of Optimax's PP&E.

Pro-rata share of Optimax's net income	$87,500	[$250,000 × 35%]
Less: Additional depreciation from PPE	7,000	[($200,000 / 10 years) × 35%]
Equity income	$80,500	

Wayland's investment account on the balance sheet increased by its equity income and decreased by the dividends received from the investment.

Beginning investment account	$300,000	
Equity income from Optimax	80,500	
Less: Dividends received	35,000	[$100,000 dividends × 35%]
Ending investment account	$345,500	

(Study Session 6, LOS 22.b)

57. **A** Since all of the profit from the intercompany transaction is included in Optimax's net income, Wayland must reduce its equity income of Optimax by the pro-rata share of the unconfirmed profit. Since half of the goods remain, half of the profit is unconfirmed. Thus, Wayland must reduce its equity income $2,625 [($15,000 total profit × 50% unconfirmed) × 35% ownership interest]. (Study Session 6, LOS 22.b)

58. **B** Proportionate consolidation and the equity method both lead to the same net income and the same shareholders' equity. COGS are higher under proportionate consolidation as compared to the equity method. Under proportionate consolidation, the investor recognizes its pro-rata share of each income statement account. Under the equity method, the investor recognizes its pro-rata share of the investee's earnings in one line of the income statement. (Study Session 6, LOS 22.c)

59. **A** IFRS typically does not allow reclassification of investments into and out of fair value through profit or loss category and reclassification of investments out of held-for-trading category. U.S. GAAP does permit securities to be reclassified into or out of held-for-trading or designated at fair value. (Study Session 6, LOS 22.a,b)

60. **B** The change in market value for the period and dividends received from the investment are recognized in the income statement for trading securities. In 2008, there was a $25,000 unrealized gain on the original 25,000 shares [25,000 shares × ($76 – $75)] and a $10,000 unrealized loss on the shares purchased in 2008 [5,000 shares × ($76 – $78)]. Wayland received $30,000 in dividends from Vanry (30,000 shares × $1 per share). For 2008, the income statement impact is a $45,000 profit ($25,000 unrealized gain on original shares – $10,000 unrealized loss on increase in shares + $30,000 dividends received). (Study Session 6, LOS 22.a,b)

©2011 Kaplan, Inc.

Exam 2
Afternoon Session Answers

To get valuable feedback on how your score compares to those of other Level II candidates, use your Username and Password to gain Online Access at schweser.com and choose the left-hand menu item "Practice Exams Vol. 1."

61. B	81. A	101. A
62. B	82. A	102. C
63. C	83. A	103. B
64. C	84. B	104. C
65. C	85. A	105. C
66. A	86. C	106. A
67. B	87. C	107. B
68. A	88. A	108. B
69. A	89. C	109. A
70. C	90. C	110. A
71. A	91. A	111. A
72. B	92. C	112. B
73. C	93. C	113. B
74. A	94. A	114. C
75. B	95. A	115. A
76. C	96. C	116. B
77. B	97. A	117. C
78. A	98. A	118. A
79. A	99. C	119. C
80. A	100. B	120. C

EXAM 2
AFTERNOON SESSION ANSWERS

61. **B** Invested capital in the fund was $20 million + $100 million = $120 million. Committed capital was $120 million + $100 million = $220 million. Since the fund was sold for $180 million, the fund earned a profit of $180 million – $120 million = $60 million.

    Under the total return using invested capital method, carried interest is paid to the GP only after the portfolio value exceeds invested capital (by 30% as specified by IGS). Since the $180 million exceeds ($120 million)(1.3) = $156 million, the GP is entitled to carried interest. Carried interest is calculated as:

    $180 million – $120 million = $60 million. 20% of $60 million is $12 million.

    (Study Session 13, LOS 46.h,i)

62. **B** The DCF method and relative value approach would be less appropriate for Sverig. Given that Sverig is a startup venture capital firm, it would be difficult to assess its future cash flows and there are likely few comparables to benchmark against. Given that L'Offre has been in existence for over a century, it likely has relatively stable and predictable cash flows. Several comparables would also likely exist in the same industry. This would make either the DCF method or relative value approach an appropriate valuation technique. (Study Session 13, LOS 46.i)

63. **C** Market risk is the uncertainty in long-term macroeconomic factors, such as changes in interest rates and foreign exchange rates. If these changes adversely affect the private equity fund firms, both the fund's investors (limited partners) and the firms' managers could see their equity stake and investment declining. Agency risk refers to the possibility that the managers of the portfolio (investee) companies may place their personal interests ahead of the interests of the firm and of private equity investors. (Study Session 13, LOS 46.g)

64. **C** The GP's share in profits is referred to as carried interest and is generally set at 20% of net profits after fees. A tag-along, drag-along clause would give management the right to buy an equity stake upon sale by the private equity owners.

    Ratchet specifies the equity allocation between the limited partners (LPs) and management. Distribution waterfall specifies how profits will flow to the LPs and also the conditions under which the GP may receive carried interest. (Study Session 13, LOS 46.b)

©2011 Kaplan, Inc.

65. **C**   First, the $400 million terminal value must be discounted two years at 30% to the second round of financing:

$$POST_2 = \frac{\$400 \text{ million}}{(1.3)^2} = \$236.686 \text{ million}$$

The second-round pre-money valuation (PRE_2) is calculated by netting the $40 million second-round investment from the $POST_2$ calculation:

$$PRE_2 = POST_2 - INV_2 = \$236.686 \text{ million} - \$40 \text{ million} = \$196.686 \text{ million}.$$

Finally, the PRE_2 valuation must be discounted back 4 years at 40% to arrive at the $POST_1$ valuation:

$$POST_1 = \frac{\$196.686 \text{ million}}{(1.4)^4} = \$51.199 \text{ million}$$

(Study Session 13, LOS 46.j)

66. **A**   Calculating the number shares for Sverig's first-round investors requires a three-step approach where:

- f_1 is the fractional ownership for first-round investors.
- INV_1 is the initial investment in Sverig by the private equity partners.
- S_e is the number of shares owned by Sverig's founders.
- S_{pe} is the number of shares owned by the private equity LPs.

Step 1: Determine the fractional ownership for first-round investors (f_1):

$$f_1 = \frac{INV}{POST_1} = \frac{\$20 \text{ million}}{\$51.199 \text{ million}} = 39.06\%$$

First-round investors thus own approximately 39.06% of the firm.

Step 2: Determine the number of shares first-round investors need to receive their fractional ownership:

$$S_{pe1} = S_e\left(\frac{f_1}{1-f_1}\right) = 5,000,000\left(\frac{0.3906}{1-0.3906}\right) = 3,204,792$$

To obtain a 39.06% stake in Sverig, first-round investors would have to receive 3,204,792 shares.

Step 3: Determine the stock price after the first round of financing (P_1):

$$P_1 = \frac{INV_1}{S_{pe1}} = \frac{\$20 \text{ million}}{3,204,792} = \$6.24$$

(Study Session 13, LOS 46.j)

67. **B** Fisher should take the natural log of the dependent variable so that the data in Exhibit 1 are transformed and can be better modeled using a linear regression. From the plot, it appears that the data follow a log-linear trend. If the natural log is taken of the dependent variable, the data will be more linear so that it is readily modeled in a regression. The transformed data will plot as follows:

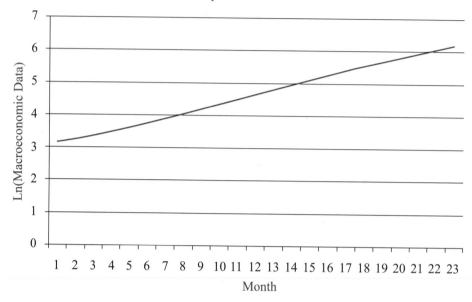

(Study Session 3, LOS 12.i,j and 13.a)

68. **A** The most likely problem in Fisher's regression of the emerging market data is that the error terms appear to be positively correlated in Exhibit 2. The first few error terms are positive, then negative, and then positive. This indicates serial correlation, which is common in trend models. As Fisher regresses the macroeconomic data against a time variable, she is using a trend model. In a trend model, the Durbin Watson statistic can be used to detect serial correlation. (Study Session 3, LOS 12.i)

69. **A** The use of the Durbin Watson statistic is inappropriate in an autoregressive regression, which is what Weatherford is using. The Durbin Watson statistic is appropriate for trend models but not autoregressive models. To determine whether the errors terms are serially correlated in an autoregressive model, the significance of the autocorrelations should be tested using the t-statistic. (Study Session 3, LOS 13.d)

70. **C** Weatherford is using an autoregressive first-order regression model in which this period's silver price is regressed on the previous period's price. The regression is of the form:

$$X_t = b_0 + b_1 X_{t-1}$$

The most likely problem in this regression is that the data is not covariance stationary. In the plot of the data, the mean of the data does not appear to be constant (it is much higher in the middle period.) The estimate of the lag one slope coefficient is close to 1.0, which also suggests that the data is nonstationary.

To definitively test this, the Dickey Fuller test should be used, where the null hypothesis is that $b_1 - 1$ is equal to zero. If the null hypothesis is not rejected, we say that the data has a unit root and is nonstationary. (Study Session 3, LOS 12.j and 13.f,k,n)

©2011 Kaplan, Inc.

71. **A**   Weatherford should use the first differences of the data in the regression. That is, instead of using the actual price levels, she should use the change in the data rather than levels:

$$Y_t = X_t - X_{t-1}$$

Then the appropriate regression will be:

$$Y_t = b_0 + b_1 Y_{t-1}$$

The transformed time series data will have a mean reverting level and be covariance stationary. (Study Session 3, LOS 13.j)

72. **B**   To determine the mean reverting level, we divide the intercept by one minus the slope coefficient:

$$\text{mean-reverting level} = \frac{b_0}{1-b_1} = \frac{2.00}{1-(-0.09)} = 1.83$$

The one-step-ahead predicted value is calculated by substituting the current value into the regression equation:

$$\hat{y}_{t+1} = b_0 + b_1\left(y_t\right) = 2.00 + (-0.09)(-0.80) = 2.072$$

The two-step-ahead predicted value is then calculated by substituting the one-step-ahead predicted value into the regression equation:

$$\hat{y}_{t+2} = b_0 + b_1\left(\hat{y}_{t+1}\right) = 2.00 + (-0.09)(2.072) = 1.81$$

(Study Session 3, LOS 13.d,e)

73. **C**   Investments in financial assets are classified as held-to-maturity, held-for-trading, designated at fair value, and available-for-sale. Held-to-maturity applies to debt securities only. Held-for-trading securities are debt or equity securities that are expected to be sold in the near term. Since the investment in Odessa is long-term, the securities are classified as available-for-sale. (Study Session 6, LOS 22.a)

74. **A**   Since Iberia owns 40% of Midland (5 million shares owned / 12.5 million total shares outstanding), the equity method is used. Under the equity method, Iberia reports its pro-rata share of Midland's net income (€5 million loss × 40% = €2 million loss). Changes in market value are ignored under the equity method.

Iberia's investment in Odessa is classified as available-for-sale since the investment is considered long-term. Dividend income from available-for-sale securities is recognized in the income statement (€3 dividend × 1 million shares = €3 million). The changes in market value are reported in shareholders' equity.

Investment income from Midland and Odessa is €1 million (€3 million dividend income from Odessa − €2 million pro-rata loss from Midland). (Study Session 6, LOS 22.a)

75. **B** Under the equity method, the balance sheet carrying value is increased by the pro-rata earnings of the investee and decreased by the dividends received from the investee. The balance sheet value at the end of 2008 is €88 million [€80 million + (€30 million Midland 2008 net income × 40%) – (€10 million dividend × 40%)]. The balance sheet value at the end of 2009 is €84.4 million [€88 million – (€5 million loss × 40%) – (€4 million dividend × 40%)].

    Available-for-sale securities are reported on the balance sheet at fair value. Thus, the fair value of Odessa is €17 million (€17 × 1 million shares).

    As a result of its investment in Midland and Odessa, Iberia will report investment assets of €101.4 million (€84.4 million book value of Midland + €17 million fair value Odessa). (Study Session 6, LOS 22.a)

76. **C** Profit from intercompany transactions must be deferred until the profit is confirmed through use or sale to a third party. Since all of the goods purchased from Midland have been sold to third parties, all of the profit from the intercompany sale has been confirmed. Thus, no adjustment is needed. (Study Session 6, LOS 22.a)

77. **B** Under U.S. GAAP, the equity method is required in accounting for a joint venture. Proportionate consolidation is not allowed except in very limited situations. Proportionate consolidation is the preferred method for joint venture accounting under International Financial Reporting Standards (IFRS). Therefore, the statement is not correct. (Study Session 6, LOS 22.b)

78. **A** In a profitable year, net profit margin (net income/sales) will be higher under the equity method because sales are lower under the equity method. Acquisition includes the sales figures for both the parent and subsidiary, while the equity method only includes the sales figure for the parent company. Net income is the same under both methods. Therefore, the statement is correct. (Study Session 6, LOS 22.c)

79. **A** Statement 1: Employers often face onerous disclosure requirements—incorrect; the accounting is quite simple and the onerous disclosure requirements are more characteristic of defined benefit plans.

    Statement 2: Employers often bear all the investment risk—incorrect; benefits received by each individual employee on retirement depends on the investment performance of each individual's personal retirement fund. Thus, the employees bear the investment risk.

    Therefore, both statements are incorrect. (Study Session 6, LOS 23.a)

80. **A** Under current U.S. GAAP pension accounting rules, which apply to firms with fiscal year ends after December 2006, Samilski will report the funded status of the plan on its balance sheet.

    funded status = fair market value of plan assets less PBO
    = $316 million less $320 million
    = $4 million underfunded

    Therefore, Samilski will report a $4 million liability on its balance sheet. (Study Session 6, LOS 23.b)

©2011 Kaplan, Inc.

81. **A**   A lower discount rate increases the PBO. It also increases the overall pension expense by increasing the service cost and, most likely, the interest cost. (For mature plans, a lower discount rate might decrease interest costs. In rare cases, interest cost will decrease by enough to offset the increase in the current service cost, and pension expense will decrease.) (Study Session 6, LOS 23.c)

82. **A**   A higher rate of compensation increase will increase the PBO. It will also increase the overall pension expense by increasing both the service and interest costs.
(Study Session 6, LOS 23.b,c)

83. **A**   As a result of consolidating SPEs that were previously accounted for using the equity method, assets and equity will increase but net income won't change. Therefore, return on assets as well as return on equity will decrease. (Study Session 6, LOS 22.c)

84. **B**   An actuarial loss results from a change in actuarial assumptions. In the case of a loss, the amount of pension benefits payable in the future would increase, thus increasing the PBO. Actuarial gains have the opposite effect.

The amortization of prior service costs results in pension expense being increased gradually over a number of years, rather than all at once in the year of occurrence. In contrast, the expected return on plan assets is an "income" component in calculating pension cost (service cost and interest cost being the expense components), so recognition of expected return on plan assets would decrease pension expense.
(Study Session 6, LOS 23.b)

85. **A**   The variance for an equally-weighted portfolio approaches the average covariance of the assets in the portfolio as the number of assets in the portfolio increases. Of the four portfolios, Fund W's variance is closest to its average asset covariance. While not necessary to answer this question, we could derive the exact number of assets in each portfolio using the formula for the variance of an equally weighted portfolio:

$$\sigma_P^2 = \frac{1}{n}\overline{\sigma}_i^2 \;+\; \frac{n-1}{n}\overline{COV}_{ij}$$

where $\overline{\sigma}_i^2$ is the average variance of all assets in the portfolio, and $\overline{COV}_{ij}$ is the average covariance of all pairs of assets in the portfolio. Note that the equally weighted portfolio variance equals the sum of two components, each of which is affected by the size of the portfolio:

* $(1 / n) \times \overline{\sigma}_i^2$ gets closer to zero as n gets large.
* $[(n-1) / n] \times \overline{COV}_{ij}$ gets closer to the average covariance as n gets large.

Therefore, the variance of an equally weighted portfolio approaches the average covariance as n gets large. (Study Session 18, LOS 60.d)

86. **C**   The expected return on a portfolio of two assets equals:

$$E(R_P) = w_Y E(R_Y) + w_Z E(R_Z)$$

Alverson asks about the expected return on an equal-weighted combination of Funds Y and Z, implying $w_Y = w_Z = 50\%$.

$$E(R_P) = 0.50E(R_Y) + 0.50E(R_Z) = \frac{E(R_Y) + E(R_Z)}{2}$$

Therefore, the expected return on the combination equals the arithmetic average of Fund Y and Fund Z expected returns.

The portfolio standard deviation equals:

$$\sigma_P = [w_Y^2 \sigma_Y^2 + w_Z^2 \sigma_Z^2 + 2w_Y w_Z \rho_{YZ} \sigma_Y \sigma_Z]^{1/2}$$

Assuming $w_Y = w_Z = 0.50$, this will equal the average of the two standard deviations *only* if the correlation between Funds Y and Z equals +1. MI already determined that the correlation of returns between Funds Y and Z is less than +1. Therefore, the equally weighted portfolio combination of Funds Y and Z will have a standard deviation that is less than the arithmetic average of the Fund Y and Z standard deviations. (Study Session 18, LOS 60.a)

87. **C**   Statement 1 is not correct. A minimum variance portfolio is one that has smallest variance among all portfolios with identical expected return. The minimum-variance frontier is a graph of the expected return, variance combinations for all minimum variance portfolios. The minimum variance frontier (in risk-return space) has a bullet shape. Along the upper section of the minimum variance frontier, all portfolios have expected returns that exceed that of the global minimum variance portfolio, and returns increase as risk increases. Along the lower section, however, all portfolio returns are *less* than the global minimum variance portfolio return, and expected returns worsen as risk increases. Clearly, portfolios lying on the lower section of the minimum variance frontier are not desirable.

Statement 2 also is not correct. MI uses mean-variance analysis to select an appropriate investment combination of the risk-free asset and the optimal risky portfolio lying along the capital allocation line (CAL). The CAL dominates the minimum variance frontier (the efficient frontier comprising exclusively risky assets). Therefore, the expected return along the CAL will exceed that of the global minimum variance portfolio (which is on the minimum variance frontier) for the same level of risk. Also, the risk along the CAL will be less than that of the global minimum variance portfolio for the same level of expected return. (Study Session 18, LOS 60.b,d)

88. **A**   Note that the MI-5000 Fund is the "market portfolio" that applies relative market value weights across assets in the portfolio. The Government Securities Fund has a standard deviation of zero, so it is the risk-free asset. Therefore, the data reported in Exhibit 2 provide the inputs needed to derive the capital market line. The intercept of the capital market line equals the risk-free rate (0.05), and the slope of the capital market line equals the Sharpe ratio for the optimal risky portfolio, the MI-5000:

$$\text{Sharpe ratio} = \frac{0.12 - 0.05}{0.20} = 0.35$$

(Study Session 18, LOS 60.d,f)

89. **C** The highest returns for each level of risk are provided along the capital market line:

$$E(R_C) = R_F + \left[\frac{E(R_M) - R_F}{\sigma_M} \right] \sigma_C$$

where $E(R_C)$ is the expected return on Alverson's investment combination, $E(R_M)$ is the expected return on the market portfolio (the MI-5000), and σ_C is the standard deviation on Alverson's investment portfolio (12%). Therefore,

$$E(R_C) = 0.05 + \left[\frac{0.12 - 0.05}{0.20} \right] (0.12) = 0.092 = 9.2\%$$

The appropriate weighting can be determined by recalling the formula for the standard deviation of an investment that combines a risky asset (i.e., the MI-5000) and a risk-free asset (i.e., government bonds):

$$\sigma_C = w_M \sigma_M$$
$$\sigma_C = 0.12 = w_M (0.20)$$
$$w_M = \frac{0.12}{0.20} = 0.60 = 60\%$$

(Study Session 18, LOS 60.d)

90. **C** Assuming all investors agree on all asset return, variance, and correlation expectations, then the market portfolio has the highest Sharpe ratio. The Sharpe ratio for the market portfolio equals the slope of the capital market line:

$$\text{market portfolio Sharpe ratio} = \frac{E(R_M) - R_F}{\sigma_M} = \frac{0.12 - 0.05}{0.20} = 0.35$$

All other risky portfolios will have a smaller Sharpe ratio, so the maximum expected return for all other risky portfolios must satisfy the following equation.

$$\frac{E(R_P) - 0.05}{\sigma_P} < 0.35$$

The variance of the returns on Fund W is 0.25, so the standard deviation of the returns on Fund W is:

$$\sigma_W = \sqrt{0.25} = 0.50$$

In order for Fund W to have a Sharpe ratio less than 0.35, its expected return must be less than 0.225.

$$\frac{E(R_W) - 0.05}{0.50} < 0.35$$

$$\Rightarrow E(R_W) < 0.225$$

Fund Z has the same variance as Fund W, so its expected return must also be less than 0.225. (Study Session 18, LOS 60.d,f)

91. **A**   The equity risk premium is estimated as:

$$ERP = [1 + i] \times [1 + REg] \times [1 + PEg] - 1 + Y - RF$$

where:

i	= the expected inflation rate	= 2.6%
REg	= expected real growth in GDP	= 3.0%
PEg	= relative value changed due to changes in P/E ratio	= −0.10
Y	= yield on the market index	= 1.7%
RF	= risk-free rate of return	= 2.7%
ERP	= (1.026) × (1.030) × (0.97) − 1 + 0.017 − 0.027 = 0.015	= 1.50%

Note: We do not add the risk-free rate because we are computing the equity risk premium and not the required rate of return. Conversely, we can compute the required rate of return and then subtract the risk-free rate to obtain the equity risk premium.

(Study Session 10, LOS 35.b)

92. **C**   Historical estimates are subject to survivorship bias. If the data are not adjusted for the effects of non-survivors, returns (based only on survivors) will be biased upwards. (Study Session 10, LOS 35.b)

93. **C**   Using CAPM, the required return is:

required rate of return = risk-free rate + (beta × equity risk premium)

required return for NE = 2.7% + (0.83 × 5.2%) = 7.02%

(Study Session 10, LOS 35.c)

94. **A**   With the Fama-French model, the required return is:

required rate of return = risk-free rate + β_{MKT} (market risk premium) + β_{size} (size risk premium) + β_{value} (value premium)

required rate of return for NE = 2.7% + 0.83(5.2%) + (−0.76)(3.2%) + (−0.04)(5.4%) = 4.37%

(Study Session 10, LOS 35.c)

95. **A**   adjusted beta = (2/3)(0.83) + (1/3)(1.0) = 0.89. (Study Session 10, LOS 35.d)

96. **C**   The recommended method for estimating the beta of a nonpublic company from the beta of a public company is as follows: (1) Unlever the beta for the public company, using the public company's debt/equity ratio. (2) Relever (adjust upward) this beta using VixPRO's debt/equity ratio to get the estimated equity beta for VixPRO. (Study Session 10, LOS 35.d)

97. **A**   Hinesman's comment is correct. Studies have shown, that on average, companies with strong corporate governance systems have higher measures of profitability and generate higher returns for shareholders.

Randall's comment is also correct. The lack of an effective corporate governance system increases risk to an investor. Four main risks of not having an effective corporate governance system include asset risk and liability risk, as well as the two risks described by Randall: financial disclosure risk and strategic policy risk. (Study Session 9, LOS 31.a,g)

98. **A** According to corporate governance best practice, the audit committee should consist only of independent directors; it should have expertise in financial and accounting matters (for purposes of the exam, at least two members of the committee should have relevant accounting and auditing experience); the internal audit staff for the firm should report directly to the audit committee; and the committee should meet with external auditors at least once annually without management present. (Study Session 9, LOS 31.e)

99. **C** Using a target debt-to-equity ratio of 1:1, the $150 million in capital spending for 20X1 will be financed with $75 million in internal equity and $75 million in debt. The total dividend is the remaining internal equity of $112.5 – $75 = $37.5 million, or $37.5 / 56.25 = $0.67 per share. (Study Session 8, LOS 30.j)

100. **B** FCFE = cash flow from operations – FcInv + net borrowings

    20X0: FCFE = 115 – 43 + 22 = 94

    20X1: FCFE = 132 – 150 + 75 = 57

    FCFE coverage ratio = FCFE / (dividends + share repurchases)

    20X0: 94 / (42.88 + 42) = 1.11

    20X1: 57 / (45 + 3) = 1.19

    (Study Session 8, LOS 30.i)

101. **A** Kazmaier received a score of 25% because it was in compliance with global best practice with respect to only one of the four criteria.

    Criterion 1: Global best practice recommends that three-quarters (75%) of the board members be independent. Of the nine total board members, only five are independent. Kazmaier fails this criterion.

    Criterion 2: Global best practice recommends that the Chairman of the Board be independent. Since Kazmaier's Chairman is also the CEO, Kazmaier fails this criterion.

    Criterion 3: Global best practice recommends that the entire board of directors stand for reelection annually. Since it appears that Kazmaier has staggered board elections, Kazmaier fails this criterion.

    Criterion 4: Global best practice requires independent board members to meet in separate sessions at least annually. Although quarterly meetings between independent directors are preferable, the fact that they happen annually means Kazmaier passes this criterion.

    (Study Session 9, LOS 31.e)

102. **C** Nagy's three rationales all correctly describe common advantages of share repurchases. (Study Session 8, LOS 30.g)

The complete solution to Questions 103 to 108 is as follows (in thousands):

		Years		
Cost Item	0	1	2	3
Cost	(400)			
Sale of old*	30			
Revenue		175.0	175.0	175.0
Less: operating cost		25.0	25.0	25.0
Less: depreciation (400,000 × MACRS%)		132.0	180.0	60.0
EBT		18.0	(30.0)	90.0
− Tax (40%)		7.2	(12.0)	36.0
NI		10.8	(18.0)	54.0
+ Depreciation		132.0	180.0	60.0
+ Sale				10.0
+ Sale tax shield**				7.2
= CF		142.8	162.0	131.2

NPV (@ 20%) = −62,574

IRR = 8.796%

Therefore, REJECT, because the NPV < 0, FRR < 20%.

Using the calculator: CF0 = −370, C01 = 142.8, C02 = 162, C03 = 131.2, I = 20, CPT → NPV = −62,574, CPT → IRR = 8.796.

** Sale tax shield		*Sale of old
BV =	28 (= 400 × 0.07)	BV = 0
−sale	−10	Sale = 50
Loss	18	Gain = 50
Tax shield = loss × tax rate = 18 × 0.4 = 7.2		Tax (40%) = 20
Net impact of sale = $10 sale proceeds + $7.2 tax shield = 17.2		Net proceeds = 30

103. **B** See solution above. Alternatively, initial outlay = $FCInv + WCInv − Sal_0 + T(Sal_T − B_0)$ = $400 + 0 − 50 + 0.4(50 − 0) = 400 − 50 + 20 = \$370$. (Study Session 8, LOS 28.a)

104. **C** See solution above. Alternatively, $CF_1 = (S − C)(1 − T) + DT = (175 − 25)(0.6) + (0.4)(0.33)(400) = 90 + 52.8 = \$142.8$. (Study Session 8, LOS 28.a)

105. **C** See solution above. Alternatively, $CF = −(175 − 25)(0.4) + 400(0.45)(0.4) = −60 + 72 = +\$12$. (Study Session 8, LOS 28.a)

106. **A** See solution above. Alternatively, $CF_3 = (175 − 25)(0.6) + (400)(0.15)(0.4) = 90 + 24 = \$114$. $TNOCF = Sal_T + WCInv − T(Sal_T − B_T) = 10 + 0 − 0.4(10 − 28) = 10 + 7.2 = \$17.2$. $CF_3 + TNOCF = \$114 + \$17.2 = \$131.2$ (Study Session 8, LOS 28.a)

107. **B** NPV will be underestimated because the reduction in inventory should reflect a cash inflow at the beginning of the project. Even if the inventory builds back up to its previous level at the end of the project (resulting in a cash outflow), the cash inflow will be larger than the present value of the cash outflow. (Study Session 8, LOS 28.a)

©2011 Kaplan, Inc.

108. **B** If the NPV is less than zero, the IRR must be less than the discount rate of 20% (so 8.8% is the only possible answer), and the project should be rejected. The actual calculations of NPV and IRR are shown in the solution, but these calculations are not necessary to answer the question. (Study Session 8, LOS 28.a)

109. **A** Nolte is long in the underlying stock, so she should short call options, and she can use any of the options to delta hedge. The hedge ratio (the number of calls per share) is (1 / delta), so any of these four short call positions will hedge her long position in the stock:

$$\frac{1}{0.54} \times 5,000 = 9,259 \text{ 1-month call options}$$

$$\frac{1}{0.58} \times 5,000 = 8,621 \text{ 3-month call options}$$

$$\frac{1}{0.61} \times 5,000 = 8,197 \text{ 6-month call options}$$

$$\frac{1}{0.63} \times 5,000 = 7,937 \text{ 9-month call options}$$

(Study Session 17, LOS 56.e)

110. **A** The hedge must be continually rebalanced, even in the unlikely event that the stock price doesn't change, because the option's delta changes as time passes and the option approaches maturity. If she simultaneously buys an equivalent amount of put options, the overall position (including the calls, the puts, and 5,000 shares of Pioneer) will no longer be delta hedged. (Study Session 17, LOS 56.e)

111. **A** The $40 call option is at-the-money, and gamma is largest for at-the-money options. Therefore, the gamma on the $40 call is greater than a $20 call, a $30 call, and a $50 call. (Study Session 17, LOS 56.f)

112. **B** The delta of a put option is equal to the delta of the comparable call option minus one:

1-month put delta $= 0.54 - 1 = -0.46$

6-month put delta $= 0.61 - 1 = -0.39$

Therefore her estimate of the 1-month put delta is correct, but her estimate of the 6-month put delta is incorrect. (Study Session 17, LOS 56.e)

113. **B** Both the 3-month and the 9-month put options are correctly priced according to put-call parity. Note that you are given the continuously compounded risk-free rate, so you have to use the continuous version of put-call parity.

$$P_0 = C_0 - S_0 + \frac{X}{e^{R_f^c \times T}}$$

$$P(3\text{-month}) = \$5 + \frac{\$40}{e^{0.05 \times 0.25}} - \$40 = \$4.50$$

$$P(9\text{-month}) = \$8.81 + \frac{\$40}{e^{0.05 \times 0.75}} - \$40 = \$7.34$$

Therefore, she's correct that the 3-month put is not mispriced, but incorrect in her conclusion that the 9-month put is mispriced. (Study Session 17, LOS 56.a)

114. **C** Put-call parity for futures options is:

$$P_0 = C_0 + \frac{X - F_T}{e^{r \times T}} = \$1 + \frac{\$22 - \$20}{e^{0.05 \times 0.5}} = \$2.95$$

(Study Session 17, LOS 56.i)

115. **A** The semi-annual fixed payment is calculated as

$$\frac{1 - 0.9285}{0.9840 + 0.9676 + 0.9488 + 0.9285} = 0.01867 \text{, which, when annualized, is 3.73\%.}$$

(Study Session 17, LOS 57.c)

116. **B** The amount owed by the fixed payer of the swap would be (0.038 / 2) × $30,000,000 = $570,000. (Study Session 17, LOS 57.c)

117. **C** The value of the fixed rate bond for $1 of notional principal is calculated as:

($0.038 / 2) × (0.9945 + 0.9760 + 0.9510 + 0.9246) + [$1 × (0.9246)] = $0.99768

The value of the floating rate note for $1 of notional principal is calculated by looking at the floating rate when the swap was created. $R_{180\text{-day}}$ = 3.25% and the 60-day discount factor as of today is 0.9945; therefore, the calculation is:
{$1+ [$0.0325 × (180 / 360)]} × 0.9945 = $1.01066.

(Study Session 17, LOS 57.c)

118. **A** The value of the swap to the floating rate payer would be (0.99000 − 1.01000) × $30,000,000 = −$600,000. In this case, the floating rate payer would need to pay $600,000 to terminate the swap, based on the value of the swap to the fixed rate payer. (Study Session 17, LOS 57.c)

119. **C** A long position in a payer swaption decreases in value as rates decrease, and a short position increases. A long position in a receiver swaption increases in value as rates decrease, and a short position decreases.

Therefore, to exploit the anticipated drop in rates, Black should go short in the payer swaption or long in the receiver swaption. (Study Session 17, LOS 57.f)

120. **C** Statement 1 is not correct. At the initiation of an interest rate swap, both parties are exposed to some potential credit risk, although the exposure is relatively low.

Statement 2 is correct. The long position in a payer swaption (and, indeed, in any option) is exposed to potential credit risk because of the likelihood that the counterparty will default if the swaption expires in-the-money. The short position, however, is not exposed to credit risk because they will not receive a payment at maturity no matter if the swaption expires in or out-of-the-money. (Study Session 17, LOS 57.i)

©2011 Kaplan, Inc.

Exam 3
Morning Session Answers

To get valuable feedback on how your score compares to those of other Level II candidates, use your Username and Password to gain Online Access at schweser.com and choose the left-hand menu item "Practice Exams Vol. 1."

1. A	21. C	41. C
2. C	22. B	42. B
3. A	23. A	43. C
4. C	24. A	44. A
5. B	25. B	45. B
6. C	26. A	46. C
7. A	27. B	47. C
8. B	28. A	48. C
9. B	29. A	49. C
10. A	30. C	50. C
11. A	31. B	51. C
12. C	32. A	52. C
13. B	33. B	53. A
14. A	34. B	54. B
15. B	35. C	55. C
16. B	36. B	56. B
17. B	37. B	57. C
18. C	38. C	58. B
19. A	39. B	59. B
20. B	40. B	60. B

Exam 3
Morning Session Answers

1. A   FCFE = NI + depreciation − FCInv − WCInv + net borrowing
           = 7.0 + 3.5 − 3.2 − 0.4 + (2.4 − 2.0)
           = LC7.3 million, or LC7,300,000
    (Study Session 12, LOS 40.d)

2. C   FCFF = FCFE + Int(1 − tax rate) − net borrowing = 7.3 + 5.0(1 − 0.34) − (2.4 − 2.0) = LC10.2 million, or LC10,200,000. (Study Session 12, LOS 40.d)

3. A   Given the assumptions stated in the problem, this is a simple single stage valuation. Using the firm's modified build-up methodology, the real required rate of return is 8% (= country real rate + industry adjustment + firm adjustment = 3% + 3% + 2%). The real growth rate is $\left[\left(\dfrac{1.12}{1.08738}\right)-1\right]=3\%$. FCFE is LC7,3000,000 from an earlier question.

    Hence, the value of PCC equity is:

    $$V_0 = \frac{\text{FCFE}\times(1+g)}{r-g} = \frac{7,300,000\times1.03}{0.08-0.03} = \text{LC150,380,000}$$

    (Study Session 12, LOS 40.j)

4. C   *Dividend policy change*: A change in dividend policy will have no direct impact on future FCFE. Note that dividend payments are a use of equity cash flows, not a reduction in FCFE. It is possible that an increase in dividends could reduce the long-term growth rate of the firm, thus reducing firm value. However, holding all other factors constant, an increase in dividends will not affect FCFE forecasts.

    Net change in debt: The increase in debt, LC400,000, will increase future interest expense and decrease future FCFE, but the amount is small, relative to net income of LC7,000,000. (Study Session 12, LOS 40.g)

5. B   Since the company's capital structure is reasonably stable and FCFE is positive, FCFE is a simpler approach to valuation than FCFF, EVA, or residual income, and is preferred in this case. (Study Session 12, LOS 40.a)

6. C   Both statements are correct. EBITDA is in fact a poor proxy for FCFF because it does not incorporate the cash taxes paid by the firm. EBITDA also fails to reflect the investment in working capital and the investment in fixed capital. EBITDA is an even worse proxy for FCFE than as a proxy for FCFF. EBITDA does not reflect after-tax interest costs or other cash flows that shareholders care about, such as new borrowing or the repayment of debt. (Study Session 12, LOS 40.h)

©2011 Kaplan, Inc.

7.   **A**   Free cash flow to the firm can be calculated in various ways. One approach to calculate FCFF is to start with net income:

FCFF = NI + NCC + Int(1 − tax rate) − FCInv − WCInv
NI = $164,497   (income statement)
NCC = Noncash charges = $56,293   (income statement)
Int = Interest = $20,265 + $5,223 = $25,488   (income statement)
FCInv = Fixed capital investment = $143,579   (additional information)
WCInv = Working capital investment = $7,325   (additional information)

Putting it all together:

FCFF = $164,497 + $56,293 + $25,488(1 − 0.3) − $143,579 − $7,325 = $87,728
(Study Session 12, LOS 40.d)

8.   **B**   FCFE can be expressed in terms of FCFF as follows:

FCFE = FCFF − Int(1 − tax rate) + net borrowing

Therefore, the amount by which FCFF exceeds FCFE can be written as:

FCFF − FCFE = Int(1 − tax rate) − net borrowing

Int = $25,488

Net borrowing = $5,866 − $33,275 = −$27,409 (additional information)

Therefore: FCFF − FCFE = $25,488(1 − 0.3) − (−$27,409) = $45,251
(Study Session 12, LOS 40.d)

9.   **B**   The cost of equity can be determined from the capital asset pricing model. We get:

r = R_f + beta[market risk premium] = 4.5% + 1.10[5%] = 10%.

The sustainable growth rate can be found from: g = ROE × b

$$\text{ROE} = \frac{\text{net income}}{\text{beginning total equity}} = \frac{\$164,497}{\$1,019,869} = 0.16129$$

b = retention rate = 1 − ($82,248.50 / $164,497) = 0.5

g = 0.16129 × 0.5 = 0.0806 = 8.06%

(Study Session 11, LOS 39.n)

10.   **A**   When depreciation is the only noncash charge, FCFF can be estimated from:

FCFF = EBIT(1 − tax rate) + Dep − FCInv −WCInv

$EBIT_{2009}$ = $4,052,173 × 1.06 × 0.064 = $274,899

Therefore: $FCFF_{2009}$ = $274,899 (1 − 0.3) + $60,000 − $36,470 − $24,313 = $191,646

(Study Session 12, LOS 40.d)

11. **A** This is a two-stage FCFE model. The required return on equity is 10% (from problem 21), and the long-term growth rate after 2 years is 5%.

$$\text{value of equity} = \frac{\$0.21}{1.1} + \frac{\$0.23}{1.1^2} + \left(\frac{\$0.23 \times 1.05}{0.1 - 0.05} \times \frac{1}{1.1^2} \right)$$

$$= \frac{\$0.21}{1.1} + \frac{\$0.23}{1.1^2} + \left(\$4.83 \times \frac{1}{1.1^2} \right) = \$4.37$$

Financial calculators can perform this calculation more quickly and accurately. The appropriate keystrokes are:

CF0 = 0; C01 = $0.21; C02 = $0.23 + $4.83 = $5.06; I = 10.0; CPT → NPV = $4.37

Notice that the second cash flow combines the FCFE for the second year with the present value of the series of constantly growing FCFE terms that begin at the end of the third year. This approach is valid since the timing of these two cash flows is the same (i.e., the end of the second year). (Study Session 12, LOS 40.j)

12. **C** Dividends, share repurchases, and changes in the number of shares outstanding do not have an effect on either FCFE or FCFF. Therefore, only the new convertible debt offering will have a significant influence on the current level of FCFE because net borrowing changes FCFE. (Study Session 12, LOS 40.i)

13. **B** Statement 1: Correct, although not all the shares will be offered.
Statement 2: Incorrect because shares are not automatically issued to existing shareholders under a carve-out.
Statement 3: Correct since the results of the business sector will be more easily identifiable once the sector represents a separate company.
Statement 4: Correct for all strategies under consideration.
Statement 5: Incorrect—with a carve-out the "selling" corporation may (usually does) maintain some control of the business that has been split out into a separate company.

(Study Session 9, LOS 32.n)

14. **A** Debian s/h gain = gain_T = TP = $P_T - V_T$ = $90m – $85m = $5m

Fedora s/h gain = gain_A = S – TP = 8 – 5 = $3m.

Synergies are not directly given, but you are given that Fedora's value post merger (after paying the $5m takeover premium) increases by $3 million. Synergies must then be $5m + $3m = $8m.

Alternatively, the change in Fedora's value post merger, ($135m – $132m) = $3m, would give the gains to the acquirer in the case of a cash merger.

Note: The total gains = value of combined entity – value of both companies prior to merger

($135m + $90m) – ($85m + $132m) = $8m

Note: The value of the combined entity in a stock merger must include the $90 million in cash that was paid by Fedora to Debian. For computing the total gains to merger in a cash transaction, we need to add the $90 million that would be paid out to the seller. (Study Session 9, LOS 32.k)

15. **B** Value of shares received based on their likely post-acquisition price = [($135m + 90m) / 8m] × 3m = $84,375,000.

Gain to Debian's shareholders is therefore $84,375,000 – $85,000,000 = –$625,000.

(Study Session 9, LOS 32.k)

16. **B**
New value of their 5m shares = ($225m / 8m) × 5m = $140,625,000
Old value of their 5m shares = $132,000,000
Gain = $8,625,000

(Study Session 9, LOS 32.k)

17. **B** Attribute 1: This attribute is incorrect. An effective corporate governance system defines the rights (not the responsibilities) of shareholders and other stakeholders.

Attribute 2: This attribute is correct. An effective corporate governance system provides for fairness and equitable treatment in all dealings between managers, directors, and shareholders.

(Study Session 9, LOS 31.a)

18. **C** Using comparable company analysis:

Using P/E ratio: 25 × 1.50 = 37.50
Using P/B ratio: 2 ×18 = 36.00
Average 36.75
Add: 30% premium 11.03
Estimated takeover price $47.78

Using comparable transaction analysis:
Using P/E ratio: 30 × 1.50 = $45.00
Using P/B ratio: 2.80 × 18 = 50.40
Average $47.70

Note: No additional premium is applied for comparable transactions.

(Study Session 9, LOS 32.j)

19. **A** External factors that are important in an industry analysis are technology, government, social, demographic, and foreign. (Study Session 11, LOS 37.d)

20. **B** Apart from external factors, a thorough industry analysis depends on an industry classification, an analysis of demand, an analysis of supply, and a profitability analysis. (Study Session 11, LOS 37.a)

21. **C** The inference in Statement 1 relates to demand, not supply. In Statement 2, the inference relates to supply, not demand. Hence both statements regarding inferences are incorrect. (Study Session 11, LOS 37.e)

22. **B** The U.S. government has taken an active stance against the tobacco industry by declaring it to be a drug and decreeing that the FDA should have jurisdiction over the industry. (Study Session 11, LOS 37.d)

23. **A**   The four factors that contribute to pricing as listed in the relevant topic review are: product segmentation, degree of industry concentration, ease of industry entry, and price changes in key supply inputs. Galloway has correctly identified all four. (Study Session 11, LOS 37.f)

24. **A**   The four phases that correspond to the order of the listed statements are mature, decline, pioneer, and growth. (Study Session 11, LOS 37.b)

25. **B**   Since the required return (12%) as determined by CAPM is greater than Lear's expected return (10%), then Taylor's stock is overvalued. (Study Session 10, LOS 35.a)

26. **A**   Required return under FFM = risk-free rate + market beta (equity risk premium) + size beta (small-cap return premium) + value beta (value-return premium)

    = 3.4% + 0.7(5.5%) + −0.3(3.1%) + 1.4(2.2%) = 9.4%

    Note: The liquidity factor is only applicable to the Pastor-Stambaugh (PS) model. The PS model is otherwise the same as the FFM, save for the addition of the liquidity factor. (Study Session 10, LOS 35.d)

27. **B**   The Gordon growth model is a popular method to generate forward-looking estimates using current information and expectations concerning economic and financial variables.

    A historical estimate of the equity risk premium consists of the difference between the historical mean return for a broad-based equity market index and a risk-free rate over a given time period.

    A macroeconomic model estimate of the equity risk premium is based on the relationships between macroeconomic variables and financial variables. (Study Session 10, LOS 35.b, c, d)

28. **A**   The build-up method is usually applied to closely held companies (such as Densmore) where betas are not readily obtainable.

    The risk premium approach requires betas for its calculations; betas are generally not readily available for closely held companies.

    The bond-yield plus risk premium method is appropriate only if the company has publicly traded debt. The method simply adds a risk premium to the yield to maturity of the company's long-term debt. (Study Session 10, LOS 35.d)

29. **A**   Neither of Saunder's statements is correct. *Confidence risk* represents the unexpected change in the difference between the return of risky corporate bonds and government bonds. *Business cycle risk* represents the unexpected change in the level of real business activity. (Study Session 10, LOS 35.d)

30. **C**   A weakness (not strength) of the CAPM is its low explanatory power in some cases. Multifactor models usually have higher explanatory power than the CAPM since they use more than one factor, whereas CAPM uses only one factor.

    A weakness (not strength) of multifactor models is that they are typically more complex to use. (Study Session 10, LOS 35.f)

              ©2011 Kaplan, Inc.

31. **B**   The Eurodollar contract is a more effective instrument to hedge LIBOR-based investments because the Eurodollar contract is a LIBOR-based contract. The T-bill contract is based on T-bill rates, which are not perfectly correlated with LIBOR rates, so hedging a LIBOR investment with a T-bill futures contract results in a less effective hedge. Reichmann should take a long position in the Eurodollar contract. If interest rates decrease, his yield on the LIBOR-based security will fall, but the decrease will be offset by gains on a long position in a Eurodollar futures contract. (Study Session 16, LOS 55.g)

32. **A**   The interest rate cap pays off when interest rates rise above the cap rate, so a long position in a cap will hedge the risk of an increase in interest rates. A call option on an interest rate also pays off when the index rate at maturity is greater than the strike rate, so a long position in the call option will also hedge the risk of an increase in interest rates. (Study Session 17, LOS 56.a and 58.a)

33. **B**   floor payoff = \$30,000,000 × (0.060 − 0.058) = \$60,000

   (Study Session 17, LOS 58.b)

34. **B**   The value of the 2-year floor is equal to the value of a comparable 1-year European put option (a 1-year "floorlet") plus the value of a comparable 2-year put option (a 2-year "floorlet"). A 1-year floorlet with an annual payoff is the same as a 1-year put option on annual LIBOR. Therefore the value of the 2-year put option is equal to the value of the 2-year floor less the value of the 1-year put option: \$285,000 − \$90,000 = \$195,000. (Study Session 17, LOS 58.b)

35. **C**   To hedge his fixed income portfolio using an interest rate collar, Reichmann should sell the 6% floor and buy the 12% cap. Reichmann is hedged partially against interest rate increases because when rates rise above 12% and the value of the fixed-income portfolio falls, the cap will pay off. Selling the floor reduces his upside potential if rates fall below 6%, but he can offset some or all of the cost of the cap with the proceeds from the floor. (Study Session 17, LOS 58.b)

36. **B**   The last part of the first comment is incorrect. If a firm anticipates a floating rate exposure at some future date (e.g., it will be issuing bonds or getting a loan), a payer swaption would *lock in* a fixed rate and provide floating-rate payments for the loan. It would be exercised if the yield curve shifted up to give the investor (effectively) a loan at the fixed rate on the swaption. The second comment is correct. Swaptions also can be used to speculate on changes in interest rates. The investor would buy a payer swaption if he expects rates to rise, or buy a receiver swaption if he expects rates to fall. (Study Session 17, LOS 57.f)

37. **B**   For two up-moves, $45(1.15)^2 = \$59.51$. For two down-moves,

   $45(1/1.15)^2 = 34.03$.

   For two up-moves, the intrinsic call value is \$59.51 − \$40 = \$19.51.

   For two down-moves, the call is out-of-the-money, intrinsic value = \$0. For an up and a down-move the stock price is unchanged at 45, so the intrinsic value of the calls is \$45.00 − \$40.00 = \$5.

   The risk neutral probabilities for the decision tree: $\pi_U = \dfrac{1.04 - 0.87}{1.15 - 0.87} = 0.607$ and $\pi_D = 1 - \pi_U = 0.393$.

The probability weighted present value of the option payoff if there are two up-moves is $\dfrac{0.607^2(19.51)}{1.04^2} = \$6.65$.

For up-down and down-up (which are equal probabilities), the probability weighted present value of the payoff is $\dfrac{(2)(0.607)(0.393)(\$5.00)}{1.04^2} = \$2.21$.

Sum these to get the option value, \$8.86. (Study Session 17, LOS 56.b)

38. **C**   To form a delta neutral portfolio Loper needs to write $\dfrac{1,000}{0.83}$ = 1,204.82, or 1,205 calls. (Study Session 17, LOS 56.e)

39. **B**   The payoff is zero for a down-move and 11.75 for an up-move. Since the probability of an up-move is 0.607, the present value is $\dfrac{(0.607)11.75}{1.04} = \$6.86$. (Study Session 17, LOS 56.b)

40. **B**   The possibility of early exercise is not valuable for call options on non-dividend paying stocks, so the value of the American call is the same as the value of the European call, and the difference in value is zero. (Study Session 17, LOS 56.b)

41. **C**   The first assumption listed in the vignette should read, "The volatility of the return on the underlying stock is known and constant." The other listed assumptions are correct. (Study Session 17, LOS 56.c)

42. **B**   Dividends on the underlying stock decrease the value of call options and increase the value of put options, all else equal. By ignoring them in his valuation, Loper will likely overvalue a long call option and undervalue a long put. (Study Session 17, LOS 56.g)

43. **C**   We are told that IMI uses the CAPM to determine the degree to which securities are mispriced. The equation for the CAPM (using the S&P500 market index and treasury bill to proxy for the market index and risk-free asset) is:

CAPM expected return = $R_{TBILL} + \beta_{CSA}[E(R_{S\&P500}) - R_{TBILL}]$

Hendricks derives his beta forecast by using the adjusted beta formula:

forecast beta = 0.33 + 0.67 × (historical beta)

The historical beta equals the slope in the market model, provided in equation (1): slope = 1.75. Therefore, the forecast beta for CSA equals:

forecast beta = 0.33 + 0.67 × (historical beta) = 0.33 + 0.67(1.75) = 1.50

Substituting the forecast beta into the CAPM:

CAPM expected return for CSA = $R_{TBILL} + \beta_{CSA}[E(R_{S\&P500}) - R_{TBILL}]$

CAPM expected return for CSA = 0.04 + 1.50(0.12 - 0.04) = 0.16 = 16%

According to Exhibit 2, Hendricks forecasts that the CSA alpha will equal 4%. The alpha equals the difference between Hendricks' forecast return and the required return:

alpha for CSA = forecast return − CAPM required return

or,

forecast return = alpha + CAPM required return = 0.04 + 0.16 = 0.20 = 20%

(Study Session 10, LOS 35.e and Study Session 18, LOS 60.e,h)

©2011 Kaplan, Inc.

44. **A** The Treynor-Black formula for the CSA weight within the IMI-Active Portfolio equals:

$\dfrac{\alpha_{CSA}}{\sigma^2(\varepsilon_{CSA})}$ divided by the sum of the $\dfrac{\alpha_i}{\sigma^2(\varepsilon_i)}$ for all securities included in the

IMI-Active portfolio. Notice that $\dfrac{\alpha_{CSA}}{\sigma^2(\varepsilon_{CSA})} > \dfrac{\alpha_{MD}}{\sigma^2(\varepsilon_{MD})}$ because the MD alpha is twice

as large as the CSA alpha, but the MD unsystematic variance is more than twice as large as the CSA unsystematic variance. Therefore, CSA should receive larger weight than MD. (Study Session 18, LOS 63.b)

45. **B** The Treynor-Black model selects optimal combinations of the passive portfolio (e.g., the S&P 500) and the actively managed portfolio (the IMI-Active portfolio). By selecting an optimal combination of the two portfolios, the new capital allocation line (CAL) will have the same intercept, but higher slope than the CAL associated with the S&P 500. The intercept of the CAL is the risk-free rate (4%, Exhibit 1), and the slope of the CAL is the Sharpe ratio for the tangency portfolio. The tangency portfolio consists of the optimal combination of the S&P 500 and the IMI-Active portfolio. The tangency portfolio is the optimal portfolio, implying that its Sharpe ratio exceeds that of any other portfolio (including the S&P 500). Therefore, the slope of the optimal portfolio will exceed the S&P 500 Sharpe ratio:

$$\frac{\left([E(R)]_{S\&P}\right) - R_f}{\sigma_{S\&P}} = \frac{0.12 - 0.04}{0.20} = 0.40 = 40\%$$

Therefore, the CAL for the optimal portfolio (combination of the S&P 500 market index and the IMI-Active portfolio) will exceed 40%.
(Study Session 18, LOS 60.d and 63.b)

46. **C** The formula for the information ratio for the IMI-Active portfolio is:

$$\frac{\alpha}{\sigma(\varepsilon)} = \frac{0.0533}{0.30} = 0.178$$

(Study Session 18, LOS 60.m)

47. **C** The formula to adjust alphas for forecasting ability equals:

adjusted alpha = $R^2\alpha$

where R^2 is the square of the correlation between past realized alphas and the past forecast alphas derived by Hendricks. A perfect forecaster will have an R^2 equal to 1.

Therefore, there is no adjustment to be made for the CSA alpha because Hendricks has exhibited perfect forecast ability for the CSA stock. An adjustment should be made for the MD stock:

adjusted alpha for MD = $(0.50)^2(0.08) = 0.02 = 2\%$

(Study Session 18, LOS 63.c)

48. **C** Hendricks is incorrect with regard to Statement 1 and is correct with regard to Statement 2. The Treynor-Black model weights the active portfolio according to its alpha and its unsystematic risk. Keeping alpha constant, a higher unsystematic risk makes the portfolio less desirable—adding unsystematic risk to the overall investment. The Treynor-Black model is based on the premise that markets are "nearly" efficient—that there are only a limited number of meaningfully mispriced securities. Alternatively, the Treynor-Black model assumes that the investment management firm can thoroughly examine only a limited number of securities. (Study Session 18, LOS 63.b)

49. **C** The investment process requires consideration of risk and return concurrently. While maximization of returns is always preferable, an investor's risk tolerance must also be determined and included in the investment decision. Recall that risk and return objectives are closely related to one another because of the trade-off between risk and return. Therefore, Statement 1 is incorrect, and Statement 4 is correct. (Study Session 18, LOS 64.c)

50. **C** Specific factors that determine an investor's ability to accept risk include required spending needs, financial strength, and long-term wealth targets. Behavioral factors affect an individual investor's willingness to accept risk. (Study Session 18, LOS 64.c)

51. **C** Strategic asset allocation requires investment managers to consider all sources of income and risk. It also requires an analysis of capital market conditions and specific risk and return characteristics of individual assets. Therefore, Statement 2 is incorrect, and Statement 3 is correct. (Study Session 18, LOS 64.e)

52. **C** Responses A and B are appropriate considerations related to tax considerations. Although investors should rely on accountants and other advisors for tax advice, portfolio managers also need to pay attention to the tax consequences of their investment recommendations and relay those consequences to the investor so proper tax planning can occur. (Study Session 18, LOS 64.c)

53. **A** The most important portfolio constraints faced by individual investors include liquidity, investment horizon, and unique needs. Legal and regulatory factors are less important for individual investors than they are for institutional investors. (Study Session 18, LOS 64.c)

54. **B** Investment policy statements should be transportable, foster discipline, and discourage short-term strategy shifts. (Study Session 18, LOS 64.d)

55. **C** Instruction 3 is consistent with the new Prudent Investor Rule, because avoidance of excessive trading costs is one of its principles. The other statements are consistent with the old Prudent Man Rule. (Study Session 2, LOS 10.c)

56. **B** Standard III(A) Loyalty, Prudence, and Care. Unusual proposals, such as hostile takeovers and executive changes, may require more review than routine matters such as renewing stock-repurchase agreements. Money managers should provide a means to review complex proxies. Establishing evaluation criteria and disclosing the firm's proxy voting policies and procedures to clients are basic elements of a proxy-voting policy. Client wishes regarding proxy voting should always be followed. (Study Session 1, LOS 2.a)

©2011 Kaplan, Inc.

57. **C**   The priority of transaction Standard holds that a financial professional's personal transactions must wait until both her employer and her clients have had a chance to act. The Standard holds that all client accounts should be treated equally, regardless of whether the client is a family member. Members and candidates should limit personal participation in IPOs in order to give preference to clients who wish to participate. There is no need to limit client participation to satisfy Standard VI(B). It is quite possible to be loyal to pension-plan beneficiaries without following Standard VI(B). (Study Session 1, LOS 2.a)

58. **B**   Commissions from both internal and external brokerage operations are considered soft dollars, so Statement 2 is false. Statement 1 is true. CFA Institute Soft Dollar Standards are voluntary, though firms that wish to claim compliance with the Standards must follow them completely. Client brokerage can be used to pay for mixed-use research with the caveat that the research must be reasonable, justifiable, and documentable, and that the client brokerage is only used to pay for the portion of the research that will be used in the investment decision-making process. While research paid for by client brokerage should directly benefit the client, it does not have to do so immediately. (Study Session 1, LOS 3.b)

59. **B**   Standard III(B) Fair Dealing requires firms to notify clients of changes in investment advice before executing trades that go counter to that advice. While equal dissemination is usually impossible, it is an admirable goal. Firms should establish dissemination guidelines that are fair to all clients. Trading disclosures and confidentiality regarding investment rating changes are sensible precautions that meet the spirit of the fair dealing Standard. Maintaining client lists that detail client holdings will simplify the process of deciding how to best disseminate a change in investment recommendation. (Study Session 1, LOS 2.a)

60. **B**   Method 2 is the best answer. Quintux should cover the cost of the trading error, and if Borchard is willing to accept investment research in lieu of cash, that's all the better for Quintux. If Quintux compensates Borchard with extra trades, its clients are covering the costs of the error, which may violate Standard III(A) Loyalty, Prudence, and Care if directing future trades to Borchard is not in the clients' best interest. By accepting the CBX shares it did not request and allocating the shares to all client accounts rather than paying for the error, Quintux is violating Standard III(C) Suitability, since the shares are not likely to be appropriate for all of its client accounts and may not be suitable for any accounts since the shares were obtained as a result of a trading error, not an intentional investment action. Passing on client names is a violation of Standard III(E) Preservation of Confidentiality. (Study Session 1, LOS 2.a)

To get valuable feedback on how your score compares to those of other Level II candidates, use your Username and Password to gain Online Access at schweser.com and choose the left-hand menu item "Practice Exams Vol. 1."

61. A	81. B	101. C
62. C	82. B	102. C
63. C	83. B	103. B
64. C	84. C	104. C
65. B	85. C	105. C
66. A	86. B	106. C
67. A	87. B	107. C
68. C	88. B	108. C
69. C	89. C	109. A
70. C	90. A	110. B
71. B	91. C	111. B
72. B	92. B	112. B
73. C	93. C	113. B
74. B	94. C	114. A
75. C	95. A	115. A
76. B	96. A	116. B
77. A	97. C	117. C
78. A	98. C	118. A
79. C	99. B	119. B
80. C	100. A	120. A

©2011 Kaplan, Inc.

Exam 3
Afternoon Session Answers

61. **A** By presenting one client account as a representative composite of United's past performance, as well as implying that it is representative of future performance, Burton is in violation of Standard III(D) Performance Presentation. A member or candidate should give a fair and complete presentation of performance and not state or imply that clients will obtain or benefit from a rate of return that was generated in the past.

    Burton's references to the CFA program in his marketing materials were acceptable according Standard VII(B) Reference to CFA Institute, the CFA Designation, and the CFA Program. The Standard states that members and candidates may make references to the rigor of the program and the commitment of members and candidates to ethical and professional standards. However, statements must not exaggerate the meaning or implications of the designation, membership in CFA Institute, or candidacy. (Study Session 1, LOS 2.a)

62. **C** According to CFA Institute Soft Dollar Standards, research paid for by client brokerage is the property of the client, and the research should benefit the client. If the research is for the benefit of other clients, in this case Crossley, disclosure must be made to the client, and prior permission must be obtained. (Study Session 1, LOS 3.b)

63. **C** Standard VI(C) Referral Fees states that members and candidates must disclose to their clients and prospective clients any compensation or benefit received for the recommendation of services. In this case, Burton may accept a referral fee if he discloses it to the client so that the client may evaluate any partiality shown in the recommendation. (Study Session 1, LOS 2.a)

64. **C** According to Requirement 4.0 Investment Banking of the CFA Institute Research Objectivity Standards, firms must prohibit communication between members of the research and investment banking divisions. Recommended compliance procedures for Requirement 4.0 include prohibiting analysts from participating in marketing road shows. Therefore, while Security Bank complies with all of the requirements of the Standards, it does not comply with all of the recommendations.

    Under Requirement 10.0 Disclosure, firms are required to disclose all conflicts of interest to which the firm or its covered employees are subject, including whether the firm engages in any investment banking or other corporate finance activities. Therefore, "publicly revealing" the relationship is not a violation of the client's confidentiality. (Study Session 1, LOS 4.b)

65. **B** Standard V(A) Diligence and Reasonable Basis states that the member or candidate must exercise diligence, independence, and thoroughness before making an investment recommendation. The Standard also requires that members and candidates have a reasonable and adequate basis supported by research and investigation for any investment recommendations or actions. Burton made his purchase recommendation to Crossley purely on the basis of the Security Bank road show and did not perform his own evaluation to determine whether or not the SolutionWare IPO was a good investment opportunity. Burton has therefore violated Standard V(A).

Standard III(C) Suitability was also violated because there is no indication that Burton made any effort to determine if the investment was appropriate for Crossley's portfolio. Burton should have determined that the investment was consistent with Crossley's written objectives and constraints before he recommended the investment. Even though he later determined that the investment was suitable, he did not know this was the case before he told Crossley that he should purchase shares in the IPO. Standard III(B) Fair Dealing (and not I(B) Independence and Objectivity) would also be violated if Burton did not afford all the clients for whom the IPO was suitable to participate in the offering. Standard III(B) Fair Dealing (and not standard I(B)) would also be violated if Burton did not extend IPO participation to all portfolios meeting suitability criteria. (Study Session 1, LOS 2.a)

66. A   Standard VI(B) Priority of Transactions clearly states that investment transactions for clients must have priority over members' and candidates' transactions. Members and candidates can profit from personal investments as long as the client is not disadvantaged by the trade. By taking a portion of the IPO shares for his own account, Burton has ensured that Crossley's order will not be completely filled. It does not matter that the trade allocation was done on a pro-rata basis; Burton should have placed his client's transaction ahead of his own. (Study Session 1, LOS 2.a)

67. A   Hoskin's statement is likely to be correct. If the Maldavian government is considering restrictions on further stock market growth, then this will limit future economic growth. Economic growth is dependent in part on markets, because markets facilitate business transactions between buyers and sellers. The establishment of a securities regulator may or may not be neutral for the economy, but this is not explicitly mentioned in the topic review as a factor influencing economic growth.

Lanning's statement is also likely to be correct. If the president of Petria nationalizes the oil industry, then private property will be seized and property rights will not have been respected. Without property rights, firms and individuals have little incentive to make investments that could lead to future economic growth. The diversification of the economy, while perhaps good for the long-term health of the economy, is not explicitly mentioned in the topic review as a factor for economic growth. (Study Session 4, LOS 14.d)

68. C   Hoskins's reasoning is incorrect because although labor productivity will increase, the increase will result from a movement along the productivity curve. An upward shift in the productivity curve requires an advancement in technology. (Study Session 4, LOS 14.d)

69. C   The figures for taxes and fiscal spending are distracters. To calculate the growth in labor productivity, calculate a growth rate using the beginning and ending figures for real GDP per labor hour: ($21.50 − $20.00) / $20.00 = 7.50%.

The one-third rule states that a 1% increase in capital per labor hour will result in a one-third of 1% increase in labor productivity. The growth in capital per labor hour was: ($36.80 − $35.00) / $35.00 = 5.14%. This 5.14% increase will result in a 1.71% [(1/3) × (5.14%)] increase in labor productivity. The remaining 5.79% (7.50% − 1.71%) growth in labor productivity is due to improvements in technology. (Study Session 4, LOS 14.d)

70. C   Hoskins implies that population growth is independent of economic growth because, although women are having fewer children, people are living longer. He also believes that after a period of growth, the returns to capital will decline and real interest rates will fall. Both of these statements are consistent with the neoclassical growth theory. (Study Session 4, LOS 14.d)

   ©2011 Kaplan, Inc.

71. **B** Under the classical growth theory, the Tiberian economy will settle at a subsistence level. The high growth in the economy will result in a higher population. The higher population will eventually result in decreased returns to labor and decreased labor productivity. No permanent increase in labor productivity will result and per capita GDP will settle at a subsistence level. (Study Session 4, LOS 14.d)

72. **B** Under the endogenous growth theory, the Tiberian dividend growth rate can continue to increase because technological advances will be shared by many sectors of the economy. The benefits of technological advances cannot be captured entirely by a single firm. As these benefits flow to other firms, the economy becomes more productive and the long-term economic growth rate and dividend growth rate can continue to increase. Under the endogenous growth theory, the economy does not necessarily settle at a long-run equilibrium growth rate as it does under the neoclassical model, which posits a diminishing marginal productivity of capital. (Study Session 4, LOS 14.d)

73. **C** The balance sheet accrual ratio is the year-over-year increase in net operating assets divided by average net operating assets. An increase in payables (a liability) will tend to decrease (reduce the change in) net operating assets, while an increase in inventory will tend to increase (increase the change in) net operating assets. Cash is not an operating asset and does not affect the ratio. (Study Session 7, LOS 27.e)

74. **B** The unadjusted interest coverage ratio is calculated as follows:

$$\text{interest coverage} = \frac{\text{EBIT}}{\text{interest expense}} = \frac{10{,}876.00}{693.00} = 15.69$$

To adjust the interest coverage ratio for the operating lease, we need to take EBIT and add back the lease/rental expense (the lease payment amount) and subtract an estimate of depreciation for the machinery. Then, we need to add the appropriate interest expense for the operating lease to the overall interest expense.

To compute the interest expense and depreciation for the operating lease, we must first calculate the present value of the operating lease as follows:

PMT = 2,000
I/Y = 9
N = 5
FV = 0
CPT→PV = 7,779.30

Depreciation and interest expense are then calculated as:

$$\text{depreciation} = \frac{7{,}779.30 - 3{,}000.00}{5} = 955.86$$

$$\text{interest expense} = 7{,}779.30 \times 0.09 = 700.14$$

The adjusted interest coverage ratio is:

$$\text{interest coverage}_{(\text{adjusted})} = \frac{\text{EBIT} + \text{operating lease rent expense} - \text{depreciation}}{\text{interest expense} + \text{interest expense}}$$

$$\text{interest coverage}_{(\text{adjusted})} = \frac{10{,}876.00 + 2{,}000.00 - 955.86}{693.00 + 700.14} = 8.56$$

(Study Session 7, LOS 27.c)

75. **C** The elimination of the securitization of receivables as an off-balance-sheet item would result in Konker having to report the transaction as securitized borrowing, replacing the receivables on the balance sheet, and reporting a liability equal to the proceeds of the securitization transaction. The impact on Konker's balance sheet would be an increase in assets, and an increase in liabilities. The change in equity from reporting the transaction in this way is likely to be small. Financial leverage would increase, and the consequent increase in interest expense from the liability would decrease the interest coverage ratio. (Study Session 7, LOS 27.d)

76. **B** Removing the effects of the income reported under the equity method involves removing the income and the equity asset reported on the balance sheet. The decrease in total assets will increase the asset turnover ratio. The tax burden term is net income divided by earnings before tax so that the decrease in net income from removing the equity income will decrease the term (an apparently greater reduction in ROE due to taxes). Neither interest expense nor operating earnings (EBIT) are affected by the appropriate adjustments, so the interest coverage ratio is unaffected. (Study Session 7, LOS 27.b)

77. **A** The fact that Konker is growing the Industrial division most rapidly (highest capex percent to asset percent ratio) is a likely cause for concern and further investigation, since this division has the lowest operating return on assets. The decrease in the operating ROA for the Capital division is not particularly troublesome as it mirrors the pattern for the other divisisions and likely just reflects year-to-year variation in profitability. The fact that the percent of capex for the Defense division is less than its percent of total assets is not a primary cause for concern since that division has a lower operating ROA, and growth in capital assets likely follows contract awards in the defense industry, rather than drives business. Also, the apparent overinvestment in the Industrial division will decrease the capex percent for other divisions, other things equal. (Study Session 7, LOS 27.b)

78. **A** Volatile accruals ratios are an indicator that a firm may be manipulating earnings. Additionally, increasing accruals ratios may be a sign that a firm may be manipulating earnings. Lower accrual ratios represent higher earnings quality. (Study Session 7, LOS 27.e)

79. **C** The first step is to determine the tax rate from Exhibit 1.

net income = (after tax cash flow – depreciation), so net income
$$= (\$375,600 - \$264,000) = \$111,600$$

net income = EBT – taxes, so taxes = EBT – net income
$$= (\$186,000 - \$111,600) = \$74,400$$

tax rate = taxes / EBT = ($74,400 / 186,000) = 0.4000 = 40%

initial investment outlay
= purchase price + increase in net working capital
+ shipping and installation costs
= $700,000 + ($50,000 - $20,000) + $100,000 = $830,000

terminal year after-tax non-operating cash flow (TNOCF)
$$= Sal_T + NWCInv - T(Sal_T - B_T)$$
$$= 75,000 + 30,000 - 0.4(75,000 - 0)$$
$$= 75,000$$

after-tax operating cash flow (Year 4)
$$= (S - C)(1 - T) + DT$$
$$= (\$750,000 - \$225,000 - \$75,000)(1 - 0.4) + (0.4)(\$56,000) = \$292,400$$

The book value at the end of Year 4 is $0 because total depreciation over the four years was $800,000.

total CF (Year 4) = $292,400 + $75,000 = $367,400

(Study Session 8, LOS 28.a)

80. **C**   Both recommendations are incorrect. The $100,000 is a sunk cost and is thus not a relevant cash flow. Using straight-line depreciation will reduce the present value of the depreciation tax shield and reduce the NPV. (Study Session 8, LOS 28.a)

81. **B**   By ignoring the initial $30,000 cash inflow (recall that you are asked to assume it is an inflow), he has underestimated project NPV by $30,000. By ignoring the terminal cash outflow of $30,000, he has overestimated the project NPV by $\dfrac{\$30,000}{1.08^4} = \$22,050$

The net effect is to underestimate NPV by $30,000 – 22,050 = $7,950.

(Study Session 8, LOS 28.a)

82. **B**   The overall NPV of Project 1 = project NPV – option cost + option value

overall NPV = –$7 million – $3 million + $9 million = –$1 million

Without the option, the NPV of the production facility is negative, and the real option does not add enough value to make the overall project profitable.

Holbrook is incorrect that he needs to wait for more information to make the decision on Project 2. If the NPV of the project without the option is positive, the analyst knows that the project with the option must be even more valuable, and determining a specific value for the option is unnecessary. A real option adds value to a project, even if it is difficult to determine the monetary amount of that value. (Study Session 8, LOS 28.f)

83. **B**   economic income = cash flow – economic depreciation

economic depreciation = beginning market value – ending market value

market value at time t = present value of all remaining cash flows discounted at the WACC

$$\text{Year 3 beginning market value} = \frac{CF_3}{(1+\text{WACC})^1} + \frac{CF_4}{(1+\text{WACC})^2}$$

$$= \frac{\$318,000}{(1.08)^1} + \frac{\$367,400}{(1.08)^2} = \$294,444 + \$314,986 = \$609,430$$

$$\text{Year 3 ending market value} = \frac{CF_4}{(1+\text{WACC})^1} = \frac{\$367,400}{(1.08)^1} = \$340,185$$

Year 3 after-tax operating cash flow (given) = $318,000

Year 3 economic depreciation = $609,430 – $340,185 = $269,245

Year 3 economic income = $318,000 – $269,245 = $48,755

(Study Session 8, LOS 28.h)

84. **C** Comment 1 is incorrect. Interest should not be included in a project's cash flows when conducting NPV analysis because it is a financing cost that is reflected in the discount rate use to compute NPV.

   Comment 2 is incorrect. In theory, when discounted at the WACC, the present value of the economic profits from a project equals the NPV of the project. For a given period, economic profit = NOPAT – $WACC, where NOPAT is net operating profit after taxes and $WACC is the dollar cost of the capital used during the period. Economic profit reflects the income earned by all capital providers. (Study Session 8, LOS 28.a,i)

85. **C** Since MBS have an embedded option (prepayment option) that is typically exercised and is path dependent, the appropriate valuation model is Monte Carlo simulation. Credit card ABS do not have an embedded option, so neither valuation model is needed. A simple discounted cash flow model is sufficient. (Study Session 15, LOS 53.i)

86. **B** Statement 1 is incorrect. The *Z*-spread is the appropriate spread measure for option-free corporate bonds. Statement 2 is also incorrect, as it should say option-adjusted spread or "option-removed spread." Statement 3 is correct. (Study Session 15, LOS 53.i)

87. **B** The MCPPS is the difference between the conversion value and the bond's current market price, on a per share basis.

$$MCPPS = \frac{920}{10} - 40 = \$52 \text{ per share}$$

   Regarding the stock price increase, the convertible bond is essentially a straight bond (i.e., no conversion privilege), plus a call option on the underlying common stock. In this case, the option is far out of the money. So, while the increase in the stock price will have a positive impact on the bond, the impact will be small because the delta is close to zero for options that are far out of the money. (Study Session 14, LOS 53.i)

88. **B** IO investors want prepayments to be slow and, thus, are more concerned with contraction risk.

   Interest-only strips: An interest-only (IO) strip receives all interest payments from the underlying mortgage pool. If market interest rates increase, prepayments will fall. This results in larger than expected principal balances and, thus, larger than expected interest payments. Hence, IO strips have higher realized returns when interest rates increase. If interest rates fall, the pool tends to prepay and interest payments fall, resulting in lower returns to the IO strip.

   Principal-only strips: A principal-only (PO) strip receives only the principal payments (both scheduled and prepayments) from the underlying pool of mortgages. If interest rates fall, prepayments increase. Since the PO strips are discount securities, larger than expected prepayments result in the early return of principal and, thus, a higher return on the security. Increasing interest rates result in lower than expected prepayments (i.e., extension risk) and lower actual returns.

   Volatility: Both IOs and POs have greater price volatility than the passthrough from which they were derived. This occurs because the IO and PO returns are negatively correlated (they respond in opposite directions to changes in interest rates), but the volatility of the combined IO and PO strips equals the price volatility of the source passthrough.

   (Study Session 15, LOS 51.i)

©2011 Kaplan, Inc.

89. **C** Excess servicing spread funds (a type of reserve fund) and overcollateralization are internal credit enhancements. Letters of credit and bond insurance are external enhancements. (Study Session 15, LOS 52.d)

90. **A** $SMM = 1 - (1 - 0.07)^{0.0833} = 0.00603$ (Seasoning just means that the pool is older than 30 months).

   The estimated prepayment for the month = $0.00603 \times (\$500,000 - \$150) = \$3,014$. (Study Session 15, LOS 51.c)

91. **C** Market extraction method:

   The capitalization rate = R_0 = NOI/MV, where NOI and MV represent the net operating income and market value of properties that are comparable to the property being valued.

   The NOI for comparable properties is given as $135,000 per unit.

   The MV for comparable properties is given as $1,250,000 per unit.

   So, the capitalization rate may be computed as:

   R_0 = NOI/MV = $135,000 / $1,250,000 = 10.80%

   Built-up method:

   The capitalization rate under the built-up method is expressed as:

   R_0(BU) = pure rate + liquidity premium + recapture premium + risk premium.

   The components of the built-up capitalization rate are provided, so R_0(BU) may be computed as:

   R_0(BU) = pure rate (5%) + liquidity premium (2.5%) + recapture premium (1.25%) + risk premium (3.0%) = 11.75%

   (Study Session 13, LOS 45.b)

92. **B** Direct income capitalization:

   Market value under the direct income capitalization approach is computed using the formula:

   $MV_0 = NOI_1 / R_0$

   where:
   MV_0 = the estimated current market value
   NOI_1 = net operating income over the first period of the investment

   NOI_1 is given for Riviera Terrace as $4,200,000.

   The capitalization rate may be computed as:

   $R_0 = NOI_1 / MV$ = $135,000 / $1,250,000 = 10.80%

   So, $MV_0 = NOI_1 / R_0$ = $4,200,000 / 0.108 = $38,888,889

   (Study Session 13, LOS 45.c)

93. **C**

Selling price	$60,000,000	
Cost of sale (7%)	(4,200,000)	
Net selling price		$55,800,000

Purchase price	$40,000,000	
Less accumulated depreciation*	(6,250,000)	
Adjusted basis (book value)		$33,750,000
Realized gain on sale		$22,050,000
Recaptured depreciation**		($6,250,000)
Long-term capital gain		$15,800,000

Tax on recaptured depreciation ($6,250,000 × 0.28)	$1,750,000
Tax on long-term capital gain ($15,800,000 × 0.15)	$2,370,000
Total tax due on property sale	$4,120,000

*Accumulated depreciation = 5 × $1,250,000 = $6,250,000

**When net selling price > original cost, recaptured depreciation = accumulated depreciation

(Study Session 13, LOS 44.c)

94. **C**

Selling price	$45,000,000	
Cost of sale (7%)	(3,150,000)	
Net selling price		$41,850,000

Purchase price	$40,000,000	
Less accumulated depreciation*	(6,250,000)	
Adjusted basis (book value)		$33,750,000
Realized gain on sale		$8,100,000
Recaptured depreciation**		($6,250,000)
Long-term capital gain		$1,850,000

Tax on recaptured depreciation ($6,250,000 × 0.28)	$1,750,000
Tax on long-term capital gain ($1,850,000 × 0.15)	$277,500
Total tax due on property sale	$2,027,500

*Accumulated depreciation = 5 × $1,250,000 = $6,250,000

**When net selling price > original cost, recaptured depreciation = accumulated depreciation

Net selling price	$41,850,000
Outstanding mortgage balance	($32,000,000)
Pre-tax sales proceeds	$9,850,000
Less total tax on property sale	(2,027,500)
Equity reversion after tax	$7,822,500

(Study Session 13, LOS 44.c)

95. **A**   Hint: Once you compute net operating income (NOI) for Year 3, the Year 3 cash flow after tax (CFAT) computation may be made independently of the other years. This will save some valuable time on the exam. (Study Session 13, LOS 44.c)

©2011 Kaplan, Inc.

Table 1: Tax Computation

Year	1	2	3	4	5
Net operating income	4,200,000	4,410,000	4,630,500	4,862,025	5,105,126
Depreciation	(1,250,000)	(1,250,000)	(1,250,000)	(1,250,000)	(1,250,000)
Interest expense	(2,240,000)	(2,240,000)	(2,240,000)	(2,240,000)	(2,240,000)
Taxable income	710,000	920,000	1,140,500	1,372,025	1,615,126
Tax rate	0.4	0.4	0.4	0.4	0.4
Income tax payable	284,000	368,000	456,200	548,810	646,051

Table 2: CFAT Computation

	1	2	3	4	5
Net operating income	4,200,000	4,410,000	4,630,500	4,862,025	5,105,126
Debt service	(2,240,000)	(2,240,000)	(2,240,000)	(2,240,000)	(2,240,000)
Pretax cash flow	1,960,000	2,170,000	2,390,500	2,622,025	2,865,126
Income tax payable	284,000	368,000	456,200	548,810	646,051
Cash flow after tax	1,676,000	1,802,000	1,934,300	2,073,215	2,219,076

96. **A**   To compute the IRR, we must determine the initial cash outlay CF_0, and the subsequent three cash flows after tax, CF_1, CF_2, and CF_3.

CF_0 is the initial equity investment, which is 20% of the purchase price, or $0.2 \times 40,000,000 = \$8,000,000$.

$CF_1 = \$1,676,000$, which is CFAT for Year 1.

$CF_2 = \$1,802,000$, which is CFAT for Year 2.

$CF_3 = CFAT_3 + ERAT$

ERAT = \$4,934,000 (given in vignette)

So, $CF_3 = CFAT_3 + ERAT = \$1,934,300 + \$4,934,000 = \$6,868,300$.

Using a TI BA II Plus, the IRR can be computed as follows:

[CF][2nd][CLR WORK]
[8,000,000][+/-][ENTER][↓]
[1,676,000][ENTER][↓][↓]
[1,802,000][ENTER][↓][↓]
[6,868,300][ENTER]
[IRR][CPT] = 11%

Since the IRR of 11% is less than Sentry Property's required rate of return of 20%, the investment is not acceptable under the assumption that it will be liquidated in three years. (Study Session 13, LOS 44.b)

97. **C** The best formulation for Smith's retail sales data would include the intercept, the lag one coefficient, and the lag twelve coefficient. First, note that in the second regression, all of these are statistically significant, with a p-value of less than 1%. Also, the second regression that included the lag twelve term has a higher adjusted R-square at 0.92 compared to 0.83 in the first regression that omits the lag twelve term. Lastly, we should suspect that the lag twelve term is appropriate because this is seasonal, monthly data.

We could have also looked at the significance of the autocorrelations if they had been provided. If any are significant in either regression, another lag term would be added to the autoregressive model. (Study Session 3, LOS 13.d,l)

98. **C** To forecast the sales this month, we first calculate the change in the log of sales last month:

$$\Delta \ln \text{sales}_{t-1} = \ln(6{,}270) - \ln(6{,}184) = 8.7435 - 8.7297 = 0.0138$$

Next, use this change in the regression model to obtain the forecasted change for this month:

$$\Delta \ln \text{sales}_t = 0.052 + 0.684(0.0138) = 0.0614$$

Add the forecasted change to last month's log sales to obtain this month's forecasted log sales:

$$\ln \text{sales}_t = 0.0614 + 8.7435 = 8.8049$$

Lastly, convert the forecasted log value to a dollar value by taking its antilog:

$$\text{sales}_t = e^{8.8049} = \$6{,}667$$

(Study Session 3, LOS 13.d)

99. **B** Smith is correct. The first step in testing for an ARCH process is to take the residuals from the original autoregressive model and then square them.

Sims is incorrect. The next step in determining whether an ARCH process exists is to regress the squared residuals from this period against the squared residuals from the previous period as follows:

$$\varepsilon_t^2 = b_0 + b_1 \varepsilon_{t-1}^2$$

If b_1 is statistically different from zero, then we conclude that the regression model contains an ARCH process. (Study Session 3, LOS 13.m)

100. **A** Neither the lag two term nor the lag four term should be included. To determine the significance of the autocorrelation of the residuals, we need the standard error, which is calculated as one over the square root of the number of observations. There are 36 quarters of inflation data. One quarter is lost because we have a lag one term, so there are 35 observations in the regression. Therefore, the standard error is $\dfrac{1}{\sqrt{35}} = 0.1690$.

©2011 Kaplan, Inc.

The *t*-statistics are the autocorrelations divided by the standard error which results in:

Lag	Autocorrelation	Standard Error	t-Statistic
1	0.0829	0.1690	0.49
2	0.1293	0.1690	0.76
3	0.0227	0.1690	0.13
4	0.1882	0.1690	1.11

The critical *t*-value is 2.03 for a two-tail test, so none of the *t*-statistics indicate that the autocorrelations are significantly different from zero. Therefore, we do not need to include additional lag terms. (Study Session 3, LOS 13.d)

101. **C** In the first regression, the Federal Funds rate in the United States has a unit root, but the bond yield in the European Union does not. So the former data series is not covariance stationary, but the latter is. In this case, the regression results will not be valid.

In the second regression, both the Federal Funds rate in the United States and the bond yield in Great Britain have a unit root. So both data series are not covariance stationary. However, because they are cointegrated, the regression results will be valid.

To sum up the possibilities you may face on exam day:
- If neither data series has a unit root, the regression results are valid.
- If only one data series has a unit root, the regression results are invalid.
- If both data series have a unit root and they are cointegrated, the regression results are valid.
- If both data series have a unit root and they are not cointegrated, the regression results are not valid.

(Study Session 3, LOS 13.k,n)

102. **C** To test whether two variables are cointegrated, we regress one data series on the other and examine the residuals for a unit root using the Dickey-Fuller/Engle-Granger test. If we reject the null hypothesis, the error terms of the two data series are covariance stationary and cointegrated. The regression results will be valid. (Study Session 3, LOS 13.n)

103. **B** The assets and liabilities of the purchased firm are included on the balance sheet of the acquiring firm under either method. Under the pooling method, there is no adjustment of balance sheet asset and liability values to their fair values. Under the acquisition method, assets and liabilities acquired are reported at fair value at the time of the purchase. There is no goodwill reported under the pooling method; the purchase price is not reflected on the balance sheet of the acquiring firm. (Study Session 6, LOS 22.a)

104. **C** Under the proportionate consolidation method, the proportionate share of the purchased firm's revenue and expenses would be reported on Fisher's income statement, increasing both expenses and revenues. Under the equity method, Fisher's revenue and expenses are reported without adjustment, and the proportion of income from the purchased firm is reported separately, so that net income is the same under either method. (Study Session 6, LOS 22.a)

105. **C** Goodwill is no longer amortized under IFRS or U.S. GAAP. The test for impairment is different under IFRS than under U.S. GAAP. (Study Session 6, LOS 22.b)

106. **C** All business combinations (e.g., merger, purchase, or consolidation) are reported under the acquisition method. Identifiable assets and liabilities must be reported at fair value at the time of the acquisition. Under IFRS, Fisher has the option of calculating the goodwill for the acquisition under either the full goodwill or partial goodwill methods. Goodwill is less under the partial goodwill method. (Study Session 6, LOS 22.b)

107. **C** U.S. GAAP requires that unrealized gains and losses on available-for-sale securities be reported in comprehensive income as part of shareholders' equity. The appropriate adjustment to Fisher's statements is to decrease net income by the amount of the gain. Lower net income will result in lower ROA and ROE (lower numerators). Lower net income results in lower retained earnings. However, the gain increases other comprehensive income; thus, total equity does not change. In summary, assets, liabilities and total equity are not affected by the adjustment; thus, asset turnover, debt-to-equity and debt-to-total capital are not impacted. (Study Session 6, LOS 22.a,b)

108. **C** The acquisition method results in higher assets and higher sales, but the same net income. Therefore, both ROA (net income divided by assets) and net profit margin (net income divided by sales) will decrease. (Study Session 6, LOS 22.c)

109. **A** Exposure under the current rate method is equity. Beginning equity is positive ($4,000) and the change in equity during the year is positive ($6,000 − $4,000 = $2,000). Because the Rho appreciated during the year, the current rate method will report a translation gain for 2008. Under the current rate method, gains and losses are reported as part of the cumulative translation adjustment in the equity section of the balance sheet. (Study Session 6, LOS 24.d,e)

110. **B** Exposure under the temporal method is cash and accounts receivable minus current liabilities and long-term debt. Beginning exposure is negative ($5,000 − $11,000 = −$6,000) and the change in exposure is also negative [−$6,300 − (−$6,000)] = −$300. Because the Rho appreciated during the year, the temporal method will report a translation loss for 2008. Gains and losses are reported on the income statement under the temporal method. (Study Session 6, LOS 24.d,e)

111. **B** If the Rho is appreciating, mixed ratios, like return on assets and total asset turnover (using end-of-period balance sheet figures), calculated from the local currency statements, will be larger than the same ratios calculated from the reporting currency statements that were translated using the current rate method. For example, under the current rate method, net income will be translated at the lower average rate ($0.42) and assets will be translated at the higher ending rate ($0.45). Therefore the original return on assets (net income divided by total assets) from the Rho statements will be higher than the ratio after it is translated into the reporting currency. (Study Session 6, LOS 24.d,e)

112. **B** With the Rho appreciating, fixed asset turnover will be lower under the current rate method. (Study Session 6, LOS 24.d,e)

113. **B** In this example, the Del is the local currency, the Rho is the functional currency (because Wayward is an independent subsidiary), and the U.S. dollar is the reporting currency. The appropriate application of U.S. GAAP is to first remeasure the Del receivables from Del to Rho using the temporal method. (Study Session 6, LOS 24.c)

©2011 Kaplan, Inc.

114. **A** The quick ratio (cash and receivables divided by current liabilities) is a pure balance sheet ratio, which means both numerator and denominator will be translated at the current exchange rate and the ratio will be the same before and after translation. The result is the same for the interest coverage ratio (EBIT divided by interest expense) because it is a pure income statement ratio; both the numerator and denominator will be translated at the average rate over the reporting period and the ratio will be the same before and after translation. (Study Session 6, LOS 24.d,e)

115. **A** Since inventory prices are rising, COGS is higher under last-in, first-out (LIFO) than under first-in, first-out (FIFO). Therefore, net income and taxes are lower under LIFO. Since taxes are lower under LIFO, cash flows will be higher. Working capital would also be lower under LIFO. (Study Session 5, LOS 20.a)

116. **B** Over an inflationary period, older layers of inventory will have been purchased at lower prices than more recently purchased inventory. Since older layers of inventory that are liquidated were purchased at lower prices, the cost of goods sold will be lower and earnings will be higher. (Study Session 5, LOS 20.b)

117. **C** FIFO COGS is equal to LIFO COGS minus the change in LIFO reserve. Therefore, $30,757 – ($5,750 – 3,250) = $28,257. (Study Session 5, LOS 20.c)

118. **A** Under the double-declining balance method of depreciation, the deductions in assets and net income are greatest in the early years and decline over time. This means that return on investment will increase over time as net income increases. (Study Session 5, LOS 21.b)

119. **B** Remaining useful life = (gross investment – accumulated depreciation) / depreciation expense.

13.94 = ($32,268 – $9,769) / $1,614

(Study Session 5, LOS 21.d)

120. **A** Under U.S. GAAP, long-lived assets are reported on the balance sheet at depreciated cost less any impairment losses ($525 million original cost less $182 million accumulated depreciation and less $43 million impairment loss, for a net amount of $300 million). Increases are generally prohibited with the exception of assets held for sale. Since these assets are currently in use, this exception does not apply. Therefore, Project Depot may not revalue the assets upward. (Study Session 5, LOS 21.c)